BAYONET
BATTLE

TIM RIPLEY

BAYONET BATTLE

Bayonet Warfare in the 20th Century

SIDGWICK & JACKSON

First published 1999 by Sidgwick & Jackson

an imprint of Macmillan Publishers Ltd
25 Eccleston Place, London SW1W 9NF
and Basingstoke

Associated companies throughout the world

ISBN 0 283 06323 8

1 3 5 7 9 8 6 4 2

A CIP catalogue record for this book is available from
the British Library.

Typeset by SX Composing DTP, Rayleigh, Essex
Printed and bound in Great Britain by
Mackays of Chatham plc, Chatham, Kent

CONTENTS

INTRODUCTION

'Fix bayonets' has been a feared war cry for almost 400 years. It is more than just an order for soldiers to attach an edged weapon to their rifles. Commanders use the order to boost the aggression of their troops and get their adrenalin flowing as they advance close enough to the enemy to impale him with their bayonet. Once soldiers have fixed bayonets, they know hand-to-hand combat is near and they should steel themselves to either kill or be killed. There is no going back.

In the twentieth century the bayonet has remained one of the infantryman's key weapons of war. Almost all rifles or assault weapons have been provided with either fixed or detachable bayonets. Infantrymen the world over spend days in basic training perfecting the art of stabbing mannequins, while shouting blood-curdling curses.

Early in the First World War, bloody battles led to a dramatic change in the tactical use of the bayonet. At the start of the war senior commanders on all sides had little under-standing of the effect of modern weapons, such as the machine-gun and artillery. They were still keen for infantry to charge the enemy in the hope that the sight of glinting bayonets would put them to flight. 'They don't like it up 'em' may have been the slightly jokey catchphrase later popularized in British television comedy, but most commanders of the

First World War era were firm believers in the psychological impact of 'cold steel'.

In the grim reality of the Western Front, the 'myth of the bayonet' faded for ever. The bayonet was now the infantryman's weapon of last resort, used only in close combat after artillery, mortars, machine-guns, sub-machine-guns and grenades had failed to do their work.

There was a brief renaissance of the bayonet in the Far East during the Second World War, where the Japanese put great store in the bayonet charge. Well-sited and determined defences, however, usually thwarted these banzai charges, often at great cost to the attackers.

Even so, looking back through the history of warfare in the twentieth century, it becomes clear that the bayonet has had a far greater impact than is often thought. This book goes some way to setting the record straight.

History of the Bayonet

During the twentieth century the bayonet has been largely seen as a weapon for use in hand-to-hand combat between infantrymen. However, the origins of the weapon go back to the age when cavalry ruled the battlefield and infantrymen were struggling to find ways of defending themselves against their mounted foes.

Most scholars attribute the antecedence of the bayonet to the seventeenth century and the small town of Bayonne in the French Pyrenees, near the border with Spain. Here a group of Basque musketeers found themselves surrounded by a superior force of Spanish cavalry. Without the usual six-metre pikes to keep the cavalry at bay, the musketeers were soon running short of ammunition and in danger of being overrun. In desperation, one of the soldiers pulled out his short knife and forced it down the barrel of his musket, instantly turning the weapon into an improvised pike. His comrades followed suit and the Spaniards were soon put to flight. The site of the battle on a ridge outside Bayonne quickly become known as 'La Bayonette'.

The exact date of the creation of the first purpose-designed and manufactured bayonet is unclear. Throughout the seventeenth century there are references in numerous journals to soldiers from the Bayonne region arming themselves with knives designed to be pushed into the end of a musket. Local worthy Jacques de Chastenet described in 1647 how his men were armed with 'bayonettes' having thirty-centimetre handles and similar length blades.

Over the next hundred years the bayonet caught on in armies throughout Europe. They saw the potential for providing musketeers with a means of fighting off cavalry. These early weapons were known as 'plug' bayonets because they effectively plugged or screwed into the barrel of the musket. By the beginning of the nineteenth century pikemen had all but disappeared as bayonets became standard equipment for infantrymen. Despite its widespread adoption, the plug bayonet had one major disadvantage: for the musket to be fired the bayonet had first to be removed.

To get round this problem, the 'socket' or 'ring' bayonet was developed. Introduced by the Swedes in 1696, it was in widespread use early in the seventeenth century: the British Army adopted its first socket bayonet in 1720. As the name implies, the socket bayonet fitted round the muzzle of the musket and allowed the weapon to be fired with the bayonet in position. Its attachment was a metal tube that passed over the end of the musket barrel and held in place by a variety of means, including studs, screws, leaf springs, or locking rings.

Early designs were far from ideal, with defective securing catches often resulting in the bayonet being propelled towards the enemy when the musket was fired. What is more, eighteenth-century breech-loading muskets were difficult to reload in the heat of battle and the attachment of a bayonet did not make this any easier, leading to many over-enthusiastic soldiers injuring themselves on their own blades.

The first socket bayonets were akin to spikes, rather than edges, swords or knives. They were also largely triangular in shape, which provided strength and killing power. They were rarely sharpened so were not very good for slashing, but when thrust into an opponent's body or face inflicted dreadful wounds.

The socket musket was to be the standard in bayonet design for over a hundred years until fashion led to a demand for so-called 'sword' bayonets, which clipped underneath or on to the side of a rifle's muzzle. There is some debate whether this trend was driven by ceremonial considerations rather than military practicality.

During the late eighteenth century and throughout the Napoleonic wars sword bayonets were mainly employed by riflemen or skirmishers, such as the British 95th (Rifle) Regiment. Their famous Baker's rifles were the first in British service to use sword bayonets. Riflemen were attracted to them largely because they were long and heavy enough to chop wood and butcher meat rather than because of their value as weapons of war.

During the latter half of the nineteenth century the threat from cavalry was still considered serious enough for the major European armies to retain long sword or knife bayonets, often up to a metre in length. Experience in colonial conflicts also reinforced the military's interest in long bayonets that allowed the infantryman to duel at some parity with spear-carrying tribesmen. There was also a feeling among high-level military commanders that the longer the bayonet, the greater the psychological advantage over the enemy. This theory was found to be fatally wanting in the first months of the First World War, when the psychological reassurance of a long bayonet proved unable to overcome the killing power of the machine-gun and repeating rifle.

During those rare occasions when hand-to-hand bayonet fighting took place in the First World War it was very clearly demonstrated that the long thin sword bayonet was a liability in the confined spaces of a trench or dugout. The soldier could not wield the weapon easily and the knife-type blade proved too prone to snapping when an opponent's torso was impaled on it.

By the start of the Second World War the British Army and others had introduced the short spike or 'pig sticker' bayonets, which were under half the length of their predecessors. The Japanese, for idiosyncratic reasons, retained their long sword bayonets, and every weapon, including heavy machine-guns, had to be capable of fielding one for the banzai charge. Likewise in Burma, because of the unique requirements of jungle combat, the British and Indian armies started to revert to knife rather than spike designs.

Short blades became the norm after the War in the form of spikes or short knives. These may have been efficient killers, but they were not pretty, so the ceremonial units such as the British Brigade of Guards adopted their own special long bayonets that looked good on parade. Russian and Chinese weapon manufacturers also came up with designs that involved folding bayonets permanently attached to rifles. This saved the resources needed for bayonet scabbards and meant that poorly educated, quickly trained conscripts were never separated from their bayonets.

The Russians also led the way in diversifying the use of the bayonet with the first combined bayonet/wire-cutter, which used the scabbard to form a cutting device. During the First World War this idea was tried and found impractical. In the post-Second World War period the Russian idea has, however, been copied by a number of armies, including the British, which used it on the SA-80 series of weapons. The SA-80 family also returned to a socket bayonet design, albeit with modern stylistic features, indicating that bayonet design is an art form somewhat lacking in originality.

Increasingly, after the Second World War, the bayonet was seen more as a multi-purpose tool rather than as simply an extension of the soldier's weapon system. Bayonets had to be useful in knife fighting, killing wild animals for food, preparing field defences or even as mechanical tools. In some cases the attachment of the bayonet to the rifle was seen as an after-thought. One major small arms manufacturer, Denel in South Africa, even stopped making bayonets for its assault rifles in the 1970s.

This has led some tacticians to consider the bayonet obsolete as a weapon. The most notable modern instance of the bayonet being used in action was during the 1982 Falklands War, since when it seems to have fallen into disuse. This opinion is, however, somewhat deceptive. During the run-up to Operation Desert Storm in 1991 the British, American and French forces trained extensively for trench-clearing operations using bayonets. Fortunately the overwhelming Coalition air power and artillery destroyed the Iraqi will to fight before the ground forces advanced, limiting the opportunity for trench clearing at bayonet point. Given this salutary lesson, few infantrymen faced with the prospect of hand-to-hand combat were able to suggest that the bayonet is redundant.

The Bayonet Charge in History

The bayonet charge is at the heart of many military legends, from the British 'thin red line', through Napoleon's Imperial Guard to Pickett's Charge at Gettysburg in the American Civil War.

INTRODUCTION

However, it was as a defensive weapon for keeping cavalry at bay that the bayonet, in the seventeenth and eighteenth centuries, first made its name. The famous infantry squares that defeated Napoleon's cavalry at Waterloo in 1815 would not have been possible without the bayonet. In the first years of its existence the bayonet was not considered an offensive weapon; cavalry were the decisive arm and offensive action was not the job of the infantry.

In the gentlemanly battles of the eighteenth century, the infantry's main job was to trade volleys of musket fire with the enemy's infantry. Armies would present themselves in long lines and blast hell out of each other until one side decided to give in. It was very rare for hand-to-hand combat to take place.

The aggressive use of the bayonet was largely a British development, in the aftermath of the defeat of the Jacobite Highlanders at Culloden in 1745. Experience during the American War of Independence further reinforced the British belief in the bayonet, but only when used in combination with firepower. The enemy first had to be weakened by accurate rifle fire from skirmishers and a quick volley by a regiment's main body before being put to flight by a swift charge. Rarely did the enemy stand and fight. The first major battle of the war for America's freedom was a bloody affair. On 7 July 1775, some 2,600 British troops twice stormed up Bunker Hill opposite Boston harbour. On their third attempt the Redcoats got among the Rebels, bayoneting any they found, but by that time over 1,000 British soldiers lay dead or wounded. The British bayonet was again ascendant at the Battle of Princeton in January 1777. To the fore was the 17th Regiment of Foot, which alone broke a whole brigade of Continental Regulars before being shot to pieces by overwhelming enemy fire.

Revolutionary France was also keen on the bayonet. When fighting the old armies of central Europe, the sight of a determined column of French soldiers pressing down upon them was usually enough to force the enemy back in panic. Time after time, Austrian, Prussian, Russian, Spanish and other European armies fled in terror in the face of determined French columns brandishing bayonets, though it was more the threat of hand-to-hand combat that broke the enemy rather than bayonet fighting itself.

The British and French tactical systems first met in open battle in continental Europe at Maida, in southern Italy, in 1806. This was the first occasion when the famous British line first stood its ground against French columns, before putting Napoleon's troops to flight at bayonet point. The same story was repeated throughout the Peninsular War and culminated in the dramatic defeat of the French Imperial Guard at Waterloo. In the final hours of the battle, Napoleon threw in his Old Guard to batter through what was left of the British line. They dropped down into a valley and then moved up towards the ridge line held by the British Brigade of Guards and the 52nd Regiment of Foot. At the crest of the hill the Duke of Wellington personally ordered his troops to fire. The volley stunned Napoleon's elite and a swift bayonet charge by the British sent them fleeing, so ending the French Emperor's career for good.

If the bayonet only had a psychological impact in open battle during the era of 'horse and musket' battles, in sieges and close-quarter fighting in buildings the bayonet proved decisive. Once two groups of soldiers were locked in combat, there was no time to reload muskets, so the killing had to be done by bayonet. Also, during the Peninsular War, British assault teams, regarded as forlorn hopes, stormed Spanish fortresses at Badajoz and Ciudad Rodrigo at bayonet point. At Fuentes de Onoro, in the street battle of 1811, French and British troops traded bayonet slashes for a whole day. During the Battle of Waterloo, the farm of La Haye Sainte and the château of Hougoumont became charnel houses after hours of hand-to-hand fighting.

The last hurrah for the British bayonet was during the Crimean War, at the Battle of Balaklava in October 1854, when the Sutherland Highlanders, standing in line, fought off Russian cavalry, fighting bayonet to sabre. This won the regiment eternal fame as 'The Thin Red Line'.

Developments in small arms over the next fifty years dramatically altered the part played by the bayonet. Rapid-firing rifles and machine-guns made it foolhardy to try to manoeuvre across open battlefields in Napoleonic-style formations. This, however, did not dampen military commanders' desire for Napoleonic-style glory. The 1866 Austro-Prussian War and the 1870-71 Franco-Prussian wars saw futile bayonet charges that ended in wholesale slaughter without purpose or result. But it was across the Atlantic during the American Civil War that the effect of this new firepower was most cruelly felt. Again senior commanders exhorted their troops to close with the enemy and put him to flight with the bayonet. In engagement after engagement this proved a recipe for disaster. The Battle of Fredericksburg on 13 December 1862 saw one of the most pointless examples of this school of tactics, when Union troops made a river crossing and then attempted to storm the Marye's Heights above the town. Deadly accurate Confederate small-arms and artillery fire swept down on the Union columns with slide-rule precision. Fourteen times the Union troops attempted to attack and each time the result was the same. They got nowhere near the enemy positions. By the end of the day some 12,900 Union soldiers lay dead or wounded in front of the Confederate lines. In the face of this appalling slaughter their commander, Major-General Ambrose Burnside, called off the battle, despite the urging of some senior officers to carry on.

The influence of such overwhelming firepower forced rival commanders to extremes. There were those who favoured manoeuvre to outflank the enemy, while others wanted their troops to dig in behind field defences, protected by massed artillery. Confederate generals Robert E. Lee and Stonewall Jackson epitomized the manoeuvrist approach and scored some notable victories. At Chancellorsville, in May 1863, at Lee's command, Jackson's troops succeeded in taking a large Union force in the flank and turfing them out of their emplacements at bayonet point.

Barely two months later, the Civil War reached a climax at Gettysburg in a dramatic charge by Confederate troops under Major-General George E. Pickett. In a massive set-piece attack, Lee, the Confederate commander-in-chief, hoped to break a two-day deadlock and punch a hole through Union lines by launching ten brigades of infantry straight into the centre of the enemy's position. Immortalized as 'Pickett's Charge', the Confederate soldiers stormed forward across two and a half kilometres of open country, swept by fire from scores of Union guns. Miraculously, they made contact with the Union line, but reinforcements under Major-General George C. Meade counter-attacked and threw back the Confederates. Some 7,000 Confederate soldiers were killed or wounded; almost half of those who attacked were killed by Union artillery, rifles, or bayonets.

Colonial warfare saw a renaissance of the bayonet towards the end of the nineteenth century, as small units of European troops sought to subdue Africa. Here the bayonet again became a defensive weapon as outnumbered European armies sought to keep hordes of spear-carrying natives at bay by adopting tight Napoleonic-style squares. Usually, though, artillery and machine-guns were enough to win the fight, as was the case at Omdurman in 1898, when 12,000 British troops behind entrenchments killed 15,000 Sudanese tribesmen.

INTRODUCTION

When firepower was not available, however, the Europeans had to rely on their bayonets to hold back the enemy. At Isandhlwana in South Africa, on 22 January 1879, 10,000 Zulu tribesmen surrounded 1800 British troops, mainly from the 2nd Battalion, the 24th of Foot (later the South Wales Borderers) Regiment. In a fearful charge, the Zulus closed with the British and were not halted by the weight of rifle fire. The British line broke, and the battle turned into a massive mêlée in which the British soldiers used their bayonets to fight off Zulus wielding assegai (spears). In a hand-to-hand struggle the odds were against the British and only a handful of them managed to escape.

The following day a British garrison of just under a hundred men was trapped in the nearby mission station of Rorke's Drift. Time and again the Zulus charged. This time the British force held its ground. Each time the South Wales Borderers fought them off with the bayonet and disciplined rifle volleys. In the narrow, confined spaces of the mission yard, the British bayonets were more than a match for the Zulu assegai. In a day-long siege 400 Zulus were killed as against only 17 British.

British bayonets also won the day at Tel El-Kebir during the 1882 campaign to subdue a revolt in Egypt. Native troops defending a prepared position outside Cairo put up spirited resistance to the British until the Highland Brigade moved forward into the enemy redoubt. The battle swayed back and forth in huge trench lines until the Cameron, Gordon and Royal Highlanders, as well as the Highland Light Infantry, pushed the Egyptians out at bayonet point. Some 250 of the 400 British casualties were sustained by the Highlanders in the desperate fight.

In 1896 an Italian expeditionary force tried to invade Abyssinia (now Ethiopia) but met a similar fate to the British at Isandhlwana. On 1 March, 20,000 Italian troops tried to take on 90,000 Abyssinian tribesmen at Adowa. The four Italian brigades that advanced on the enemy were soon surrounded and cut to pieces. Of the Italian force, 4,500 were killed and 1600 taken prisoner.

The many wars in Mexico during the nineteenth century saw two classic bayonet actions. The insurrection by American settlers against Mexican rule in Texas in 1835 led to armed action to put down the revolt. General Antonio Lopez de Santa Anna marched into Texas with some 3,000 troops in February 1836, and laid siege to the 188-strong Texan garrison in the Alamo, San Antonio. Over a two-week period the Mexicans tried repeatedly to assault the fort, but on 6 March they finally broke in and put the surviving defenders to the bayonet.

By 1863 Mexico was temporarily under French Imperial rule, but the population was soon in revolt. A 65-strong French Foreign Legion detachment found itself trapped in a small farmhouse at Camerone on 30 April. Completely surrounded, they held off 2,000 Mexicans for ten hours until their ammunition was almost exhausted. Only five men were left unwounded. Facing their fate, these survivors formed up outside the farmhouse, fixed bayonets and charged the Mexicans. It was hopeless, but the Mexicans took three of the five prisoner after they had collapsed from their wounds. Inspired by this action, do or die bayonet charges were to become a Foreign Legion speciality.

In the final year of the century the British found themselves at war with the Dutch settlers in South Africa. Known as Boers, they were natural hunters and were armed with modern German-made repeating rifles. The British resorted to the tactics that had served them well against the Zulus and Sudanese. They formed line, fixed bayonets and charged. This proved to be a costly rerun of the experience of the American Civil War. In a series of battles, small groups of Boers perched on hilltops and picked off hundreds of British soldiers for minimal loss to themselves. The battles of Modder River, Magersfontein, Colenso, Spion Kop and Vaal Kranz all ended the same way, with hundreds of brave but badly led British troops dying as they charged forward with fixed bayonets. Firepower once again proved superior to cold steel.

In spite of its bitter experiences in the Boer War and the lessons offered up by the American Civil War, the British Army, along with its European counterparts, was still convinced that the bayonet would be the decisive infantry weapon in any future European war. These armies even drilled their infantry to form squares to defend themselves against enemy cavalry. When war eventually did break out in 1914, the realities of modern conflict would come as a shock great enough to transform not only traditional infantry tactics but also the role of the bayonet.

Bayonet Drills and Killing Skills

Bayonet fighting skills are taught in most armies during a soldier's basic training. Although some east European and east Asian armies have exotic bayonet-fighting techniques, the fundamental skills are fairly universal. On seeing the 1990 vintage British Army bayonet fighting manual, one First World War veteran commented that little had changed.

A soldier's first exposure to bayonet drills is usually in a rain-drenched training area early one morning. There will usually be four or five dummies attached to a wooden frame, known appropriately as a gallows. Some are firmly fixed to the frames, while others are hanging down on single strands of rope. A couple of dummies are also placed on the ground. The dummies are arranged in a circuit or course so the recruits have to pass them to complete the drill. Some of the gallows are fitted with swinging arms to simulate the enemy's own weapons and bayonets. To add to the realism the dummies are usually dressed in the uniforms of the enemy or possible foes. Second World War dummies, for example, invariably featured German 'coal scuttle' helmets and 'Hitler' moustaches. The dummies are stuffed with hay or, if the instructors are feeling particularly aggressive, blood and offal from a local butcher's shop. This trick is the nightmare of many recruits, who end up covered in blood and gore after their first bayonet training.

The four types of dummy are designed to train recruits in the basic weapon drills. Recruits are told that the bayonet is to be used in the final phase of an assault when it is not practical to shoot the enemy, such as when ammunition has run out, their weapon has a stoppage (a mechanical jam), or when they are too close to comrades and shooting would endanger them.

To enhance the 'demoralizing' effect on the enemy, recruits are taught to scream and shout as they make their bayonet charge. The noise is meant to confuse the enemy and also increases the recruit's adrenalin, making him more aggressive.

At the start of the drill the recruits are taught how to hold their weapons comfortably with the bayonets fixed. The basic position is called 'on guard'. The soldier is leaning slightly, with one foot in front of the other to provide balance and support forward, and the weapon is inclined slightly upwards. Weapons with pistol grips (such as the SA-80) are easy to hold in this position. The 'on guard' provides the most effective way of thrusting the weapon forward with good momentum.

At the start of the lesson the instructor, who is usually a senior non-commissioned officer, will walk the recruits through the different drills used with the various dummies. Each dummy is designed to test very distinct fighting skills. The gallows dummies are designed to simulate a standing enemy. Here the drill is to approach within one and a half metres, then continue the forward movement to provide momentum for the weapon as it is pushed into the enemy's torso.

The bayonet then needs to be quickly withdrawn. If necessary the enemy can be bayoneted again, otherwise the soldier should leave him to die and press on to the next position, maintaining the momentum of the advance. It is essential that the blade is withdrawn quickly from the enemy, otherwise he may grab the rifle or exploit a vulnerability elsewhere and perhaps attempt to stab with a knife. Only with the bayonet free is the attacker able to defend himself.

Next on the circuit is the dummy on the ground. This simulates bayoneting an enemy soldier in a trench or shell scrape. The thrust is essentially the same, but the soldier's feet must be kept clear of the enemy to prevent being tripped up or pulled down to the ground. The downward pressure can either be achieved by bending the knees and leaning over the enemy or by moving the hand from the weapon's pistol grip to the butt and pushing down. Again it is important to remove the blade quickly and this is best achieved by stamping a foot on the enemy and using it to hold him down as the weapon is pulled up. The advance must then be continued.

Two standing dummies are next placed close to one another in an exercise dealing with multiple enemies. The first enemy is attacked as per the drill, the weapon is withdrawn and returned to the 'on-guard' position. The soldier then steps forward and thrusts his bayonet into the next enemy. If the second enemy is very close to the first it may not be necessary to withdraw the weapon immediately and thrust again.

Defensive action is taught on the gallows with the swinging arm. Here the drill is to advance towards the enemy. As the enemy lunges forward, the recruit uses the rifle to parry the blow and push him off to one side. While he is recovering the soldier then quickly withdraws his weapon from the dummy and thrusts forward into the undefended chest.

This clean manoeuvre, however, may not be possible, so additional tactics are required. Here the hanging dummies are used. The soldier uses his weapon to strike the enemy on the chest and then push him away. Once stunned and falling backwards, the enemy is vulnerable to bayoneting and should be run through as the original drill. Another method is to use the rifle butt to hit the enemy in the face, and again bayonet him as he falls back.

After the instructor has walked the recruits through the basic skills, they will put on their full fighting order, fix bayonets and go through the motions. The first attempts will be at a slow speed, and then the pace will be increased until the recruits are going round the circuit at the double. Once a recruit's training in the basics of bayonet fighting is complete, the skills learnt are incorporated into other aspects of infantry training. Trench-clearing exercises using live ammunition nearly always culminate in a close-combat phase with fixed bayonets.

At the start of these exercises troops do not have their bayonets fixed. They first advance towards the simulated enemy. When the enemy opens fire on them they go to ground and return fire. First they win the fire fight, putting down aimed rounds on the enemy's trenches and bunkers with machine-guns and anti-tank rockets. The next phase is to assault the enemy trenches. The platoon commander will muster his assault troops in a covered forming-up point. Here he will swiftly give his battle orders and then issue the order 'fix bayonets'. In the confusion of battle, clear orders are essential; to emphasize the direction of the attack he will use his rifle, with bayonet attached, to point out the final objective of the assault.

The assault troops will now move forward in pairs. One soldier will put down covering fire as his comrade doubles forward for a few metres. In the final dash, one soldier will 'shoot-in' as his mate leaps into the enemy trench. Usually a grenade will herald his arrival.

Anyone in the trench who survives the grenade is then shot and bayoneted for good measure. During exercises, the simulated trench systems are occupied by dummies and the assaulting soldiers have to move through them, grenading, shooting and bayoneting any dummies they may find. Again a judicious use of butcher's waste inside the dummies can add to the realism.

While not quite the real thing, such exercises simulate the excitement, confusion and noise of battle. Most important they give soldiers the confidence to set off grenades and carry bayonets on their weapons for extended periods.

Drills such as these are usually the culmination of a period of work-up training in which different skills are taught and brought together into a coherent package. Bayonet training is only a small part, but soldiers nevertheless must be able to complete a number of different activities safely while having their bayonets fitted. Only regular practice firing rifles with bayonets attached will ensure that, come the big day, soldiers will fit the thing on their rifle properly and not lose it as soon as they jump out of their armoured personnel carrier. Early versions of the British SA-80 'socket' bayonet were also known to blast themselves down the range during firing practices if not secured properly. These are basic skills, but only the best-trained troops get them right when it counts.

Different armies regard the bayonet with varying degrees of importance. The Japanese took their bayonet training very seriously; during their invasion of China and later in the Second World War they provided live prisoners tied to stakes for their troops to practise on. This was designed to generate 'blood lust' and make them regard their enemies as 'inferior'. The Japanese bayonet tactics, however, usually failed them when they came up against opposition who were prepared to fight back. As a modern equivalent, Saddam Hussein's Republican Guard in Iraq have also been reported to use similar methods with new recruits to instil fighting spirit and loyalty to the ruling regime.

Modern Western armies now regard bayonet training more as a tactical skill and preparation for battle rather than an ideological preparation for war or political struggle. As we have seen, bayonet fighting is taught as part of an integrated package to prepare soldiers for a variety of tactical scenarios. Long gone are the days when the infantryman was taught to rely on the bayonet alone to sweep all before him – no matter what.

CHAPTER ONE

THE FIRST WORLD WAR

Port Arthur Prelude

In the decade before the First World War, the major powers were provided with the opportunity to observe the impact of modern weaponry during the 1904–5 Russo-Japanese War. It would be a nightmare vision into the future, but no one seemed to learn the lessons.

Since Japan's exposure to Western influence less than fifty years before, the island empire had begun a crash programme to prevent colonization by modernizing its society, industry and armed forces. By the end of the nineteenth century the Japanese were themselves a colonial power with interests in China and the Korean peninsula. This brought them into direct conflict with Imperial Russia, who had expanded eastwards to the Pacific.

The Japanese Army that went to war with Russia for control of Korea in 1904 was a curious mix of East and West. Its soldiers were armed with the 6.5mm magazine-loading Arisaka rifle which boasted the famous 50cm-long Japanese bayonet. Japanese artillery units fielded the finest weapons from Europe and North America, while the Japanese battleships used technology supplied by the British Royal Navy.

At the same time, the Japanese soldier was a product of his oriental culture. Martial honour was all to the Japanese men of this period. Victory or death in battle – the Bushido, or warrior code – was central to Japanese thinking. This would ensure that Japanese soldiers would die in their tens of thousands outside Port Arthur, the Russian stronghold on the Yellow Sea.

Port Arthur was a natural fortress at the end of a long peninsula, and Russian engineers constructed a series of forts on the hills approaching the port city. Each fort had concrete casements and artillery positions, but most importantly kilometres of pre-prepared trenches overlooking open fields of fire for machine-guns. Barbed-wire entanglements were spread out in front of the forts to channel attackers into killing zones, while searchlights were positioned to reveal any night attacks.

To overrun these defences, the Japanese assault tactics were far from sophisticated. Infantry regiments simply formed close column, fixed bayonets and charged the enemy. In the first probing attack on 7–8 August 1904, Japanese *élan* allowed them to seize a series of outposts for little loss. Eleven days later they tried the same tactics against the main Russian position.

In the ensuing slaughter Japanese troops managed to overwhelm one fort but lost 15,000 men in the process. On 15 September, the Japanese formed up again and tried to assault the Russian fort of 203 Metre Hill. For two weeks the Japanese charged forward. There was some hand-to-hand combat in the outer trenches, but the main position remained in Russian hands. At one point the Japanese got to within 300 metres of the Russian fort, only to be cut down in a hail of bullets and shrapnel. Japanese soldiers piled up the bodies of their comrades for protection, but whenever they rushed forward to bayonet-killing distance, the Russians opened fire once again. In all, 4,000 Japanese died in the assault. A month later the Japanese again formed up in column to attack at bayonet point. This time the attack lasted only two days before it was called off with the loss of 1,000 men.

By 26 November the Japanese had changed tactics and

brought up massive siege guns to blast the Russian defences. After a full day-long bombardment, the Japanese columns stormed forward along the length of the Russian perimeter. In this attack 12,000 men were killed in a day. The day after the slaughter, the Japanese began to concentrate their attack on 203 Metre Hill. For over a week wave after wave of Japanese stormed forward only to be cut down. Now the thousands of dead bodies in front of the Russian positions were to prove useful as they created a ramp over the barbed wire. Russian counter-attacks twice drove the Japanese back at bayonet point, but the Japanese just kept coming. Some 11,000 Japanese died. On 5 December the fort was in Japanese hands and they began to move up artillery to dominate what remained of the Russian defences and port below. On 2 January 1905 the Russian garrison was forced to surrender.

During the siege 57,780 Japanese were killed – most in suicidal bayonet charges – and 31,306 Russian defenders were killed or wounded. Western military observers were invited by the Japanese to watch the campaign, but their reports were not given much consideration in the chancelleries of Europe. White men did not fight like orientals; that at least is what conventional wisdom said.

When the Great Powers of Europe went to war in the summer of 1914 infantry tactics were at a turning point. Some enlightened officers had seen the potential of machine-guns and indirect artillery fire in the American Civil, Boer and Russo-Japanese wars. They were, however, in a minority. What tactical advances there had been had largely been aimed at improving the defensive firepower of infantry.

The Boer War had taught the British Army some important points in defensive infantry tactics, but there were still some serious lessons to be learnt. To begin with, the British now saw the benefit of setting up defensive positions with overlapping fields of fire. This meant that the area in front of a unit could be covered from two or more directions, thus preventing the enemy from approaching over dead ground or from out of line of sight. Extended lines or skirmish lines were now the norm for defensive battles; however, entrenching tools were not universally issued, so if caught in the open by an enemy, troops could not easily dig in.

While the redcoat was now a thing of the past, replaced by khaki cloth, there were still no steel helmets to protect soldiers from artillery shrapnel. Unlike the careful study given to infantry in defence, offensive operations by infantry were the subject of less clarity of thought. The pre-1914 British Army still believed that the massed bayonet charge was the way for infantry to deliver the decisive blow on the battlefield. And this idea was by no means unique among European armies of the era. British offensive action was centred around a tactical concept called 'fire and movement'. This involved the infantry gradually advancing against the enemy position in extended formation, with long-range rifle fire being used at first to help kill as many of the enemy as possible. Artillery fire over open sites, in much the same kind of direct fire role as that employed at Waterloo, would assist this softening-up process. Once a regiment had advanced to within 200 metres of the enemy, a firing line would be established to win the firefight with fifteen rounds a minute, in a so-called 'mad minute' of rapid rifle fire. The shock effect of this weight of fire at close range would soon lead to the enemy faltering. A swift bayonet charge would then finish them off.

To conduct these dramatic bayonet charges the British 'Tommy' was provided from 1902 onwards with the famous Short Magazine Lee Enfield (SMLE) rifle. By 1914 every infantryman carried the 1907 pattern sword bayonet with a 42cm-long blade, a weapon which was modelled on the Japanese Arisaka blade.

Senior British commanders recognized that a single charge

might not be enough to finish off a determined enemy, so the idea of the wave attack was born. These lines of bayonets would sweep forward one after the other until the enemy could take no more and broke. Brigadier-General Ivor Maxse, a noted British tactician of the period, went on record, saying that: 'A single line will fail; two will usually fail; three lines will sometimes fail, but four will usually succeed.' It is not surprising that the British were soon to embark upon a succession of costly headlong charges against German defences, and then attempt repeated attacks in exactly the same place.

The French had similarly fanciful ideas, basing their infantry tactics on closing to within fifty metres of the enemy and then charging home. The twenty seconds it took to charge was supposedly not enough time for the defenders to take aim and fire.

The Germans had also set their minds on massed infantry attacks, which in their way were even more anachronistic. The German idea was to press home the attack with massed columns of troops whose *élan* – combined with sheer weight of numbers – would be enough to maintain the momentum of the advance.

The need to press home attacks quickly was important to the Germans because their famous Schlieffen Plan called for rapid strategic advances to surround the French Army. However, the Germans also had the foresight to regard the machine-gun as an offensive weapon and used it in large numbers from the very start of the war.

War of Movement – 1914

The reality of war was very different from the gracious tactical drills envisaged by pre-war theorists. In August 1914 Europe was ablaze. Germany invaded Belgium in the hope of outflanking the main French Army, before turning to the Eastern Front and the Russians. Germany's Schlieffen Plan called for a rapid lunge through Belgium to reach Paris before the French could organize their defences. The small Belgian Army was quickly pushed aside by the massive German sledge-hammer. French troops and the small British Expeditionary Force (BEF) raced to head off the Germans, but soon found themselves hopelessly outnumbered. Retreat was the only option if they were not to be comprehensively defeated.

There then followed a series of rearguard actions by the BEF as it raced to keep one step ahead of the Germans. The British Army was small by continental standards, because of its reliance on long service professionals and volunteer reservists called Territorials, rather than massed units of conscripts and recalled reservists. Indeed the German Kaiser mocked its small size when he called the BEF a 'contemptible little army'. Soon, however, the Germans would come to fear their khaki-clad enemy.

The first units of the BEF to arrive were almost all regular army units, manned by professional soldiers with many years' service under their belts. They were almost all armed with the Short Magazine Lee Enfield (SMLE), which sported the 1907 pattern sword bayonet.

The infantry battalions of the BEF were the best equipped and trained units in the British Army. Each soldier was expected to fire fifteen rounds a minute from his SMLE. The fire was so rapid that in the coming battles the Germans would mistake it for machine-gun fire. When it came to hand-to-hand combat, the British also had an advantage. The officers and soldiers of the BEF had all served together for many years, so discipline and morale were very high. When an officer ordered a bayonet charge, his men would be right behind him. All the men were keen to kill as many of the enemy as possible and bring home a German *pickelhaube* helmet.

On 23 August 1914 the BEF made its first determined stand against the Germans at Nimy, just to the north of the Belgian town of Mons. The British 3rd Division took up defensive positions along the south bank of the Mons-Condé canal. The 4th Battalion, The Royal Fusiliers, held the section of the canal to the north of Nimy and to the right of them were the 4th Battalion, The Middlesex Regiment.

At 09.00 hours the Germans began a preliminary bombardment of the defences. Soon afterwards two huge columns of grey-coated Germans advanced towards the two battalions. Time and again they charged the two bridges over the canal, only to be turned back by withering British rifle fire. The Germans in response brought up their machine-guns and artillery to open the way for a bayonet charge, but their efforts were to no avail. To the west of the town in the village of Tertre, the German 12th Brandenburg Grenadiers charged the Royal West Kent Regiment. More than 500 were cut down without even getting near the British defenders.

The British line held and there was no clash of cold steel at Mons.

By late afternoon, with casualties mounting from artillery and machine-gun fire, the British broke contact from the Germans and retreated to the south. More than 5,000 Germans had been killed or wounded in their attempt to get close to bayonet-fighting range.

The following day at Elouges, the British 5th Division, in the face of the German IV Corps, was not to be so lucky. After a heroic but disastrous British cavalry charge against the advancing Germans, the British started to pull back. The order, unfortunately, did not get through to the 1st Battalion, The Cheshire Regiment. They kept an entire enemy division at bay with their superb rifle fire until the Germans brought up a machine-gun. In response, the Cheshires' own machine-gun returned fire and a sergeant and ten men charged forward with fixed bayonets to clear out the remaining enemy. They were only to win a brief respite. Soon the Cheshires' colonel was killed and the battalion was being split up into small groups, which were slowly being pushed back. To cover the withdrawal, three captains mustered fifty men from A and B Companies for a 'forlorn hope' bayonet charge. The charge, just after 17.30, so surprised the enemy that they were temporarily stopped in their tracks. However, the German advance soon began again, and by nightfall the Cheshires were out of ammunition. It was then that those left alive decided to surrender. In the battle more than 800 men of the Cheshires had been killed, wounded, or captured.

On 26 August, Lieutenant-General Smith Dorrien, commander of the British II Corps, controversially decided to stand and fight at Le Cateau in northern France. The action was to be a repeat on a larger scale of Mons and Elouges. Both the British and Germans deployed in lines and columns respectively, and had field guns forward with their infantry. It could have been Waterloo. The Germans charged forward and were slaughtered by the thousand, but the British withdrew when the enemy's superior numbers began to tell. The Germans had been dealt a bloody blow and they were unable to pursue with any vigour. The BEF would live to fight another day.

The fate of the 2nd Battalion, The King's Own Yorkshire Light Infantry, encapsulates the bitter fighting at Le Cateau. During the morning the battalion was bombarded by German artillery fire, and then just after 13.00 two battalions of enemy troops advanced in column, with fixed bayonets, towards the Yorkshiremen. They held their fire until the enemy were within 600 metres and then let loose a massive rifle volley. Hundreds of Germans were cut down and the rest fled.

For the rest of the afternoon the battle degenerated into a raging firefight. Scores of men were cut down by machine-guns and shell fire because the troops had not had time to dig in properly. A general order to withdraw was issued, but never reached the Yorkshiremen, who were soon surrounded on three sides by Germans. Ammunition was now almost exhausted and British fire was beginning to falter. Now the Germans surged forward. Major Charles Yates ordered the nineteen surviving men of his company to 'fix bayonets' and charge out of their improvised trenches towards the Germans. All of them were either killed or wounded. It was a brave but futile effort. The battalion was just overwhelmed. Those the Germans did not kill were kicked and punched to the ground and stripped of their weapons. Some 290 men were killed and 310 captured, of whom 170 were wounded. For his bravery, Major Yates was awarded the Victoria Cross, but he was later to die during an escape attempt from a German POW camp.

With the Germans no longer snapping at their heels, the British were able to withdraw southwards and move into a blocking position with the French to defend Paris. Soon British bayonets would be in action in large numbers.

On 1 September, the brigades of the British 2nd Division were carrying out a leapfrog retreat to the north of Villers-Cotterets. There was no sign of the enemy, so the brigades stood rearguard in turn to cover the withdrawal of their comrades. Just after dawn, the five-battalion-strong Guards Brigade was using the cover of the morning mist to withdraw into a huge forest, when German artillery started to bombard its positions. Soon large columns of Colonel-General Alexander von Kluck's 1st Army appeared on the ridge line across the valley.

The 3rd Battalion, The Coldstream Guards, took up positions to the left, the 1st Battalion, The Irish Guards, and 2nd Battalion, The Coldstream Guards, were in the centre, slightly forward, while 2nd Battalion, The Grenadier Guards, were on the right. The wood was a far from ideal defensive position; it was dark with a thick plantation of trees, and the only way to move through it was along straight rides or firebreaks. The brigade's main defensive position was astride a straight path through the forest, with groups of riflemen covering the rides facing in the direction of the enemy. The Irish Guards and 2nd Coldstream fell back in good order as the Germans appeared and took up reserve positions. The main action now began as the Germans crept forward through the woods towards the 3rd Coldstream. Hundreds of Germans were within a few metres of the Guardsmen, trading fire and setting up machine-guns. Trees were being sliced apart by the weight of fire. It was a flanking movement, and it would be only a matter of time before the Germans would be behind the Coldstream Guards.

Watching this action from a few hundred metres away, the Grenadiers saved the day when their No.4 Company were ordered to fix bayonets and charge the Germans from behind. Major George Cecil drew his sword, and, shouting at the top of his voice, led his men forward in a mad dash that took the Germans by surprise. He managed to stab and slash several Germans before he was machine-gunned. His men bayoneted scores of Germans, who fled the scene in confusion. The charge of the Grenadiers turned the tide of the battle and the brigade was soon able to break clear of the wood and retreat southwards. The German regiments were hopelessly dis-organized by the bayonet charge, and spent the rest of the day trying to rally their confused and demoralized troops.

By October the crisis for Paris had passed. Von Kluck's troops had been defeated by the French on the Marne. The Germans now turned their attention to Flanders, where they aimed to capture the Channel ports to cut off the BEF from its supplies. This move resulted in the so-called 'Race for the Sea', with the British and Germans manoeuvring troops in attempts to head each other off. The two armies clashed at the Belgian border town of Ypres, or 'Wipers' as it would be known to the thousands of British soldiers who would fight there over the next four years. German casualties over the previous ten weeks had been horrendous, and they were relying increasingly on recalled units manned by reservists, or volunteers who had joined up on the wave of patriotic fervour that had followed the outbreak of war. Formed only on 16 August, the Volunteer Reserve Corps was made up largely of young seventeen- and eighteen-year-old students from Germany's great universities. The brigades and divisions were each formed by students from the same universities. In October 1914 they spearheaded the 'Race for the Sea' and soon clashed with the veterans of the BEF at Ypres.

This was a brutal battle as each side sent battalion after battalion into murderous artillery and machine-gun fire. In the third week of October the battle swayed back and forth around Polygon Wood. Eventually German numbers began to tell and the British line was breached. A counter-attack was ordered on 24 October and the 2nd Battalion, The Worcestershire Regiment, was given the job. Its colonel had long since been put out of action and the battalion was under the command of a Major Hankey. There were still pockets of British soldiers holding out in and around the wood so the major decided not to go in firing. They would instead go in with the bayonet: 'cold remorseless steel' was the battle cry of the Worcesters. Major Hankey formed up his men in the open a few hundred metres from the wood. With his sword drawn he gave the order to charge, and the battalion moved forward at the trot. Before long they were running and cheering. The German student soldiers heard them coming but they held their ground to await the British.

Within minutes the Worcesters were in the wood, bayoneting the Germans without mercy, even though some of the unshaven and haggard old sweats of the BEF clearly felt some sympathy for the fresh-faced youngsters they found. Under the ferocity of the attack, the Germans broke and fled, and the Worcesters charged after them, still cheering and shouting. At the far end of the wood the German reserves were waiting and met the Worcesters with a hail of machine-gun fire, stopping them in their tracks. Major Hankey's men now dug in to hold the wood and bring up their own machine-guns. They had saved the British line but at a cost of 200 casualties.

Rather than adopt conscription to provide the manpower for its army, the British adopted a system of volunteer soldiering. Farmers, factory workers, bank clerks, dockers, teachers and lawyers all signed up to train as soldiers at week-ends, in what became known after 1908 as the Territorial Force or Army. One particular unit, the London Scottish, were a Territorial battalion formed from Scotsmen resident in the capital. They were one of the first British units to cross the Channel to support the BEF, but it was not until October that they had sight of the hated 'Boche'. On 31 October 1914, Hallowe'en night, they were to be the first Territorial infantry regiment to go into action: the deficiencies of their rifles meant it was to be at bayonet point.

German pressure on Ypres had continued during the remainder of October and their push to the south of the city was threatening to break through near Messines Ridge. Unit after unit was thrown in to hold the line. Finally it was the turn of Lieutenant-Colonel G. A. Malcolm's London Scottish to hold the Germans. The British line was in a state of confusion, with orders and counter-orders being issued, so when the London Scottish got into position to advance they had little idea of where the enemy was or what they were supposed to do. They saw a flanking unit apparently moving forward to engage the enemy and immediately followed suit, fixing bayonets and charging up the ridge in close formation. Some men got so carried away they charged over the crest and on towards the Germans on the other side. Now disaster struck.

Over half the battalion's rifles jammed when a newly modified magazine spring refused to feed in bullets. The battalion was reduced to manually loading each round, and in the firefight a third of the part-time soldiers were killed or wounded.

As darkness fell the remnants of the London Scottish cowered in a series of shallow trenches. There was bright moonlight, which gave the battlefield a ghostly feel. Then at 22.30 the Germans began to march forward. They came at a slow deliberate pace with a band playing 'Deutschland über Alles'. For three hours the London Scottish turned them back, but by now the weight of their fire was diminishing as more rifles jammed. Just after 02.00 the German 21st RIR and 122nd Fusilier Regiments came forward again. The attack was again repulsed and Colonel Malcolm decided to counter-attack. 'We're charging! Get ready to join in,' he shouted. His men rose out of their trenches with bayonets fixed and pushed forward, just as the Germans themselves were putting in a new attack. Hundreds of men clashed bayonets in the moonlight. For several hours the fight swayed back and forth along the top of the crest line. In the confusion a haystack caught fire. It was a scene from hell that few would forget. The London Scottish eventually were ordered back and the Germans were too weak to pursue. The bodies of several hundred British and German soldiers were strewn over the ridge, one of the dead being the battalion's medical officer, Captain MacNab, who had been bayoneted to death by a Bavarian soldier while attending to a wounded soldier. Only 300 soldiers of the London Scottish answered the roll call the following morning.

Earlier on 31 October the Germans piled on the pressure to the north of Ypres, again pushing in the British line near Polygon Wood. The Germans were streaming forward in columns towards the British 5th Brigade. Accurate rifle fire picked off German officers and the attack bogged down in front of the British position. Brigadier-General Bulfin quickly organized a counter-attack, after a 'mad minute' of rapid fire. Six British battalions were to attack, including the 2nd Battalion, The Gordon Highlanders; 2nd Battalion, The Oxfordshire and Buckinghamshire (Oxon and Bucks) Light Infantry; 1st Battalion, The Northamptonshire Regiment; 2nd Battalion, The Royal Sussex Regiment; and dismounted cavalrymen of The Royal Dragoons.

The rifle fire stunned the Germans and within minutes several hundred British soldiers were on top of the German positions, bayoneting left and right. The Germans fled in chaos. Hundreds of enemy were killed and the 5th Brigade swept forward for 800 metres. The Oxon and Bucks Light Infantry suffered nine dead and thirty-six wounded. This success stabilized the front for a few precious days.

German pressure, however, was soon growing again, and it reached a climax on 11 November when the 17,500-strong Prussian Guard Corps – 25 battalions – formed on either side of the Menin road, outside Ypres. Only some 7,850 worn-out and tired British Tommies waited to meet them, with fewer than 2,000 held in reserve behind the line.

After a massive artillery bombardment the Prussian Guards steamrollered forward at 09.00, bayoneting the defenders of Verbeck Farm. By midday the German 1st and 3rd Guards Foot Regiments, and the 2nd Guard Grenadiers, under the command of Prince Eitel Friedrich of Prussia, were firmly established in Nonnebosschen and Polygon woods. All seemed lost.

The only thing that stood between the Prussian Guards and the British corps headquarters was a single under-strength infantry battalion, plus the disorganized remnants of several engineer and administrative troops who had been scraped together to plug the gap. Lieutenant-Colonel H.R. Davies of the Oxon and Bucks Light Infantry formed up his 300 men on the western edge of Polygon Wood to attack the Germans in the flank. Two British artillery batteries were brought up and blasted the Germans, while the two lead companies of the Light Infantry moved forward to join the attack just after 14.00. Small groups of other British soldiers cowering in trenches nearby, seeing the advance, joined the movement. Some 600 men were now charging forward with fixed bayonets into the elite of the German Army. The Prussian Guards did not know what hit them. A Company under Captain Dillon was first into the enemy, with B Company close behind. The two companies then swept forward in extended line through the wood.

The officers dispatched any Guardsmen they saw hiding in the undergrowth with pistol shots. The soldiers bayoneted any Germans they found. Sergeant Tom Hudson shouted biblical quotes as he sent Germans to their maker. Those that were not bayoneted or captured fled out of the woods, where they were gunned down by other British troops on the flanks. Hundreds of Germans were taken prisoner.

The charge broke the back of the German offensive, and the plan to punch through to the Channel was dropped. Trench warfare had begun. Both sides were now exhausted and reverted to digging into defensive trench systems and rebuilding their shattered armies.

The Oxon and Bucks Light Infantry were justifiably proud of their part in defeating the Prussian Guard, likening the feat to their role in halting Napoleon's Imperial Guard at Waterloo a century before. The defeat of the Prussian Guard was perhaps the last decisive bayonet charge of the First World War. The bayonet fighting of 1914 would not be repeated, in spite of the wishes of senior commanders.

BAYONET BATTLE

1915 – Nemesis of the Bayonet Charge

The spring of 1915 saw the Allied High Command in France convinced that offensive action on the Western Front would achieve a decisive breakthrough and hence the defeat of the German Empire. 'Just one more push' was the clarion call. The British and French armies would take the war to the Germans in a series of coordinated offensives involving massive artillery barrages. The infantry would then go in with fixed bayonets to finish off any remaining enemy.

Unfortunately the Germans were not going to oblige the Allies by repeating the mistakes of 1914. They dug deep bunkers to protect their soldiers from Allied artillery, strung huge barbed-wire entanglements to delay enemy infantry, brought up hundreds of machine-guns to sweep no man's land, and positioned artillery observers to overlook their front line ready to call down fire on any threatening Allied movements.

In the British and French armies, the 'myth of the bayonet' still ruled. Offensive tactics were rigid and flawed. Artillery was to blast enemy positions for hours, destroying bunkers and flattening wire. Then the infantry were to rise out of their trenches and walk briskly – not run – towards the enemy lines. There was to be no ducking or diving into shell holes for cover or returning fire. This would just break up the line, slow down the advance and increase the time the infantry would spend in no man's land. Breaking formation to take cover was in fact made a court martial offence. As long as the infantry kept advancing it was taken for granted that enemy morale would falter, his fire would fall away and he would flee. If the first attack didn't work, then a second, third and even fourth wave would be sent 'over the top'. It would be Polygon Wood all over again. 'The Boche have no backbone,' or so the red-tabbed staff officers at GHQ said. The British Army's Manual of Bayonet Training stated:

The bayonet is essentially an offensive weapon. In a bayonet assault all ranks go forward to kill or be killed, and only those who have developed skill and strength by constant training will be able to kill. The spirit of the bayonet must be inculcated into all ranks, so that they go forward with the aggressive determination and confidence of superiority born of continued practice, without which a bayonet charge will not be effective.

By March 1915 the worst of the winter weather had passed and the campaign season had begun in earnest. On 10 March the British launched their first major offensive of the war to crush the German salient at Neuve Chapelle. This was to set the precedent for the remainder of the year. In total, forty-eight infantry battalions were mustered for the attack against what was termed a 'weakly held' sector of the German front line.

Along the southern flank of the salient, the 25th Brigade's artillery support did indeed blast the enemy bunkers as predicted, and its battalions sliced through the German line almost unopposed. There was no serious fighting during this lightning advance, in which only a few dozen soldiers were killed, and the attack achieved a breakthrough into the undefended German rear area. Unfortunately they received orders to halt and wait for flanking units to catch up. This was when disaster struck.

Along the northern flank, the artillery preparation was nowhere near as succesful, and the Germans were ready for the British. The 2nd Battalion, The Middlesex Regiment, went over the top in three successive waves with bayonets fixed. Morale was high at the prospect of getting at the enemy; but neither morale nor bayonet would do them any good. Nearly a thousand were killed or wounded in no man's land, cut down by machine-guns and artillery. Of those who did make it back, not a single soldier was left unwounded.

The neighbouring unit, the 2nd Battalion, The Scottish

Rifles, went over the top at about the same time. They suffered a similar fate. More than 90 per cent of the battalion were killed or wounded. Their commanding officer was killed as he attempted to rally his men in no man's land. Two more battalions were sent in behind the Scottish Rifles and were also cut down.

Supporting the advance was the Indian Corps; its Gharwali Rifles lost all its British officers in the opening few minutes of the advance. The attack bogged down quickly. More infantry were ordered forward overnight, ready to press home the attack in the morning. Confusion reigned and it was not until midday that the first orders were sent out to units. The 1st Battalion, The Worcestershire Regiment, arrived in a front-line trench occupied by the survivors of the previous day's slaughter. The colonel of the regiment in the trenches refused to join the Worcesters in their attack, saying any advance would get no further than twenty metres. The first two companies of the Worcesters went over the top and were all killed within minutes. Further attacks went in the following day with the same result. It was now the Germans' turn to attack. They were not, however, going to repeat the mistakes of the British, and to carry their attack through deployed a new secret weapon – chlorine gas. French troops holding the northern shoulder of the Ypres salient were the target of the German experiment, which got under way during the afternoon of 22 April 1915. Some 15,000 French troops were doused in the poison gas and fled, while 5,000 died painful and lingering deaths. Another 5,000 surrendered to the advancing Germans.

British and Canadian troops were ordered to turn back the German advance along a string of low hills known as 'Mauser Ridge'. The Germans had a small outpost occupying 'Kitchener's Wood' on its northern end.

In the early hours of 23 April, in its first offensive action of the war, the 3rd Canadian Brigade moved out to counter-attack, bayonets glinting in the light of flares fired into the pre-dawn by alert German sentries. A few hundred metres from the wood the Germans spotted the Canadians and opened fire. The Canadians charged forward. Hundreds were mown down, but they reached the wood and chased out the small German contingent. Half the Canadians had been killed or wounded.

The battles of the 10th Canadian Battalion that night were particularly violent and bloody. It was forced to rely on the bayonet during its action because the Canadian Mark III Ross rifles had been made inoperable by encrusted mud and dirt. Just before midnight on the 23rd, the 1000-strong battalion formed up for their three-wave attack. They got to within 200 metres of the Germans undetected when they ran into a thick hedge threaded with barbed wire. As they tried to chop through it, the Germans heard the noise and opened fire. Now the Canadians surged forward in a hail of bullets. Hundreds died before they got into the enemy trenches and started bayoneting, kicking, punching and grenading. In less than ten minutes the position was captured and two German battalions routed. The Canadians now held their positions during a night of shelling, but by dawn less than 300 men were fit for action.

All through the night the British had been trying to bring up their reserves. The high command was in a state of confusion, and no one was sure where the Germans were or what the French were doing in their sector. Troops marched and countermarched all night. They were not fed or watered and had no protection against the German gas.

To bring some order to the battlefield, a scratch brigade of 4,000 men under Colonel A. D. Geddes of the 2nd Battalion, The Buffs (East Kent Regiment), was mustered behind Hill Top Ridge opposite Mauser Ridge. Colonel Geddes formed his battalions in long lines behind the shelter of the hill crest and at 05.30 on 23 April sent them forward one at a time. As dawn broke The Buffs, the 3rd Battalion, The Middlesex, 5th Battalion King's Own (Royal Lancaster) and 1st Battalion, The York & Lancaster Regiments, all took their turn to charge the Germans. There was no artillery support of any consequence, and the attacks soon stalled. As soon as they moved into the open the battalions were mown down by German machine-guns. A few score survivors got to within a hundred metres of the German front, but were pinned down in shell holes with no food or water. They then made a terrifying dash back to British lines only to find their battalions had ceased to exist.

Another attack was ordered by the BEF's commander-in-chief Sir John French. This time the 13th Brigade under Brigadier-General Wanless O'Gowan was ordered forward. It boasted five infantry battalions – 5,000 men – all long-service regulars or Territorial veterans of 1914. This time an artillery barrage would support the attack. Unfortunately, the troops were delayed in getting to their forming-up points and so 'Zero Hour' was put back from the planned 15.00 to 16.25. But no one, though, could get the message through to the artillery, which on schedule fired its barrage. When the delayed attack did go in, there was no ammunition left to support it.

Each of the attacking battalions was given 500 metres in which to form up. The 2nd Battalion, The King's Own Scottish Borderers; 1st Battalion, The Royal West Kents; 2nd Battalion, The Duke of Wellington's; 2nd Battalion, King's Own Yorkshire Light Infantry; and 9th Battalion, The London Regiment, all formed up abreast, in six lines. They moved forward at a slow deliberate pace over the debris left from the morning's ill-fated attack. Adding to the gloom of the day were the large numbers of gas casualties still littering the battlefield and the brigade's approach route. When the officers blew their whistles to open the attack, their men had

38

only a few minutes before they were within machine-gun range. The first two lines were killed to a man. The following waves passed through them and got close to the German outpost line before being brought to a halt by machine-gun fire and a well-directed artillery bombardment. By 19.00 the attack had run its course and 3,000 men lay dead. They had never even got close to crossing cold steel with the 'Boche'.

On the 24th the Germans tried to extend their position on Mauser Ridge, hitting the badly depleted Canadian units hard. Three times they charged the 10th Canadian Battalion, now under 200 men strong, but each time they were driven back after hand-to-hand fighting. The Ross rifles continued to fail, so the Canadians could not stop the Germans with firepower – only bayonets.

In the early hours of 25 April the British 10th Brigade under Brigadier-General Hull was ordered forward into the Ypres Salient to do the job the previous attacks had failed at. The same mistakes dogged this attack. The troops were late and the artillery were unable to coordinate their fire plan. Watching staff officers were suitably impressed by the drill of the troops as they formed up to advance across the hellish no man's land. In the two hours of the attack, no ground was recaptured and 73 officers and 2,346 other ranks were killed without coming anywhere near the enemy.

The following day, Sir John French ordered the Indian Corps's Lahore Division and the British Territorial 149th (Northumberland) Brigade forward to attack Mauser Ridge again. This time 15,000 troops would surge forward over the same ground to break the ever-strengthening front of the German 27th (Reserve) Corps. The result was the same: thousands of British and Indian soldiers were killed, but as the assault came to a halt on the German wire the enemy responded immediately with a gas attack. Small groups of troops still cowered in shell holes and ruined buildings as surviving officers and sergeants tried to rally them together. Here and there *ad hoc* units made determined charges to gain a few more metres of territory while dodging the rain of machine-gun fire from the German lines. Then the gas was released from cylinders at the western edge of the German position. It wafted over the battlefield in a thick cloud, poisoning hundreds of men in its path. Faced with all this, the Lahore Division broke and ran.

The 149th Brigade fared even worse. It was supposed to advance alongside the remnants of Hull's brigade. Its commander refused to budge out of his trench, telling Brigadier-General Riddell that to advance was futile. Riddell led his brigade over the top at 15.40 and within a few minutes his entire brigade was shot to bits. For the rest of that night the survivors spent their time pinned down in no man's land and only escaped back to safety the following afternoon. In just a day it had lost nearly 2,000 men or two-thirds of its strength.

The Second Battle of Ypres was over. During the ten-day period some 2,150 officers and 57,125 other ranks were casualties in a futile attempt to push the Germans back. The British troops showed admirable courage, but the bullet was proving to be more powerful than the bayonet.

In May 1915 the British opened their second major offensive of the year with the aim of capturing the Aubers Ridge to the south of Ypres. A thirty-minute artillery barrage was supposed to destroy the German wire and bunkers. As the bombardment progressed, however, the British assault troops watched the results through their periscopes with horror – it barely caused a scratch, and within minutes they were to go over the top.

At 05.30 hours on 9 May the Indian Dehra Dun Brigade walked forward in neat lines and were scythed down. Its Seaforth Highlander and Gurkha battalions could only advance a few metres before hundreds of men dived for cover back in the trenches. All the officers of the Seaforths were killed as they stood on the trench parapet trying to get their men to restart the attack. Some of the Gurkhas did make it to the German trench and a small group fought their way through with bayonets and kukri knives. The German 57th Regiment killed them all.

Along the line, the 1st Battalion, The Northamptonshire, and 2nd Battalion, The Royal Sussex Regiments were wiped out within minutes of going over the top, suffering more than a thousand casualties. Small groups pressed forward and only twenty Northamptonshire soldiers made it into the German lines, where they set to bayonet fighting with the enemy. The Munster Fusiliers were the most successful British unit. The commanding officer led them through the machine-gun fire to the German wire, where he was killed. A few dozen men made it through the wire into the German trenches, but the enemy brought up more machine-guns to sweep no man's land and successfully prevented any reinforcements exploiting the success.

Another artillery barrage was ordered for 07.00 and the Munsters' few remaining officers were ordered to lead their men forward again. This bombardment only served to kill more of the British wounded who were lying helpless in no man's land. The second attack got nowhere. On the northern flank of the offensive, the British attack was equally unsuccessful. The 1/13th London Regiment, aided by a 2,000lb mine exploded under the German line, was able to make a major breakthrough, but its flanking moves were soon bogged down. Flanking fire swept no man's land and prevented reinforcements exploiting the success. An hour after 'Zero Hour', the 2nd Battalion, The Lincolnshire Regiment, succeeded in making its way through no man's land to help the Londons. For twenty minutes they fought hand-to-hand with the German defenders as they spread out through the winding trench system. Acting Corporal C. Sharpe won himself a Victoria Cross as he led a 250-metre advance along a communication trench to link up with the Londons.

Another push was ordered by the British high command late in the morning, to be undertaken by three battalions from the Queen's and Middlesex Regiments. By 14.00, 2,000 men were dead for the gain of not a metre of ground. Two hours later a further attack was ordered, and the Black Watch went forward to the sound of bagpipes. Hundreds of them were cut down, but fifty men made it into the German trenches. Corporal J. Ripley and Lance Corporal D. Finlay both won Victoria Crosses in the confused bayonet fighting that lasted for an hour, until the brave Highlanders were almost all killed or captured.

This fate awaited the other British soldiers who had made their way into the German line. By the following morning all had been driven out or killed. Just under 12,000 British soldiers had been killed or wounded in a single day's fighting.

During the summer the British regrouped and prepared to have another go at the Germans. This time their attack was preceded by a massive poison gas cloud. The wind was far from favourable, and so the German defenders did not receive a major dousing. As a result, they put up stiff resistance when, at 06.30 on 25 September 1915, the British advance began. The Scottish regiments of the 15th (Scottish) Division, through heavy fire, pressed home their attack to the swirling sound of bagpipes. The 7th Battalion, The King's Own Scottish Borderers, was to spearhead the charge of Loos village.

At 'Zero Hour', the battalion's trenches were swept by enemy fire and gas was making many men skulk under cover. Piper D. Laidlaw immediately climbed on to the parapet of the trench to play 'Scotland the Brave'. His example got his comrades' blood up and within minutes they were out of the trenches and among the Germans. The piper was awarded the

Victoria Cross for his leadership and bravery. The battalion stormed into the village and had destroyed the German garrison by 08.00. An observer called it 'a magnificent spectacle'. Most of the senior officers had become casualties by this time, and it fell to a few subalterns to lead the attack onwards and take a German redoubt behind the village on Hill 70. They took the position at bayonet-point but by the afternoon it was back in German hands. Five more counter-attacks by the 46th Brigade, led by its most senior surviving officer – a second lieutenant – failed to dislodge the Germans.

The 15th Division had lost nearly 5,400 men or 60 per cent of its strength. Lieutenant-Colonel A. Douglas-Hamilton, commanding officer of the 6th Battalion, The Queen's Own Cameron Highlanders, won the Victoria Cross for leading four bayonet charges against Hill 70.

The neighbouring 1st Division had mixed fortunes. Its 2nd Brigade was wiped out going over the top, making no headway, while the 1st Brigade fared better. The 10th Battalion, The Gloucestershire Regiment, led the advance and stormed deep into the German trench complex. In the first two hours of the attack they fought hand-to-hand with German defenders, using bayonets, rifles, spades and hand grenades. Only sixty men were left alive by 09.00. Their success opened the way for supporting battalions, from the Cameron Highlanders and Royal Berkshire Regiment to advance deep into the enemy rear.

Now the British high command fatally miscalculated. Instead of reinforcing the successful 1st Brigade, the 1st Division reserve brigade was sent in after the doomed 2nd Brigade. The reserves went over the top across the corpses of the 1st Brigade. They got no further. A German counter-attack mopped up the defenders and forced several regiments to surrender.

The scene was now set for the most disastrous attack of the

1915 campaign. The 21st and 24th British Divisions were ordered forward finally to punch a hole in the German line. These 10,000 men were all volunteers who had signed up in August 1914. During the night of 25/26 September they made their way forward through the chaos left by the earlier attacks. At 10.00 a brief artillery barrage was opened, though the gunners had little idea where the Germans actually were. An hour later the two divisions formed up in twelve massive columns and started to advance at a steady walk, led by officers on horseback. The Germans initially held their fire as they tried to make out what was happening. Once the columns were in machine-gun range, however, the Germans let rip with everything they had. Machine-guns and artillery scythed into the columns. Five times the British tried to charge forward and each time they were driven back from the German wire. Every charge ended in failure. In three hours it was all over. The Germans were so sickened by the slaughter that they held their fire as thousands of wounded men crawled back to British lines, and stretcher-bearers tried to bring back their comrades.

The two divisions had been wiped out, leaving 385 officers and 7,881 other ranks dead or wounded. There were no German casualties at all that day. The Loos offensive was effectively over, and with it British hopes for decisive victory on the Western Front in 1915. The bayonet charges of the British infantry clearly demonstrated the bravery and discipline of the Tommies, but also their generals' totally foolhardy tactics.

Gallipoli – The Charge from the Sea

As the Allied offensives on the Western Front were smashing themselves against the rock of the German defences, senior members of the British leadership advocated an alternative to trench warfare. Led by the maverick First Lord of the

Admiralty, Winston Churchill, and supported by the Minister of State for War, Field Marshal Lord Kitchener, these so-called 'easterners' proposed that a new front be opened in the Balkans to knock Germany's ally Turkey out of the war. Britain could then launch a new war of manoeuvre to march on Germany from the south.

This offensive was to be spearheaded by an amphibious landing in the Gallipoli peninsula, south of the Turkish capital Constantinople, to seize control of the Dardanelles. This narrow channel ultimately led into the Bosporus and would provide the Allies with a sea route to Russian ports in the Black Sea. Some 75,000 Allied troops were mustered in Egypt for the operation, including British Regulars and Territorials, French conscripts and colonial troops, British-officered Indian Army battalions and Gurkha regiments. The landings would be made famous by the first involvement of the Australian and New Zealand Army Corps or Anzac. The Anzac was set up in Egypt in 1915 to command units arriving from Australia and New Zealand. There would eventually be two Anzac corps, which would later serve on the Western Front. The name Anzac however became a common nickname for Australian and New Zealand soldiers in both world wars, although the Australians also liked to be known as 'Diggers'.

These fiery volunteers from the southern hemisphere, who joined up to serve King and Empire in 1914, were keen to prove that they were 'bonny fighters'. The Australians in particular wanted to prove their new country was on a par with the old country. The 'Diggers' lacked the discipline and deference to authority of the British Tommy but were almost all young, fit, healthy and used to hardship. During the Gallipoli campaign the brave but ill-trained Anzac force would hold out for almost nine months in the face of fanatical Turkish resistance. Hand-to-hand fighting would be an almost daily occurrence, with bayonet combat taking place regularly, terrifying the troops who had to participate in it. There were even cases of 'bayonet psychosis', in which victims would be traumatized by battle memories, thinking they were still in a death grip with a bayoneted Turk.

Unlike the Canadians, who were armed with the unreliable Ross rifle, the Australians wisely chose to be armed with versions of the British Short Magazine Lee Enfield (SMLE), made at the small arms factory in Lithgow, New South Wales. The bayonet used was an exact copy of the British issue 1907 pattern sword bayonet, which boasted a 42cm-long blade.

The first landing took place on 25 April 1915 with the British making for the southern beaches around Cape Helles, while the Anzac troops went ashore to the north near Ari Burnu. This area was soon dubbed 'Anzac Cove'. The landing was a disaster from the beginning to the end. Some troops landed unopposed but sat around on the beaches waiting for orders, while others went ashore opposite alerted Turkish defences and suffered terrible casualties.

The 1st Australian Division's 2nd Brigade was the first unit to cross bayonets with the Turkish defenders. The rocky terrain above the beaches was criss-crossed with narrow streams, stone walls and deep valleys, and any attempt to move in large formations was doomed to failure. The battle soon bogged down into a series of small skirmishes between handfuls of soldiers. The 'Diggers' excelled at this sort of fighting, but it was slow work and this favoured the Turks, who quickly garrisoned the high ground overlooking the beachhead. They would never be dislodged from these positions. The defenders were fighting to protect their homeland from infidel invaders. According to their commander Mustafa Kemal, 'Everyone hurled himself on the enemy to kill and to die. This was no ordinary attack. Everyone in this attack was eager to go forward to succeed or go forward with determination to die.' Five times the Turks charged against the Australians and New

Zealanders that day, and each time after bitter bayonet fighting they were stopped.

On the five British landing beaches there was pandemonium. The Turkish defences were right on the shoreline and their machine-gunners wrought terrible havoc on the trawlers, barges and small boats that were bringing in the troops. Turks were firing down on the British from clifftop positions. Royal Navy landing parties and British infantry from the Lancashire Fusiliers and South Wales Borderers charged up the beach and put small groups of defenders to the bayonet. Eleven Victoria Crosses were won that morning. Then the Turkish reserves arrived to counter-attack.

At midday the 1st Battalion, The Border Regiment, was ordered forward with bayonets fixed. For nearly 600 metres they charged, driving back the Turks. The 4th Battalion, The Worcestershire Regiment, pushed forward and staged a dramatic frontal attack on the Turkish fort at Guezji Baba. Rows of Worcesters advanced at a deliberate pace, storming through the wire and putting the defenders to the bayonet.

At nightfall, more Turkish reserves arrived and were sent straight into battle. The 1st Battalion, The King's Own Scottish Borderers, defending Y Beach on the eastern edge of Cape Helles, was on the receiving end of a fearful charge by the Turkish 25th and 26th Regiments. The Turks were supported by accurate artillery and machine-gun fire, possibly helped by the bright moonlight. Wave after wave swept forward to be met by accurate rifle fire. Eventually the wave washed over the British improvised trench line. Turks tried to bayonet the Scotsmen in their trenches below. Then the Turks surged forward against the Royal Marine Light Infantry. Hand-to-hand fighting went on throughout the night. It seemed as if the whole of Y Beach would be overwhelmed. By 09.00 on 26 April the battle had worn itself out. The beachhead was surrounded by thousands of dead and wounded men, and the British were withdrawn to the main bridgehead by the afternoon.

Over the next two days the British built up their forces and supplies in preparation for a break-out of the bridgehead. Their objective was to seize the strategically important high ground that dominated the Dardanelles. The first battle of Krithia ended in a costly failure when the three advancing brigades ran into heavy Turkish machine-gun fire. Then a Turkish regiment counter-attacked, charging across open terrain with bayonets fixed. In spite of heavy fire they kept coming. They got to within 200 metres of the British line when HMS *Queen Elizabeth*, sailing close offshore, trained her 15in guns on the Turks. A salvo of the massive shells stopped the attack, scattering body parts among the British troops nearby.

The Australians and New Zealanders were on the receiving end of equally fierce Turkish attacks in the days after their landings. Swarms of Turks crawled forward towards the Anzac beachhead on 26 April to be met by a non-stop barrage of shrapnel from the Royal Navy battleships offshore. In one attack, the Turks got to within a few hundred metres of the beachhead where they started to snipe at the defenders. There was only one answer. The New Zealand Canterbury Battalion fixed bayonets and charged time and time again to chase off the Turks.

In the chaos of the first landings, the Anzac battalions had become intermingled, and the constant Turkish counter-attacks meant small groups of leaderless Australians and New Zealanders just attached themselves to whichever unit was killing Turks in their part of the bridgehead. The Anzacs only wanted to get a crack at the enemy.

On the left of the beachhead, Lieutenant Colonel George Braund, of the 2nd Australian Battalion, gathered a mixed group of several hundred Australians and New Zealanders to hold his sector. They had great sport killing Turks and on 27 April he led them forward in a spoiling attack towards the Baby 700 hill feature. When the Turks massed for a counter-attack, Braund decided to meet force with force and led his desperate band of followers forward in a bayonet charge. It was touch and go for a while but Braund's men won the day and the Turks fell back.

Better prospects seemed to be on offer in the British sector, and in consequence two Anzac brigades were moved by ship to the Cape Helles bridgehead, in time for the offensive against Krithia on the morning of 6 May. In two days British and French attacks got nowhere, and so the New Zealand and 2nd Australian Brigades were chosen to go forward next. The New Zealanders managed to gain only 200 metres during their early morning attack on 8 May, but they were sent forward again in the late afternoon, only to be halted again. It was now the turn of the Australians. The 2,000-strong brigade came under artillery fire long before they even reached the British front-line trenches where they were to form up for the attack. Still under heavy fire they charged out into no man's land with bayonets fixed. They only got about 500 metres before being forced to go to ground. Here a fire-line was established and more reinforcements joined them. At 18.00 they charged again up a hill and got to within 500 metres of the main Turkish trench line. The Australians and New Zealanders lost 1800 men in the attack which entered Anzac legend as worse than the infamous Charge of the Light Brigade.

The Turks renewed their offensive against Anzac Cove in the early hours of 19 May. A huge force of 40,000 Turks surged towards the Australian lines. Their first attempt was driven back with hundreds of casualties. Then the Turks started to move forward in small groups in an attempt to overrun the Australian front-line positions. This was more successful, and soon all along the front Diggers from the 14th Australian Battalion were battling for their lives. In the close-quarter fighting the Australians turned to the bayonet as the most efficient weapon.

After killing two Australians with grenades, a group of seven Turks managed to occupy a key section of the Australian trench. Acting Lance Corporal Albert Jacka and five other men were left isolated. Realizing the danger, Jacka led a counter-charge along the trench, but this was defeated, with three Australians shot dead and two wounded. Jacka then came up with a cunning plan to defeat the enemy. He crawled out into the old no man's land and came up behind the Turks, while his comrades distracted them with rifle fire. Jacka's approach was successful and he jumped down into the trench. He bayoneted five of them and shot the rest to win the first Australian Victoria Cross of the war. Thousands of men now lay dead in front of the Australian positions but their line still held.

The offensive against Krithia was renewed by the British on 4 June, at first with heavy loss. The 1st Battalion, The King's Own Scottish Borderers, made it into the Turkish lines and set about bayoneting anyone they found. The Royal Naval Division and the 1st Company, 8th Battalion, The Lancashire Fusiliers, also made good progress. but they had to fight hard once inside the Turkish trenches. A counter-attack of over a thousand Turks charged the British and a furious bayonet fight developed, with hundreds of men going down. The Krithia front, however, was not going to be broken that day, or in the series of attacks which took place over the next month.

Scottish Territorials of the 156th Brigade were given the job of spearheading the offensive planned for 18 June. Turkish gunners saw the troops massing in the British front line and fired off a spoiling barrage that killed scores of troops. Two hours later the attack finally got underway, in spite of the inevitable storm of Turkish machine-gun fire as soon as the troops went over the top. The Scots ignored the temptation to open fire; instead they levelled their rifles, pointed their bayonets at the Turks and pressed on. Only the 1st Company, 4th Battalion, the Royal Scots, made it into the Turkish trenches, dispatching numerous enemy soldiers. The other three battalions in the brigade were mown down, with 1,563 men out of 2,941 killed, wounded or missing.

After a disastrous Turkish counter-attack on 5 July that left several thousand dead in front of the British lines, the Scottish Territorial soldiers of the 155th and 157th Brigades were sent into attack on 12 July. Their charge got them into the Turkish trench with little loss. The 1st Company, 4th Battalion, Royal Scots Fusiliers, and the 1st Company, 5th Battalion, The King's Own Scottish Borderers, set about fighting the defenders with any weapons to hand, including rifles, spades, pistols and the bayonet. The Scots were unable to press on further after securing their new positions.

The British high command now decided to stage a new landing further up the peninsula, to bypass the Turkish defences that had effectively pinned them down in Anzac Cove and Cape Helles bridgeheads. Before the attack Australians were to launch a major offensive along the northern perimeter of their bridgehead to take advantage of weak Turkish defences. As a diversion, the 1st Australian Brigade staged an attack on the southern edge of the beach-head during the afternoon of 6 August. The 1st, 2nd and 3rd Battalions charged forward, reaching the Turkish trenches. The enemy were still cowering in their bunkers after a naval bombardment, so the Australians had to use their bayonets to prise open doors and roofs to get at the Turks. For two days the hand-to-hand combat raged in the trench line, until the Australians drove out the defenders. Seven Victoria Crosses were won in the brutal fighting. Now the main Anzac operation began with a complex night infiltration, but the columns got lost and delayed in the difficult terrain. The Anzac commander, Lieutenant General Sir William Birdwood, needed a diversion against Turkish entrenchments on the Nek hill feature, while his troops got in position for their attack early on 7 August. That duty fell to the 8th and 10th Australian Light Horse Regiments, both made up of cavalrymen who had volunteered to serve in Gallipoli as infantrymen. They were not properly equipped for infantry fighting but were keen to prove themselves in battle.

A thirty-minute artillery barrage was laid on, but it only served to alert the Turks as it stopped seven minutes before 'Zero Hour'. The Light Horse went over the top but only got a few metres before they were cut down. Three times the high command ordered the Light Horse to fix bayonets and charge, despite their losses.

'Gentlemen, you have ten minutes to live' was the famous order. The result was wholesale slaughter, with some 375 of the 600 attackers being made casualties, including 234 killed. This episode has gone down in Anzac legend and was later immortalized in the feature film *Gallipoli*. The main attack was itself a failure and the Turks brought up reinforcements to counter-attack in strength. All hopes now rested on the new landings planned for Suvla Bay.

A fresh British corps, consisting of three so-called 'New Army' volunteer divisions, were to be put ashore at Suvla from 6 August onwards. The initial landings took the Turks completely by surprise and there was negligible resistance. The bad luck and poor judgement that had dogged the Gallipoli campaign continued, however, with the British commanders of the landing delaying their advance off the beachhead. By the time the troops were moving inland the Turks were ready for them. Nevertheless they charged forward with bayonets glistening in the August sun. The soldiers themselves complained that the act of fixing bayonets only served to alert the Turks that an attack was coming because they could see the sun glinting off the bayonets sticking up above the parapets of the British trenches.

After four days of fruitless attacks the Turks decided to counter-attack on 16 August. In a night-time charge the Turks got into the British positions and killed hundreds in the bayonet fighting, forcing the British back. Three days later the British moved in reinforcements from Cape Helles to press home the attack but they were just mown down as soon as they charged out of their trenches. More attacks continued. The 8th Battalion, The Duke of Wellington's Regiment, did make it into the Turkish trenches to set to with the bayonet, but was soon forced back by overwhelming numbers. On 22 August the 5th Battalion, The Connaught Rangers, made its legendary charge to seize the Turkish strong point on Kabak Kuyu. At 15.40 the Irishmen rose from their trenches to charge the 400 metres across no man's land. Not a single Irish soldier returned fire during this dash. Second Lieutenant T.W.G. Johnson, an Irish football star, was first into the Turkish trenches and the enemy was soon put to flight. Hot Irish tempers now got the better of the Connaught Rangers, who charged on into a wall of machine-gun fire. Legend has it that even in death the Irishmen still had their bayonets pointing towards the enemy.

The fighting continued for a week, getting ever more brutal because of the close proximity of the two lines of trenches. By 27 August only some sixty metres separated the two sides at Hill 60 above Suvla. In an appropriate finale to the offensive, a scratch force of 350 Australians, 400 New Zealanders and 250 surviving Connaught Rangers waited in the trenches for a massive barrage from the fleet to cease. At 17.00 the barrage lifted and within minutes the first wave of attacking troops was in the Turkish trenches before the defenders knew what was happening. Bayonets and grenades soon cleared the trench and the supporting wave started to move forward, but fire from the Turkish reserve positions cut them all down. The assault troops were trapped in the Turkish trench. The enemy now poured into the trench to cross bayonets with the most aggressive Allied troops left on Gallipoli peninsula. The 9th and 10th Australian Light Horse were sent in to join the fight which was still going strong at 22.30. To shouts of 'Allah' the Turks kept coming, throwing grenades and stabbing with bayonets. The defenders quickly had to build barricades along the trenches with sandbags taken down from the parapet.

By dawn the Turks gave up, so ending attempts by both sides to achieve a decisive victory at Gallipoli. Four months of stalemate followed, after which the British finally gave up and evacuated their troops. There was little to show for the bravery of the British, French, Indian, Australian and New Zealand soldiers who tried to alter the course of the war. France would now be the decisive theatre of operations.

1916 – The Somme: The Cult of the Bayonet

The defeats and heavy losses of 1915 did not immediately undermine the British Army's faith in the bayonet as a decisive weapon in infantry combat. While the realities of trench warfare increased the importance of artillery, machine-guns and hand grenades, the British Army's senior commanders saw the use of the bayonet as a means of instilling aggression and offensive spirit in their troops. There was a perpetual fear among the 'top brass' that the troops would become stale and complacent during the long periods of duty manning the trenches. At the time, this was known as 'live and let live', in which British and German troops on either side of the front would by mutual consent desist from inflicting needless casualties on each other. Firm orders were issued against local truces, such as the famous 1914 Christmas meetings in no man's land of British and German soldiers. Regular trench raids were ordered to keep the enemy on his toes and British troops killing. There was also a travelling bayonet 'road show' run by Major Ronald Campbell, of the Gordon Highlanders. He was the General Headquarters' assistant inspector of physical and bayonet training.

Campbell and his team of instructors toured all the units of the British Expeditionary Force (BEF), raising morale by instilling in the troops the 'spirit' of the bayonet. His team gave lectures on bayonet tactics as well as the necessary anatomical information to ensure that bayonet wounds were as lethal as possible.

When the lectures were completed the troops were 'invited' to participate in practical training on an assault course, where they ran around bayoneting straw dummies. Major Campbell insisted they shout their hatred of the 'Boche' and adopt what he called a 'killing face', while they went through the drills.

For the impressionable volunteers of Kitchener's New Army, Major Campbell's lectures were inspiring stuff, though the veterans of the old BEF were less than impressed. In the run-up to the great Somme offensive of 1916, however, the shows had the desired effect. The 'New Army' was formed from volunteers who had signed up at the outbreak of war in 1914. They were recruited from sections of society that had previously not been closely connected with the military, such as middle-class professionals or factory workers. Individual towns and communities raised their own battalions of local men, who served under officers recruited from the same areas. Not surprisingly they became known as 'Pals' battalions.

These units were short of trained manpower and material at first, but by early 1916 they were nearly ready for action. In the first months of the year the bulk of the New Army was on its way to France. These new troops were keen to show what they could do, and prove to old Regulars and Territorials that they were just as good soldiers. They went into action with great determination, but would suffer terrible casualties in consequence. Whole communities would be blighted for decades by the loss of the prime of their menfolk on the Somme.

For six months the British Army had been preparing for the Somme offensive. It was to be the first major offensive by the New Army and it was intended to inflict a decisive defeat on the Germans, relieving pressure on the French who were under heavy attack at Verdun. More than 500,000 British troops were concentrated near the battlefield and 100,000 would go over the top on the first day of the battle, making it in theory the greatest bayonet charge in history.

The experiences of 1915 had made the British Army reconsider its tactics. Great faith was put in a week-long artillery barrage that was to fire 1,500,000 shells. They were supposed to destroy the German front-line positions, flatten the enemy barbed-wire entanglements and drive the defenders mad. At 'Zero Hour' the infantry would rise out of the British trenches and march towards the German lines, behind a so-called 'rolling barrage', which would advance deep into the enemy rear at a pre-arranged rate. To gain the maximum benefit from the barrage, the infantry had to stick close to this pre-arranged rate otherwise they would fall behind and the advance would stall. Strict orders were issued forbidding infantry from firing during the advance, using hand grenades, and taking cover. The infantry were to fix bayonets, adopt the high port position and walk towards the enemy. Everything else would be done by the rolling barrage. The Germans would either flee at the sight of the British cold steel or be so concussed by the artillery that they would be cowering in their trenches waiting to be bayoneted.

More complex tactics were thought to be beyond the inexperienced volunteers of Kitchener's Army, while the emphasis on artillery and the bayonet was thought necessary to compensate for their poor musketry skills.

There was in any case little possibility that the British Tommies would have been able to attack the German lines at a run. Each soldier was weighed down with more than 35kg of ammunition, gas masks, entrenching tools, wire-cutters, empty sandbags, grenades, water bottle and rations. This was indeed to be a 'slow motion' charge.

Precisely at 07.30 hours on 1 July 1916 the British artillery barrage lifted off the German front line and started to move on to second-line targets. All along the British trenches whistles were being blown by platoon commanders to order their men out of the trenches into no man's land. The troops had been waiting for months for the opportunity to see action. Many were fortified with an extra large rum ration to overcome their natural fear, as battalions were able to form up and begin their advance towards the Germans. There must have been more than 10,000 men in the first wave and many participants said it was a stirring sight watching the huge mass of men rise from the trenches and advance in line towards the enemy. Some units on the other hand were immediately cut down by fire from enemy machine-guns as they emerged from their trenches. This was because the much-vaunted artillery barrage had failed to destroy the German bunkers.

As the first British units were beginning their advance, the German defenders were rushing out of their intact dugouts and starting to put down fire. Flares were fired to signal to the German artillery to start plastering no man's land with thousands of shrapnel shells.

Still the British kept coming. Wave after wave of infantry went over the top that morning. They kept moving forward, not stopping to return fire or even to tend to their wounded. Both actions were punishable by court martial. One battalion dribbled footballs as it advanced. The first soldier to score a goal in the German lines would get a prize from his company commander, who had kicked off the game! Scottish battalions advanced to the sound of bagpipes. Some officers even brandished swords. Whole companies were mowed down at a time but small groups managed to get to the German wire only to find it was intact. Stopped at the wire, the surviving infantry had to find shelter in shell holes or dips in the ground. The Germans were openly standing on their fire steps but there was no move to bring down artillery fire on them. That would have upset the generals' precise fire plan. In places where the artillery had flattened the German defences, long-range machine-gun fire from the flanks still did great execution. Many battalions lost more than half their strength in the space of a few minutes.

All through the morning the British pressed forward. Here and there on the thirty-kilometre front small groups or individuals found their way through the wire into the German trenches. In some cases the mere sight of a Tommy sporting a bayonet was enough to make German soldiers throw up their hands and shout '*Kamerad*'. Many were not so quick-thinking and were promptly run through. With only ten rounds in the magazine, the British soldiers preferred the bayonet to the bullet in close-quarter fighting, because the need to change ammunition clips left them momentarily defenceless. These small groups of brave men soon found themselves trapped and isolated in the German trench systems. With no man's land still being swept by deadly fire, reinforcements couldn't get forward to help them.

They were condemned to lonely and unequal combat until

darkness could provide them with enough cover to allow escape back to the British lines. By nightfall on 1 July more than 57,000 British troops would be casualties, of which some 20,000 were dead, for little gain. There were however some notable British successes on that day, thanks to very determined bayonet charges.

Just to the north of the town of Thiepval, the Germans built a large redoubt or bunker complex. It was garrisoned by several hundred well-armed troops but was 400 metres behind the first line of German trenches.

The 36th (Ulster) Division was given the mission of assaulting and capturing the Schwaben Redoubt, a task it set about doing with great determination and *élan*.

The division had been formed in 1914 from the paramilitary Ulster Volunteer Force (UVF), which had been set up by Protestant Irishmen opposed to home rule. They had responded to the call to arms in 1914 with great gusto on the promise that any decision about home rule would be put off until after the war. The Ulstermen had something to prove. In the attack they also had a number of advantages. The ten Ulster battalions had a forming-up point inside Thiepval Wood that was covered from German view. There was also a sunken road just in front of the British line that provided more protection; against strict orders of the high command many Ulstermen had infiltrated into it before 'Zero Hour'. The preordained kit loads were also widely ignored. Morale was sky-high. Many even wore the regalia of their Orange lodges and marching flute bands. As the soldiers waited in the trenches for 'Zero Hour', Protestant ministers led the singing of hymns and anti-Papist songs. The rum ration helped boost morale even more.

Bang on 07.30, the leading Ulster brigade rose from its trenches and ran towards the Germans, who were still inside their dugouts. The Ulstermen did not waste time forming up into lines or waves. This was a furious charge with bayonets to the fore. Before the enemy knew what was happening thousands of Ulstermen were in among them bayoneting or clubbing to death anyone they found. The position was taken in a few minutes for almost no loss. Just 370 metres further on was the division's main objective, the Schwaben Redoubt itself, now fully alerted to the advancing Ulstermen.

They continued the movement towards the redoubt, but the line was now being swept by machine-gun and artillery fire. The advance seemed to falter in the open, when one company commander, Major George Gaffikin, took off his Orange Order sash and waved it above his head, shouting the traditional Protestant war cry, 'Come on, boys! No surrender!'

The spirit of the Ulstermen returned and a mob of men surged forward after the major. Within minutes eight battalions were inside the redoubt. Bayonets flashed, grenades were dropped in dugouts, fists exchanged and knuckledusters traded. No one was controlling the fight. Captain Eric Ball won a Victoria Cross leading infantrymen into the redoubt, even though he was only a mortar officer. By mid-morning the redoubt had been taken. Some 500 Germans had surrendered and were being led away, the redoubt littered with their dead. Speed and aggression had carried the day.

The Ulstermen then set about moving forward to their next objective, the German second line of trenches and the Stuff Redoubt. Small groups of Ulstermen moved across country towards the position which was only occupied by a few dozen cooks and rear-echelon troops. They were preparing to surrender when the British pre-timed rolling barrage started to land on the position, killing and injuring many of the Ulstermen, who dived for cover. This was to be the high point of their advance. By the middle of the afternoon they would be virtually under siege inside the Schwaben Redoubt. The Germans brought up field guns and fired them over open sights directly into the position. Three times the Germans counter-attacked, but each time they were driven back by the Ulstermen's rifle fire. By dusk, however, they were out of ammunition, so the most senior unwounded officer, a major, ordered the division back to the British lines. One group, cut off from the main body, held out in the redoubt for thirty-six hours, with its leader, Corporal George Sanders, winning the Victoria Cross. During 1 July 2,000 Ulstermen were killed, 2,700 wounded and 165 captured.

On the extreme right of the British line, troops broke through the German front and pushed more than a kilometre behind the first trench line, capturing three fortified villages in tough hand-to-hand fighting. The most successful attack of the day took place south of the fortified village of Montauban. Here the attacking divisions were made up of 'Pals' battalions from Liverpool, Manchester and East Anglia. They were not very experienced soldiers but their commanders were some of the most hardened in the BEF. Major-General Ivor Maxse of the 18th (Eastern) Division did not conform to the high command's orders, and sent his troops into no man's land in the minutes before 'Zero Hour' as the barrage was still falling. At 07.30 the barrage lifted and the men surged forward. Within an hour the 8th Battalion, The Norfolk Regiment, had taken three lines of trenches with ease. Next in the British line was the 8th Battalion, The East Surrey Regiment, which crossed its start line with men dribbling a football, and by midday had achieved all its objectives.

The neighbouring 30th Division benefited from supporting fire by French 75mm rapid-fire howitzers, which collapsed many of the front-line German trenches. Four Manchester and Liverpool Pals battalions stormed into the enemy trenches at bayonet point, where scores of Germans put their hands up rather than fight. The next objective was the fortified village itself.

Three fresh battalions were then pushed through to exploit the early victory. A single German machine-gunner opened up on the advancing line, killing every company commander. He was spotted by a Manchester 'Pals' Lewis gun team and quickly put out of action. Now the advance turned into a charge with the 1st and 2nd Manchesters, and the 2nd Battalion, The Royal Scots Fusiliers, close behind. The Germans in the trench outside the village gave up as soon as the bayonet-wielding British were upon them while there was no resistance inside the village itself. By 10.05 it was secure and the troops pushed on to a large service trench and artillery position behind the village. Some 200 Germans were rounded up at bayonet point by the jubilant Pals.

All along this sector British troops were now mopping up the German trenches, calling into bunkers for the occupants to surrender or throwing in a hand grenade if there were signs of resistance. Usually the Germans put their hands up as soon as a bayonet was spotted poking through the dugout door.

Just after midday, the 4th Liverpool Pals put in a bayonet charge on the last remaining German position holding out to the south of Montauban. A quick artillery barrage sent the defenders scurrying for their bunkers, but before they could get out to man their machine-guns the Pals were among them with their bayonets. A regimental commander and a full company of infantry surrendered.

The neighbouring 7th Division was equally successful taking its objective – the fortified village of Memetz – thanks to imaginative tactics. No man's land at this point was only 200 metres wide, so using 'dash' tactics, the British were able to sweep into the German front-line trenches with little loss. Here, small groups of British soldiers moved forward with hand grenades to blast the Germans out of their bunkers, while the Germans responded by resorting to their bayonets. Hand-to-hand fighting raged until the village fell just after 15.00.

As the day progressed, fighting raged along the thirty-kilometre front as British Tommies fought for their lives in no man's land or clung to tenuous footholds within the maze-like German trench systems. The remnants of the 2nd Battalion, The Seaforth Highlanders, were holding out in the so-called Quadrilateral Redoubt against constant German counter-attacks. An enemy party was slowly edging its way up a communication trench towards the Seaforths. Their colonel decided to drive the enemy out with a five-round rapid burst, followed by a bayonet charge.

Suddenly, without orders, a Seaforth corporal charged out of the trench throwing hand grenades. He was shot down by rifle fire, but in the confusion caused by his grenades the rest of the Seaforths charged out of the trench and were upon the Germans in seconds. All the enemy were either bayoneted or shot. A Seaforth drummer boy, Walter Ritchie, won the Victoria Cross for standing on the parapet of the Quadrilateral sounding the 'charge' to inspire its defenders. Such derring-do, however, could not overcome the iron and steel of the German defences.

The Somme campaign continued for six more months, with the British continuing to slog away in the hope of relieving pressure on the French who were still being pounded at Verdun. There would be no more mass offensives along the length of the front, just localized operations to seize 'bite-sized chunks' of the German line.

The British were slowly learning from their past errors. The short charge or dash across no man's land had proved effective; time and again the British used it to good effect, either exploiting bad weather or smoke to cover their advance. Digging saps or trenches towards the enemy also reduced the distance of the charge and provided cover during the approach.

These tactics allowed units of four divisions to take a large section of line in the early hours of 14 July, the 26th

(Highland) Brigade, with the Black Watch and Argyll and Sutherland Highlanders spearheading the advance, occupying Longueval for almost no loss.

Two nights later the 2nd Battalion, The Royal Munster Fusiliers, stormed out of Contalmaison in a cloud of poison gas to bayonet their way through three lines of German trenches. In the cloud it was impossible to see very far, or to tell friend from foe. The hand-to-hand fighting went on for almost four days. It was rare for soldiers of the battalion to fire their rifles at all – the bayonet was the weapon of choice.

On 3 September, the 7th Battalion, The Prince of Wales's Leinster Regiment, surprised the Germans in Guillemont. Every man in the enemy front line was 'bombed, captured, bayoneted or brained with the butts of rifles'. A month later on 7 October, in a textbook example of the employment of the 'rolling barrage', the 1st Company, 7th Battalion, The Middlesex Regiment, stormed a large enemy section called Spectrum Trench.

Using the cover of the barrage, the battalion dashed across the 400 metres of no man's land and was on top of the Germans before they could get out of their trenches. Some men dived into the German trenches and set about bayoneting the enemy. Others took great delight in lining the parapet and gunning down Germans as they ran out of their bunkers. Some seventy-seven unwounded Germans later surrendered.

In one of the final battles of the Somme campaign, Scottish Territorials of the 51st Highland Division spearheaded an offensive to capture the 'Y' Ravine feature near Beaumont Hamel on 13 November. Heavy fog covered the battlefield at 'Zero Hour' so the Scots were able to swarm over the German positions, bayoneting and bombing the defenders into submission. Fighting then spread to the village itself and the Highlanders set to, turfing the Germans out of their fortified cellars with bayonets and hand grenades. Highland *élan* proved irresistible with some 7,000 Germans being captured and thousands more being killed or wounded in the division's charge.

A small band of the 16th Highland Light Infantry, a Pals battalion known as the Glasgow Boys' Brigade Battalion, fought a more desperate battle after breaking into a German strong point near Ancre. Three officers and sixty men from the battalion's D Company, plus a handful of men from the 11th Battalion, The Border Regiment, fought their way into the strong point called Frankfurt Trench, though the remainder of their division's attack was repulsed. For eight days the slowly diminishing band of men held off the enemy, becoming increasingly desperate, and relying on captured food and ammunition to survive.

On the sixth day the Germans mounted a massive attack. The enemy swarmed all over the small section of trench. The Scots resorted to the bayonet and the Germans fled leaving eight prisoners. The Germans sent an ultimatum to the Scots: 'Surrender or you will all be killed.' They kept on fighting. Two days later the fifteen sick and wounded survivors surrendered.

After the withdrawal from Gallipoli earlier in the year, the Australian Imperial Force (AIF) was rested, refitted and retrained ready for action on the Western Front. The 'Diggers' were not sent into action on the first day of the Somme but were soon to be in the thick of the action, as the campaign extended into the summer and autumn of 1916.

The first major AIF action took place on 19 July to the north of the Somme at Fromelles, near the site of the previous year's abortive British attacks on Aubers Ridge. It was hoped that the attack by the 5th Australian Division would draw German reserves away from the main Somme battlefield.

BAYONET BATTLE

At dawn the Australians attacked with bayonets. They suffered grievously from German machine-gun fire but captured two lines of enemy trenches. The attack was called off after a day amid much acrimony, with the Australians claiming 5,533 casualties lost for little effect. Four days later, the 1st Australian Division was committed to the Somme front at Pozières. Four attacks by British infantry on successive days had failed to dislodge the Germans but reduced the village to rubble. Now it was the turn of the Australians.

Bayonet-wielding 'Diggers' charged forward with great determination in the face of heavy fire. All along the sector small groups of Australians managed to break into the German trenches. Lieutenant A.S. Blackburn led a party of men from the 10th Australian Battalion in an attack on a German machine-gun post. Thirty men died during the advance, but the officer and his men secured 250 metres of German trench.

The Germans were using hand grenades to keep the Australians out of their trenches. This was driving Private John Leak, of the 9th Australian Battalion, mad. He crawled up on one enemy post and threw in three grenades. In the confusion, he jumped down and bayoneted the three surviving Germans.

The enemy now counter-attacked and drove back the small groups of Australians from their trenches. Leak and Blackburn each won the Victoria Cross for his efforts.

A further example of outstanding Australian prowess with the bayonet took place on 7 August when a German counter-offensive struck the Australian lines around Pozières. Albert Jacka, who had won a Victoria Cross the previous year at Gallipoli and had now been promoted to Second Lieutenant, was in command of a platoon that was isolated by the enemy advance. Some forty Australians of a neighbouring platoon were captured by the surprise enemy advance. Despite being wounded by a grenade fragment, Jacka was determined to free his comrades, so he led seven of his men after the party of prisoners and their guards. Jacka first shot a German who was about to climb into his trench, and then led his small band out in a charge towards the Germans. More Australians joined in the movement and a general counter-attack developed. The Germans were taken completely by surprise when the eight Australians dived into the shell hole where they were sheltering, stabbing with bayonets and wielding rifle butts, killing Germans all around. Jacka himself was wounded several times but kept on bayoneting his way past the guards. He killed nearly twenty Germans, many with the bayonet, and his charge freed all the Australian captives. In fact forty-two Germans surrendered to Jacka and his men. Other Australians forced back the Germans from all their gains. For his efforts Jacka received the Military Cross, although many in the AIF believed he deserved his second Victoria Cross. His action was described as 'the most dramatic and effective act of individual audacity in the history of the AIF' and he was dubbed as Australia's 'greatest front-line soldier'.

The battles around Pozières would continue for almost six weeks, in which 23,000 Australians would die for only a few kilometres of territory gained.

The British experience on the Somme broke the myth of the bayonet. No longer would infantry be expected to walk towards the enemy with only a bayonet to intimidate them. Infantry platoons were reorganized into five sections, each with a specialized combat role. The assault wave would be made up of rifle and grenade sections. It would be their job to work their way up to the enemy trenches using ground to conceal their approach. They would then launch the attack with grenades to kill the enemy. The bayoneters would finish off any survivors.

To cover the approaching assault wave would be the job of the firepower element, made up of a rifle section and a Lewis gun team. It was their job to put down suppressive fire on the enemy as the assault wave moved into position. A section of 'moppers-up' would follow up behind to clear out enemy bunkers and collect any prisoners, allowing the platoon to continue its advance.

The coordination with artillery was also improved, so forward observers could adjust fire as the battle developed. Rigid rolling barrages would be a thing of the past. Tanks and poison gas would also be used to terrorize the enemy and allow the infantry to cross no man's land uninhibited. No longer would the bayonet be the sole route to victory.

Defeat and Victory – 1917–18

Throughout 1917 Britain, France and Russia launched a series of massive offensives against the Germans which almost always broke down into bloody battles of attrition. Millions of soldiers died. On the battlefield, the decisive weapon was artillery – the 'god of war' as Napoleon once called it. No matter how brave the bayonet-wielding infantry may have been in seizing trenches in face of massed machine-guns, it was always the artillery that defeated any idea of further advances. The British and Germans both perfected their offensive infantry tactics. The British preferred the short 'dash', or charge, to surprise and overwhelm the enemy trenches, while the Germans developed infiltration or 'storm-trooper' tactics to get behind and unhinge defensive strong points. During 1917, artillery defeated all attempts to gain a decisive break through on the Western Front. Infantry were slaughtered in large numbers once enemy artillery got the range and started to blast newly captured positions. The bayonet played an important part in clearing seized positions of enemy defenders, but neither side any longer saw the bayonet as a decisive weapon.

After being blooded on the 'meat grinder' battles of attrition along the Somme in 1916, the Australian Imperial Force (AIF) was committed in strength to the Western Front for the remainder of the Great War. It remained one of the most aggressive and effective formations available to the British high command. Whenever there was a 'big push' the Australians were in the thick of the action. During the 1917 Ypres campaign the Australians regularly crossed bayonets with the Germans in the muddy trenches of northern Flanders.

During the bitterly cold winter of 1916-17, the Australians took their turn to man sections of the front line, often in very primitive conditions. This period saw regular trench raids and small-scale attacks. During the night of 4 February, the 13th Australian Battalion was ordered to seize a section of front known as Stormy Trench, near Gueudecourt, to improve their position. To achieve the objective the battalion was issued with some 20,000 grenades!

Under cover of darkness the right-hand Australian company led by Captain Harry Murray managed to get into Stormy Trench unhindered by the enemy. The 'Diggers' were then blasted by a German artillery barrage and hordes of enemy charged out of the night towards Murray and his men. Rifle-launched grenades stunned the enemy and then another barrage of grenades forced them back. But the Germans kept coming. Captain Murray fought fire with fire, regularly leading his men out of the trench to bayonet-charge the enemy infantry. The Australians always came out on top in the clash of bayonets. By morning Stormy Trench was Australian and Captain Murray had won the Victoria Cross.

That April saw the Australians committed to attacking Bullecourt alongside British tanks. The operation, however, ended in failure after the machines got bogged down in mud. A month later the Australians attacked again and seized a large section of German trench. The 1st Australian Battalion found itself holding a precarious position, surrounded on three sides by Germans, with only a narrow communication trench leading back into friendly territory. A German counter-attack pushed forward and seized part of the trench system. Corporal George Howell jumped on the parapet of the Australian-held trench and started throwing hand grenades at the enemy in a nearby position. This pushed them into panic, and Corporal Howell chased after them throwing grenades to keep them moving, but he soon exhausted his supplies. Not deterred, he resorted to the bayonet, catching up with the enemy and jabbing them with his blade. They kept on running. Corporal Howell's luck then ran out and a German sniper wounded him. His example rallied the Australian defenders and they surged out of their trenches to clear the remainder of the position. The brave corporal was awarded the Victoria Cross for his one-man charge.

On 4/5 September, Australians were committed to take Polygon Wood on the western edge of Ypres Salient. The battle started on 26 September and lasted two days. It was a slow and bloody affair, but the Australians kept pushing forward and eventually captured all their objectives. The 31st Australian Battalion's Private Budgen played a key role in the success, leading forward a handful of men to capture German machine-gun posts which were holding up the advance.

In the first position, he threw hand grenades and then his team charged in to bayonet the German defenders. Fired up, Budgen was outraged when he saw an Australian corporal being taken prisoner by a group of Germans. On his own, Budgen charged the Germans, bayoneting them and freeing the corporal. He was killed soon afterwards while rescuing wounded under fire. For his bravery during the Battle of Polygon Wood Budgen was also awarded the Victoria Cross.

By October 1917 the Australians had made two major

attempts to break out of the Ypres Salient. Their third push was to be remarkable because it saw large numbers of Australians and Germans clashing bayonets in no man's land. The British high command wanted to seize the tactically important Broodseinde Ridge, which dominated the salient, and moved three Australian divisions and the New Zealand Division for the assault. Extensive preparations were made to ensure the attack on 4 October was a success. The Australian assault troops moved into no man's land during the night to get as close as possible to German trenches before fixing bayonets and charging. They lay in old shell holes in the autumn rain until 'Zero Hour' at 06.00. Unknown to the Australians the Germans were also planning an offensive that morning and began a preliminary bombardment at 05.20. One in seven of the Australians caught in the open was killed, but the assault troops kept their nerve and stayed in position until their own artillery started firing at 06.00.

When the firing lifted, the 'Diggers' rose from their trenches and surged forward. At the same time only thirty metres in front of them, the German 212th Infantry Regiment was climbing out of its trenches to attack. The Australians were quickest into action, and began firing their Lewis machine-guns. Scores of Germans were gunned down, then the 'Diggers' were among them, bayoneting any Boche who chose to stand and fight. The enemy broke and fled.

For the next twenty-four hours the Australians cleared the remaining German positions with bayonets and hand grenades. Hundreds of Germans surrendered rather than face Australian steel. The British high command was convinced the AIF's success was decisive and the German front was on the verge of collapse. It was now raining heavily. Within days Ypres was a mud bath. Nothing would be able to shift the front line now until the following year.

At the start of 1918 the great armies of Europe were all

exhausted after almost four years of war. The only respite for the Germans was the collapse of Russia in the winter of 1917. They were able to transfer forty-two divisions from the Eastern Front to France. With the coming of spring they would strike.

The only hope for the British and French was the imminent arrival of the Americans in large numbers. Unrestricted German U-boat attacks had forced the entry of the United States into the war in April 1917 but it had taken many months to mobilize its industrial and manpower strength for the struggle ahead.

When the Germans struck on 21 March, there were some 162,000 American troops in France formed in four divisions. Each US division was 28,000-strong, making them numerically twice as strong as their European equivalent. The German offensive, Operation Michael, struck the much weakened British sector near the old Somme battlefields. Within days the front had collapsed under the weight of the German attacks, and twenty-eight British divisions had been all but destroyed.

By the high-water mark of the German offensive on 5 April Paris was once again being threatened and all available reserves were thrown into the gap. A month later the 2nd US Division would spearhead the Allied counter-offensive, in the first major action of the American Expeditionary Force (AEF).

The advance elements of the AEF were almost all drawn from the small US Regular Army, except for the 4th Brigade of the 2nd US Division which was formed around two regiments of the US Marine Corps. These were hardened veterans of America's colonial conflicts in Central America, the Caribbean and the Far East. In 1917 the corps was only 19,000 strong, so to form the brigade Marines were drafted in from remote stations and ships around the world with the 5th Regiment of Marines arriving in France in June 1917. The Marines were armed with the M1903 Springfield rifle which sported a 42cm-long thin blade, similar in style to those used by the British. From 1913 onwards some 6,000 'bolo' bayonets, which had wide 25cm-long blades, were manufactured. These pandered to the American fascination with 'Bowie'-style fighting knives.

General John 'Black Jack' Pershing, the AEF's no-nonsense commander, was a keen believer in the offensive, but he fought hard to resist attempts by the British and French to get him to commit his forces before the summer of 1918, when his million-strong army would be fully deployed. He wanted to avoid using his troops in the meat-grinder of the Western Front until they were ready to launch a concerted offensive. Pershing was a great bayonet exponent and the US Marines were ready to prove that the American soldier was able to take cold steel to the 'Boche'.

On 27 May the Germans launched their final push for Paris, routing eight divisions between Soissons and Reims. The 2nd US Division, with its Marines, was sent north to halt the Germans. Even Jack Pershing realized that the time was right for Americans to enter the war in earnest. Spearheading the advance was the 1st Battalion, 5th Marine Regiment. Just after dawn they formed up in a wood near Champillion, fixed bayonets and went after the enemy. A few hundred metres on they found them. The Marines charged forward in French style in platoon waves or lines. Heavy fire forced them to go to ground in a large wheat field. The Marines realized the French tactics left a lot to be desired and decided to improvise. Officers ordered their men to put down fire on the enemy. Fortunately the Germans did not have time to prepare their defences or bring up artillery so the weight of their defensive fire was light. The Marines then began to crawl forward, working round the German flanks in small groups. When they were a few metres from the enemy, the Marines charged into the German machine-gun posts bayoneting anyone they found. 'Bayonets flashed in, and rifle butts rose and fell.' First blood to the Marines.

In the surrounding hills Germans continued to fight on. Time and again the Marines used their rifles and bayonets to clear the remnants of a German storm-trooper battalion from the woods. Then the Marines dug in on Hill 142 to secure the line which they held until 6 June. One Marine officer put their success down to his soldiers' prowess with the bayonet.

> Trained Americans fight best with rifles. Men get tired of carrying grenades and chaut-chaut [automatic rifle] clips; the guns cannot, even under the most favourable conditions, keep pace with the advancing infantry. Machine-gun crews have a way of getting killed at the start; trench mortars and one-pounders are not always possible. But the rifle and bayonet go anywhere a man can go, and the rifle and the bayonet win battles.

The 3rd Battalion, 5th Marine and 3rd Battalion, 6th Marine, Regiments, took Belleau Wood at bayonet-point on 6 June, an attack pressed home across open country with horrendous casualties, including many senior officers. The Marines kept moving forward, driving out the Germans and securing a foothold along the edge of the wood. 'What do you wash your bayonet in? German blood' was the Marines' battle cry.

Over the next ten days the Marines defended Belleau Wood from six German counter-attacks. This would enter Marine Corps history as one of their greatest and bloodiest battles. For almost a month the Marines held the wood. Every time the Germans got into the wood, the Marines advanced with fixed bayonets and threw them out. By the time the Germans gave up trying it was a moonscape of devastation. On 30 June the French officially renamed it 'Bois de la Brigade de Marine'.

A month later the Americans were on the offensive,

advancing towards Soissons to regain ground lost to the Germans over the previous three months. The French and Americans combined forces for the offensive that was to begin on 18 July. The 1st Battalion, 5th Marine Regiment, again spearheaded the 4th Brigade, marching overnight through summer rain to its start line.

At 04.35 the Allied barrage began and the Marines waited in the ruins of a French village for the order to charge. Once the advance began they were caught by machine-gun fire as they tried to cross the German wire entanglement. Everyone went to ground. Three lines of machine-guns were spraying bullets from the woods ahead. Mustard gas shells also started landing among the Marines. The Americans still went forward; they crawled, ducked and dived until they were upon the German trenches. Then they jumped in with their bayonets. Sometimes the Marines fired volleys of rapid fire as they charged into the trenches, at other times they just lunged at their unsuspecting victims with their blades. The result was always the same – dead Germans. The lucky ones saw what was coming and raised their hands in surrender.

Working alongside the Marines was a regiment of French Senegalese colonial troops. They were also pushing forward with great *élan*, using their bayonets to great effect. Marines watching them in action noted that the slim French bayonet often broke if the victim struggled. Then the Senegalese delivered the *coup de grâce* with their long knives, which they usually used to slaughter cattle. The mere presence of the Senegalese was often enough to send whole German companies and battalions into panicked flight towards the rear. Soon the woods were clear of Germans, and the Marines then turned their bayonets on enemy soldiers holding a group of buildings just beyond the tree line.

The Marines continued to advance, taking scores of Germans prisoner as position after position was overrun. At

Vierzy ravine a Saxon regiment decided to stand and fight. They had laid low barbed-wire entanglements in wheat fields, which brought the advance to a halt and turned the Americans into sitting targets for the enemy's machine-guns. Again the Marines crawled forward through the wheat and lunged at the Germans with bayonets. The fight surged back and forth. The ravine resounded with the horrific shrieks of dying men. A French tank came up to help the Marines and a swarm of Germans attacked it. They were going berserk, poking their bayonets through any opening in the hope of killing the crew. American riflemen then cut down the Germans. This broke the defences and soon the position was in the hands of the Marines. Now the German front was collapsing and the Marines were at the forefront of the Allied general advance during September and October. On 3 October, another major French–American offensive opened with the Marines pushing towards Reims.

A furious barrage opened the attack and the Marines took the first line of German defences around the high ground of Mont Blanc, taking many prisoners. Two German infantry regiments counter-attacked out of the village of St Etienne, and the 1st Battalion, 5th Marine Regiment, went out to meet them.

A massive column of Brandenburgers surged head-on towards the Marines. For a few brief moments the two elite forces were fighting hand-to-hand, bayonet-to-bayonet. A German sergeant tried to run through the second-in-command of the Marine Battalion but a Marine intervened, parrying the German's bayonet thrust with his rifle, then shooting the German's head off. The enemy broke, hundreds feigned death or raised their hands to surrender. All further German attacks were broken by the Marines' rifle fire and a few hours later Mont Blanc was in Allied hands.

With the German spring offensive broken, the Australians

were also in the forefront of the burgeoning Allied counter-offensive that would eventually drive the Germans to seek an armistice.

At first the attacks were local in nature, such as the 6th Australian Brigade's attack on 26 March to seize high ground around Ville-sur-Ancre. The Germans fought tenaciously and intense machine-gun fire held up the 'Diggers', inflicting heavy casualties. All the officers in a company of the 22nd Australian Battalion were killed, so Sergeant William Ruthven took charge. One enemy machine-gun post was holding up the company, so he charged forward, threw a grenade into the position and then set about the occupants with his bayonet. More Germans started to move along a nearby trench and Ruthven bayoneted them as well. The remainder surrendered.

The war was becoming more fluid and the German defences were less well prepared, making it easier for infantry to fight. In a spirited action by the 29th Australian Battalion the village of Beaumetz was taken at bayonet point. Lieutenant H.A. Harrison and ten newly arrived members of the New South Wales Light Horse charged up a small hill just outside the town. On the top of the hill the Australians and Germans crossed bayonets for several minutes before the Germans fled.

This attack brought the AIF to the outer edges of the German Hindenburg Line; a series of bitter battles developed in April to seize a series of fortified villages along its outer edge. The Australians made good progress but in places the Germans fought back tenaciously. At Louveral, the 11th Australian Battalion captured the village only to be surrounded by a massive enemy counter-attack. Lieutenant Charles Pope organized the last remaining fifteen men of A Company in the village. They kept the Germans at bay until their ammunition was exhausted, then Lieutenant Pope ordered his men to fix bayonets. No one survived the charge into the mass of grey-coated Germans.

After the battle the Australians found the bodies of eight dead Germans around Lieutenant Pope's gallant band. The officer was awarded the Victoria Cross.

The Allied pressure on the Germans continued throughout the summer until 8 August, when an all-out offensive was launched around Amiens. For three weeks the Allies poured troops into the Hindenburg Line, and finally the German front collapsed. Field Marshal von Ludendorff called it 'the black day for the German Army'. Not surprisingly, the Australians were the spearhead of the offensive.

The 37th and 40th Australian Battalions were in the vanguard of the advance on 12 August, when a line of German machine-guns sparked into life. A dozen men from the 37th Battalion charged the guns but they were mown down. Sergeant Perry Statton of the 40th Battalion now led three of his mates forward against the guns. In a daredevil dash across 800 metres of open ground, Sergeant Statton moved so fast that the Germans never saw him. He got to the first machine-gun and shot two enemy soldiers with a revolver. A German lunged at him with a bayonet but the sergeant grabbed his opponent's rifle and threw him to the ground, bayoneting the man with his own rifle. The small group of Australians then charged the other machine-gun pits; the other crews, fearing the same fate as their comrades, fled, only to be gunned down by Australian troops covering their mates' charge. Two of the party were killed but Sergeant Statton and a colleague recovered their bodies. The day's action earned the sergeant a Victoria Cross.

On 29 August, the 2nd Australian Division launched its daring attack on the Mont St Quentin to capture the hill 'before breakfast'. The division's 5th Brigade led the way at bayonet point, with the 20th Battalion taking the strongly held Gottlieb trench. They bayoneted the German defenders, in what a senior British commander called the 'finest feat of the war'. The Germans then counter-attacked in large numbers and by evening the 5th Brigade had been pushed halfway down the hill. It was the turn of the 6th Brigade to fight the next day, and it too resorted to the bayonet to seize the crest. Three Australians won the Victoria Cross leading charges against the Germans during this brief battle. The Diggers' prowess with the bayonet during this battle was commemorated by a statue on the site showing an Australian soldier bayoneting a German eagle. In 1940 the Germans reoccupied France and removed the monument. It has not been seen since.

Two more months of hard fighting were to take place until the Germans threw in the towel and asked the Allies for an armistice. The enemy's resistance was collapsing and Allied soldiers only had to show their bayonets for hundreds of Germans to surrender at a time.

It had taken over four years for the bayonet to regain its place on the battlefield, but by this time the Germans were weakened by food shortages, revolution at home and war weariness. It was the determination and courage of the man wielding the bayonet that brought victory – not the blade itself. Armies around the world recognized that the bayonet could not bring victory alone. With the exception of one nation – Japan – all armies in the interwar years remoulded their infantry assault tactics around all-arms tactics.

CHAPTER TWO

THE SECOND WORLD WAR

Introduction

In a conflict that saw the first use of the atomic bomb, jet fighters and radar, the bayonet would seem to be an archaic and obsolete weapon. Politicians, generals and assorted 'mad scientists' claimed the war was won by these wonder weapons, but front-line soldiers knew that more basic items, such as the rifle and bayonet, were their preferred weapons. Infantry soldiers of the Second World War learned that their bayonet was an essential tool of the trade – it was ideal for close-quarter combat or when silent killing was required.

Although the bayonet charge had been to a certain extent discredited by the slaughter of the First World War, many nations developed and fielded new designs of bayonets in the interwar years. Learning from bad experiences during the First World War, where very long sword bayonets had proved difficult to use in confined spaces, most countries opted for short-thin designs. The British provided their Short Magazine Lee Enfield (SMLE) with a spike or 'pig sticker', while the German Airborne Forces also went for a spike when designing the bayonet for their revolutionary Fallschirmjaeger Gewehr (FG42) assault rifle. France and Russia both adopted cruci-form-spike type bayonets for their infantry rifles. In Germany, Italy and the United States, mainstream infantry rifles were all provided with short 15–25cm knife-style bayonets. The adoption of short knives and spikes showed at last that armies recognized bayonets were primarily intended for close-quarter infantry combat rather than keeping cavalry at bay, which had given bayonet design its main impetus before 1914. Only the Japanese stuck with their 37cm-long Arisaka bayonets, perhaps as a result of their 'banzai' fixation.

Western armies all saw the bayonet as a close-quarter weapon. They envisaged it being used in the final stages of assaults on enemy positions, killing enemy soldiers manning trenches or bunkers who had already been stunned by grenades or artillery fire. Bayonets were primarily used in terrain which allowed infantry to close on the enemy unseen while being protected from machine-gun fire. Throughout the Second World War bayonets were the preferred weapon inside trench complexes, in house-to-house combat, in jungles, or on mountain ridges.

The presence of armoured vehicles also played a major part in determining whether bayonets were to be used. In the giant armoured battles of the war – Kursk, Western Desert, Ardennes – close-quarter infantry fighting was an irrelevance. Where tanks were prevented from getting close to the action, for example on Crete, in the Italian mountains or the jungles of the Far East, then the bayonet came into its own as infantrymen fought for their lives hand-to-hand.

In the Far East the Japanese remained committed to the bayonet charge as their primary infantry tactic – it was if nothing had changed since Port Arthur. This was perhaps due to the Japanese not experiencing the slaughter of the Western Front. Easy successes against the Americans, British and Dutch in the first months of the war in the Pacific, after Pearl Harbor, convinced the Japanese that their opponents were not true warriors, but that they would surrender at the earliest opportunity. Time and again, they charged British and American troops only to be cut down in their thousands. They never seemed to learn and were still employing the same tactics in the defence of Okinawa in May and June 1945.

The Japanese loved the bayonet – it symbolized a link to their Samurai past. However, the bayonet became for ever associated with Japanese atrocities, such as the Rape of Nanking where tens of thousands of Chinese prisoners were butchered at bayonet point. This brutality was repeated against European POWs and civilians in Hong Kong, the Philippines, Malaya, Singapore and the Dutch East Indies.

CRETE – 1941

The spring of 1941 saw the Third Reich at the height of its strength. Western Europe, then Yugoslavia and Greece had all fallen to the German Blitzkrieg. Rommel's Afrika Korps was rampaging across the Western Desert and the German Army was massing to attack Russia. One item of unfinished business was the Greek island of Crete, which lay 320 kilometres south of German-occupied Athens. Hitler feared the island would be used as a base for air raids against his vital Romanian oil fields. Plans were therefore drawn up for its capture, immediately after Greece fell to the panzers on 24 April 1941. The attack on the island was going to be the chance for the German Luftwaffe's elite airborne forces to prove they were equal to the Wehrmacht's panzers. Lieutenant General Kurt Student's XI Air Corps was assigned 22,000 troops for the invasion, which was code-named Operation Mercury. His troops were a mix of paratroopers (*Fallschirmjaeger*), glider-landed and mountain troops, with the latter making up more than half the assault force. Over 700 fighters and bombers would support the operation, and they quickly set about bombing and strafing the island.

Defending Crete were 27,000 British, Australian and New

Zealand troops, supported by 14,000 Greek troops, and every able-bodied citizen on the island. Most of the British and Dominion troops had been part of a force sent to help the Greeks in March, which had been forced to evacuate under German pressure a month later. They had lost most of their armour, artillery and communications equipment – the latter being a problem which would prove a decisive factor in the coming battle. Crucially they also had no air cover, after the handful of Hurricanes sent to defend the island were shot out of the skies by the Luftwaffe.

Commanding 'Creforce', as the garrison was dubbed, was Major-General Bernard Freyberg, at the time the most senior field commander in the New Zealand Army. He had won the Victoria Cross in the First World War and was famously cool in a crisis. However, he was no 'rocket scientist' when it came to strategy and tactics. During the coming battle he was to be accused of making serious tactical errors, particularly for keeping thousands of troops defending Crete's beaches, because he misread ULTRA intercepts of German communications, and thought the main invasion would come by sea. By the time he realized the German paratroops were his main threat they were too well established to be beaten back.

For almost three weeks the Luftwaffe pounded Crete. Large Heinkels bombed the airfields at Maleme, Rethymno and Heraklion, as well as the port at Suda Bay. Stuka dive-bombers attacked the ships bringing in supplies, and Messerschmitt fighters made strafing attacks on troops in the open and on vehicles on roads. It was virtually impossible for the garrison to carry out any activity or movement by day. All the defenders could do was hide in their trenches and watch the aerial bombardment. The helplessness of the situation proved very bad for morale.

For the defenders, 20 May 1941 did not start any differently from other days. There were the usual German air raids, and no one was very excited until just before 08.00 when a new sound could be heard. The skies over Maleme were full of Junkers Ju-88 troop transports. Thousands of parachutes started to open over the area and scores of gliders swooped down on the airfield.

In the Maleme–Canea sector, on the north-east coast of Crete, hundreds of the German *Fallschirmjaeger* were shot by the New Zealand and British troops, as they descended in their parachutes. The slaughter went on all day as the garrison hunted down the small groups of enemy troops who were scattered all over the area. The only place where the Germans seemed to gain a foothold was on the far edge of Maleme airfield, which was held by a hard-pressed New Zealand company, and assorted Royal Air Force mechanics. Afternoon drops on Rethymno and Heraklion proved even more disastrous, with the assault forces almost all but wiped out and a number of senior officers captured. Scattered Germans found themselves easy prey to marauding groups of Cretan resistance fighters, who took great delight in hacking them to death with knives and spades. Now disaster struck the defence in the Maleme sector. The commanding officer of the New Zealand battalion defending the area decided to commit his reserve force and two tanks to clear out the enemy threat to the airfield. Determined *Fallschirmjaeger* beat off the attack, and soon communications broke down with the company fighting on the airfield. Thinking all was lost, a withdrawal was ordered from a key hill overlooking the battlefield. Capitalizing on their good luck, the Germans seized the hill during the night and were soon able to start flying in reinforcements. It was now only a matter of time before the poorly armed defenders were rolled up by the *Fallschirmjaeger* , as they swept along the north coast of Crete.

Long used to applying the sensible military maxim, reinforce success, General Student now ordered every remaining

Junkers to be packed with troops and sent to Maleme. Its runway had yet to be cleared of rubble, so more parachute drops would have to be made. Two companies were dropped on the New Zealanders' line three kilometres from the airfield. It was a bad move – ready and waiting for them was the 28th (Maori) Battalion. Recruited from the native inhabitants of New Zealand, who pride themselves on being a warrior race, the battalion to a man stood in its positions and raked the skies with bullets.

Those who reached the ground were still struggling to get out of their parachute harnesses when the Maoris raced towards them with fixed bayonets. One officer described how he led his men across the drop zone; every twenty metres or so they found a German and bayoneted him. The *Fallschirm-jaeger* had yet to get to their weapon containers, so were only armed with pistols or in a few cases Schmeisser MP-40 machine pistols. They were largely defenceless.

The Maoris continued to 'mop up' the drop zone. A few Germans tried raising their hands to surrender, but the Maoris took no chances and shot or bayoneted them anyway. By the time it was getting dark every officer and non-commissioned officer in the two *Fallschirmjaeger* companies was dead, along with 160 other ranks. The shocked remnants scattered into the hills in the hope of reaching German lines. Thanks to the Maori prowess with the bayonet this threat, at least, had been neutralized.

Now it was time for a counter-attack against the airfield. A night assault was planned by the 20th Australian Battalion and the Maoris. But they were late getting into position, their supporting tanks were knocked out by the Germans and heavy resistance slowed the advance. The assault force had yet to make much headway when the sun came up and swarms of Messerschmitts arrived to strafe them.

The poorly equipped British and Dominion troops

considered themselves lucky when they looked at the state of the 14,000 Greek troops on the island. In the build-up to the invasion, depots in Egypt had provided the British and Dominion forces with limited supplies of new uniforms, helmets, blankets and .303 rifle ammunition. The Greeks, their country occupied by the Germans, had nothing. Many of the ordinary soldiers were Cretan volunteers with no military training or combat experience; they did not, however, lack courage or hatred of the Germans.

In the first hours of the German assault on 20 May, the 6th Greek Regiment had been scattered, because its commander had not yet handed out rifle ammunition to his troops. Some 200 of them had been rallied by a New Zealand adjutant and formed into a battle group under the command of a maverick British officer, Captain Michael Forrester of the Queen's Regiment. A member of the British Military Mission in Greece, Forrester had made a daredevil escape to Crete on a fishing boat. He was an unlikely combat leader, dressed in shorts, an army jumper with brass rank insignia, fair hair and no steel helmet – just service dress cap. Forrester set about training his Greeks in the basics of soldiering. To avoid any confusion in battle he devised a basic command and control procedure based on whistles. One whistle blast was stand by; two, move forward; three, deploy into line; four, charge. They were also taught to shout 'Aiera!' which Forrester thought was a Greek battle-cry, although he was not entirely sure. Greek civilians loved watching their men drilling and soon were joining in.

During the early evening of 22 May an isolated group of Germans forced the New Zealand defenders off a key hill near Galatas. The New Zealanders were gathering to counter-attack when an 'infernal uproar' was heard nearby. Captain Forrester was seen leading a huge crowd of Greek soldiers and civilians, men and women. The soldiers had their bayonets fixed and civilians sported an assortment of improvised weapons, including one shotgun with a large serrated-edge knife tied on like a bayonet.

Forrester started issuing his commands by whistle, which led some observers to describe him as 'tooting a tin whistle like a Pied Piper'. With the captain twenty metres out in front, the Greeks charged forward across the open ground towards the Germans. The sight was too much even for the *Fallschirm-jaeger*, who just turned tail and fled down the hill. All around the New Zealanders just stood and watched the amazing sight, with one describing it later as the 'most thrilling moment of my life'.

Now a constant stream of Junkers transports were flying into Maleme. So desperate was the need for new troops to spearhead the advance westward, that General Student ordered the aircraft to crash-land on the shattered runway. This stream of reinforcements was never-ending, and soon the first German mountain troops were on Crete in strength. General Freyberg saw the writing on the wall and ordered a general withdrawal to the south coast.

The fresh 100th Mountain Regiment began to make its presence felt, and was soon pressing hard on the heels of the New Zealand rearguard that was holding the village of Galatas. Early on the morning of 25 May, the Germans put in a massive attack on the 400 tired men of the 18th New Zealand Battalion. The battle raged all day until the forward companies started to crack. The commanding officer mustered all the battalion's odds and sods – the padre, batmen, clerks and cooks – and led them on a bayonet charge. It did no good. What was left of the 18th Battalion staggered out of the village, ignoring calls by Brigadier Howard Kippenberger to 'Stand for New Zealand!' The arrival of fresh troops managed to hold the line, but only just.

An improvised defensive line was then established on a hill outside the village when two companies of the 23rd New

Zealand Battalion, with three 'I' tanks of the British 3rd Hussars, arrived. Brigadier Kippenberger sent the tanks forward to make a reconnaissance foray into the village while the New Zealanders sorted themselves out. As they fixed bayonets, stragglers started to attach themselves to the assault force. Even the famous Captain Forrester joined up armed only with his rifle and bayonet. In the space of a few minutes, men who had been running for their lives were chafing at the bit to stick bayonets into the Germans. Not surprisingly, a group of Maoris also found their way into the ranks of Brigadier Kippenberger's miscellaneous force.

The two tanks returned and the brigadier quickly turned them round to lead the assault, with the Maoris chanting their famous 'haka' war cry, which was soon taken up by the rest of the force. The show of bravery was infectious.

As the tanks moved out, the whole force set off behind them at a trot, and soon the two vintage machines were way ahead of the infantry. On reaching Galatas, one of the tanks began machine-gunning Germans in the village square, until it was badly damaged with an anti-tank grenade. The other vehicle turned around and retreated back the way it had come until stopped by the advancing New Zealanders.

The infantry pushed forward, running along the narrow streets of the village, throwing grenades into houses as they went. Any Germans who survived and staggered outside were bayoneted. At the square the Germans put up a show of resistance. Bullets were ricocheting off the burning hulk of the British tank. Lieutenant Sandy Thomas mustered his platoon and charged across the square, shouting and screaming as he ran forward. The sight was too much for the Germans, who fled. A lone machine-gunner on a roof fired down and wounded the gallant officer as he reorganized his men. Only two officers in the 23rd Battalion remained unwounded after this bloody battle.

The German advance had been checked, and Brigadier Kippenberger ordered his brave men to fall back and gain some distance from the enemy. The retreat continued.

More German reserves were brought up to keep their advance going. Two battalions of the 141st Mountain Regiment took over the lead. They soon found the Australians and Maoris defending the Suda docks area. This position held open the road south to the main evacuation beach on the south coast.

German mortars blasted the defenders, and then Messerschmitts arrived to strafe the trenches. With this massive fire support the newly arrived mountain troops were convinced the enemy were defeated, and began to advance confidently forward.

Now the 'Diggers' and Maoris turned the tables with a furious bayonet charge. For 300 metres the Maoris charged forward, firing tommy-guns and bayoneting any Germans they could catch. The Germans panicked, fleeing in a mad rush. Soon they were throwing away weapons and equipment to speed their escape. Some 121 Germans were killed in the bayonet charge and hundreds wounded in the rush to escape.

The Allied retreat now gathered pace, and by 1 June 16,000 troops were taken off the beaches by the Royal Navy. The remaining 5,000 troops surrendered. In the bitter battle for Crete, 7,000 Germans died, many of them *Fallschirmjaeger* who had fallen victim to Australian and New Zealand bayonets. Never again would the Germans launch an airborne assault on such a scale as Operation Mercury.

Desert Bayonets

Desert warfare in the Second World War was dominated by armour, artillery and aircraft. Infantry was relegated to supporting roles, and the defence or assault of prepared positions, since if caught in the open it could expect to be bombarded mercilessly and suffer heavy casualties. Infantry had to be protected and used at the decisive moment to clear the enemy's forces from bunkers or trenches. At this point in the battle the bayonet would come into its own.

The 2nd Battalion, The King's Own Royal Regiment, found itself in the Middle East in the summer of 1941. Still composed of many pre-war Regulars, the battalion was one of the best available to reinforce the hard-pressed British forces in the Middle East. In May it had been ordered to join the beleaguered garrison on Crete which was being invaded by German *Fallschirmjaeger*. Only a mechanical problem with their naval transport prevented them being put ashore at the height of that battle. Events in the Levant were to cause a more interesting diversion for the King's Own men. Since the end of the First World War, Syria and Lebanon had been administered by France. Following the fall of France in 1940 and the establishment of the pro-German Vichy regime, the British Government had started to become very concerned about Nazi influence in the French colony. German aircraft had used airfields in Syria to fly aid to anti-British rebels in Iraq, and German/Italian (Axis) spies based in Damascus were operating throughout the Middle East. After securing the approval of Free French chief General Charles de Gaulle, an Allied force was mustered to put an end to this collaborationist administration.

Free French, Indian, Australian, and a small British contingent – including the King's Own – were to take on some 45,000 Vichy French, including elements of the famous Foreign Legion. This was a strange conflict. Many of the Vichy French soldiers had been evacuated to Britain during Dunkirk, then returned to North Africa in British ships when the Vichy regime was set up.

After some surprise orders redirecting them from

Imperial Bayonets. Napoleon's famous Old Guard were the shock troop of the *Grande Armée*. The Emperor's battle tactics were very simple. His massed artillery would pound the enemy all day. When the morale started to falter his Guard would be unleashed. The sight of their bayonets was often enough to the send the enemy reeling from the battle field in disorder. (TRH Pictures)

The 'Thin Red Line'. British soldiers of the eighteenth and nineteenth centuries were masters of the bayonet, whether on European battlefields or in colonial battles. (TRH Pictures)

The US Civil War was the last time massed bodies of troops attempted to close on the enemy and 'put him to the bayonet' Napoleonic style. Heavy casualties were usually the result of bayonet charges across open country. (TRH Pictures)

Above: 'Socket' bayonets were the norm from the end of the seventeenth century through until the late nineteenth century, when 'knife' or 'sword' bayonets became fashionable. (TRH Pictures)

Below: 'The greatest bayonet charge in history' – the Battle of the Somme, July 1916. British troops advanced with fixed bayonets but were mown down by German machine guns. Few troops got anywhere near bayonet-fighting range. (TRH Pictures)

Above: Building up the 'spirit of the bayonet' was an essential part of British Army training in World War I. The aim of such training was to build up aggression so the 'Tommies' would unhesitatingly 'go over the top'. (TRH Pictures)

Below: Germans often surrendered as soon as a bayonet wielding 'Tommy' appeared over a trench parapet. Getting into German trenches was easier said than done, though. (TRH Pictures)

Above: South African troops wait to clear a house in a desert town in Libya in World War II. The lead soldier is going to 'post' a grenade, before his colleagues enter at bayonet point to clear out any surviving enemies. (TRH Pictures)

Left: Bayonets have always look good on parade! These World War II Grenadier Guardsmen maintain the reputation of the British élite regiment. (TRH Pictures)

Opposite page: A British training exercise during World War II. The bayonet was still a central part of British infantry tactics at this time. (TRH Pictures)

Above: The reality of war was very different. Firepower from Bren guns (centre) was used to keep the enemy's heads down while the bayonet men closed in for the kill. (TRH Pictures)

Below: Bayonet fighting was taught to all new recruits during their first days in uniform. Here, World War II-era Royal Marines go through the basics. (TRH Pictures)

Above: The British 'pig sticker' or 'spike' bayonet proved more practical in close-quarter fighting that long 'sword' or 'knife' bayonets. (TRH Pictures)

Below: US infantrymen prepare for action during the Battle for Normandy, 1944. In general, GI's always preferred firepower to close-quarter bayonet fighting. (TRH Pictures)

Right: A British 'Tommy' keeps Italian prisoners under control in the Western Desert in World War II. (TRH Pictures)

Below: The Bataan 'Death March' in 1942. Japanese soldiers developed a reputation for bayoneting Allied prisoners of war on occasion. Edged blades were a Japanese favourite throughout the Far Eastern theatre in World War II. (TRH Pictures)

Alexandria Docks in Egypt to Palestine – which was then British-ruled – the King's Own were assigned to the 21st Australian Brigade for the advance north into Vichy French Lebanon.

Separated from Palestine by the fertile Litani river valley, the rest of Lebanon is made up largely of high, barren mountain ridges, which make ideal defensive positions. The Vichy French had realized the natural strength of these defences and placed the bulk of their forces in them, as well as providing stone sangars (parapets) and barbed-wire entanglements. Attacking troops would have to struggle up these steep open slopes to reach the French positions.

Allied forces started their operation on 8 June 1941. At first all went well but the Vichy French were only falling back to more defensible terrain, where they fought tenaciously. The Australians seized the Merjayoun ridge after a stiff fight. Then in an amazing act of incompetence they left it unoccupied and the Vichy French moved back in. Now they were not going to be evicted so easily.

The King's Own had originally been assigned to the coastal sector, pushing northward to Damour against desultory opposition. Clearing Merjayoun became the number one priority for the Allied command, so the King's Own were ordered eastwards to spearhead the renewed efforts to clear the vital position. In circumstances of some confusion, the battalion did not arrive in its concentration area below the ridge until 16.00 on 22 June. Two hours later its commanding officer, Lieutenant Colonel Barraclough, received his orders. The King's Own were to attack in broad daylight the following morning. There was no time for detailed reconnaissance or other normal preparations. After consultations with the Australians, who attributed their two failed attempts to take the position to enemy tanks, Colonel Barraclough announced his plan. The battalion was to march round to the right and take the village of Khiam on a hill overlooking Merjayoun; it would then push down through rock-strewn terrain which would be impassable to tanks.

Because of the importance of the attack, the British Middle East Commander-in-Chief Sir Archibald Wavell turned up to observe from a nearby hill, and sent a message of good luck to the battalion before it set off. The regimental history does not record the reaction of the troops as they marched forward in the summer heat loaded down with ammunition and other supplies.

At first the flanking move was unopposed, confirming their expectations that the Vichy French had left the area unde-fended. Soon the lead company was coming under fire from enemy 75mm field guns and was pinned down. The King's Own had the sun behind them so the enemy were blinded by the glare. This fortunately lessened the accuracy of their artillery and machine-gun fire. Putting down covering fire with their Bren guns, the King's Own tried to filter round the enemy flank, but enemy troops easily countered the move.

By 15.30 promised Australian artillery support had failed to materialize, and it was clear the attack was getting nowhere. What is more, casualties were mounting. Colonel Barraclough now called off the attack and began to plan another attempt.

This time the assault would go in at 04.30 and artillery was organized to blast the enemy out of their sangars. The plan was very simple. Immediately after the artillery barrage lifted, A Company was to dash across the 150 metres separating the two sides and put the enemy to the bayonet.

Disaster, though, struck within minutes of the operation starting. The first Australian artillery salvo landed right on top of the assault company, killing and wounding twelve soldiers. There was confusion for several minutes as the artillery forward observation officer tried to correct the fire and the Vichy French started to mortar the battalion. At last the artillery got their shells on target and started to work over the enemy sangars. Then A Company surged forward to minimal resistance. The Vichy French had withdrawn rather than mix it in a bayonet fight with the King's Own.

Exhausted by the two days of battle, the men of the King's Own reacted in the only way possible. They sat on the hill and brewed up tea. Some 120 of their comrades had been killed or wounded in the battle. The King's Own now reverted to British command for the advance into Syria. Its capital, Damascus, had fallen on 21 June, so the main Allied effort was directed against the Vichy French stronghold in Beirut. British, Indian and Free French troops were to advance into Lebanon from the east, while the Australians pushed up the coast. Negotiations were already taking place for an armistice, so speed was important to ensure the Allies could gain maximum political leverage.

The King's Own were ordered to participate in a brigade attack along the Damascus–Beirut highway, which was to seize the Jebel Mazar mountain feature, at the foot of Mount Hermon. The brigade objective was a 500-metre-high rocky outcrop, criss-crossed by sharp ridges. And as if this was not bad enough, large areas of the east-facing slope were covered in treacherous scree. To many of the King's Own veterans the enemy positions looked impregnable. They had been assigned the dubious privilege of taking two peaks in the centre of the Jebel Mazar.

Again they had to go in just before dawn with limited artillery support. Only a handful of Indian mountain guns could be brought forward in time, and the battalion's own 3-inch mortars were out of range. Colonel Barraclough formed up the battalion in a three rifle company extended line and set them off at dawn towards their objectives. The going varied and soon the companies were getting intermixed. Then the Vichy French sentries spotted them. A wall of fire swept over the battalion. Scores of men were hit but the remainder kept going, finding cover under a seven-metre-high cliff, just below the enemy's positions. Here they were effectively pinned down by fire. To try to break the stalemate 2nd Lieutenant E.S. Bailey was lifted up the cliff by his men, but as soon as he emerged above the parapet a French officer raced up and bayoneted him. Locked in deadly embrace, the King's Own officer shot the Frenchman dead with his revolver. Their bodies were found wrapped around each other after the battle. In the centre of the battalion, one Bren gun team managed to secure a small piece of high ground where they were able to set up a fire base that pinned down several French positions for the remaining forty-eight hours of the battle.

With daylight breaking, the King's Own found themselves under fire from enemy positions on either side of them. The only solution was to dig in, which they proceeded to do using the only tools at hand – their mess tins and bayonets. A Vichy French tank appeared in their positions but Colonel Barraclough personally directed an Indian mountain gun to destroy it.

All through the day the battalion had to endure Vichy French fire and small counter-attacks by native colonial troops, which overran a few exposed King's Own detachments. The troops had little shelter from the sun and it was impossible to get water forward to them. Night was to be their saviour. Bringing up his reserve company, Colonel Barraclough determined to get the attack moving forward again. Captain S.C.O. Waring led the troops up to the foothill where they ran into unbroken barbed wire and fortifications.

Fortunately, he found a new route that allowed them to get round the obstacle. The captain then unleashed his troops on the unsuspecting enemy. Corporal A. Milloy led his section in a bayonet charge on the first line of sangars, personally killing four Frenchmen. Captain Waring sent his men forward twice more to clear out the remaining sangars. In all, five prisoners were taken and many casualties inflicted. The company had to go to ground when more enemy tanks made their appearance, but now the battalion position was more secure. They spent another day under French fire until the ceasefire was ordered at midnight. The following day the Vichy French signed an armistice concluding the bizarre Levant campaign.

Out on the Jebel Mazar, the King's Own were eating a hard-earned hot meal and collecting their many dead. Colonel Barraclough and his men inspected the commanding French positions, amazed that they had managed to get as far as they had.

The colonel was awarded the Distinguished Service Order for his tireless effort to visit the companies in their exposed positions. Captain Waring received a bar to his Military Cross for his company's daring bayonet charges which turned the battle. The ordinary soldiers of the battalion were content just to be alive.

Last Stand in Africa

The defeat of the German Afrika Korps at El Alamein in October 1942 set off a chain reaction that would soon lead to the final eviction of all German and Italian forces from North Africa. On 7 November British and American forces began landing in Vichy French-controlled Algeria, threatening the Afrika Korps supply lines.

Operation Torch, as the landings were code-named, provoked a furious response from the Germans who began a rapid build-up of forces in Tunisia to counter the threat to their North African army. Ships, planes and gliders were all pressed into service to move men and material to Tunisia. At the same time, Allied forces were moving out of their beachheads in Algeria and heading eastward in large numbers. The race was now on to see who could build up fastest.

The British 78th Division and elements of the US 1st Armoured Division led the Allied advance, which also involved parachute landings to seize key airfields. All seemed to be going well. Resistance was slight. American tanks overran a key airfield and succeeded in shooting up twenty Luftwaffe Stuka dive-bombers on the runway. By 29 November the Anglo-Allied 1st Army was only thirty-two kilometres from Tunis, the main Axis port and supply base.

Unfortunately for the Allies, the German commander in Tunis, Lieutenant-General Walter Nehring, was a master of improvisation. In a matter of days he had formed four armoured battle groups (*Kampfgruppe*) and had sent them off to turn back the Allies.

Tunisia's barren mountain ranges were ideal defensive terrain. Whoever held the high ground could dominate the valley floors with impunity. Unlike the Western Desert, the going in the high ground or jebels was usually impassable to tanks. It would therefore be up to highly motivated infantry to go in and clear out any resistance at bayonet-point.

On the receiving end of the German counter-offensive, at the Tunisian town of Tebourba, was the British 11th Infantry Brigade, which made a desperate effort on 30 November to hold the surrounding barren high ground and wooded valleys. Its advance guard had already been cut up badly by the Germans, so the 2nd Battalion, The Hampshire Regiment, was deployed to try to stem the enemy breakthrough.

Flanking units, however, were not so successful, and soon the 11th Infantry Brigade was holding a very exposed salient. The Hampshires were at the point of the salient and the following day the Germans moved in for the kill.

In their first attack the German *Fallschirmjaeger* of the *Kampfgruppe* Koch, were driven back with ease by the

Hampshires' deadly accurate Bren-gun fire. The next day *Kampfgruppe* Djedeida was called up to clear out the Tommies with its seven monster Tiger tanks. While the Royal Artillery's 25-pounder field guns duelled with the German panzers, German infantry worked their way through a wooded valley to close on the British. The Hampshires' X Company bayonet-charged into the wood several times to clear them out.

Enemy tanks now closed on X Company and it was soon overwhelmed. Only six men returned to the battalion lines. Drastic action was needed to restore the situation, so the Hampshires' commanding officer, Lieutenant Colonel James Lee, ordered a bayonet charge to clear out X Company's old position. Lieutenant A.W. Freemantle led his platoon forward in a ferocious attack that totally surprised the Germans. The Hampshires stormed through the wood bayoneting forty Germans and chasing off the rest. Only six Hampshires were wounded and the rest of the platoon triumphantly returned from the adventure with six cowed German prisoners in tow.

Realizing the precarious nature of their current position, Colonel Lee skilfully extracted his troops during the night and marched them silently away from the Germans to a more easily defended location. The Germans were close on their heels and early on 3 December started bombarding their new trenches. Troops of the East Surrey Regiment were hit heavily and lost a key mountain, Point 186, overlooking the Hampshires. In repeated charges the Hampshires tried to retake the hill but they could not budge the Germans.

Now the Germans made determined attacks on the Hampshires' main positions. A group of Germans who had infiltrated behind W Company were driven off by a bayonet charge led by the company commander. A similar German move against Z Company was also finished off with the bayonet. As night came on, Colonel Lee was busily planning a bayonet charge to retake Point 186, which was now blocking the battalion's communications with the rest of 11th Infantry Brigade. It quickly became apparent that the battalion was in no shape to mount such an operation. Only 200 men and 10 officers were uninjured so it was decided to break out and link up with the rest of the brigade. Weapons, ammunition and grenades were collected from the wounded, then Colonel Lee organized his final bayonet charge. Every man in the battalion was formed up into an extended line facing the wood full of Germans. Lee ordered bayonets to be fixed and the signal given to advance. It began as a slow walk, then as they closed on the wood the Hampshires broke into a run. For a few confused minutes there were isolated gunshots, grenades and the regular sound of bodies hitting the ground, along with screams as the Hampshires bayoneted any German who got in the way.

Scores of men could be seen running through the wood. They did not stop until they were on the outskirts of Tebourba. Then the battalion formed up to march into the wrecked town. Their hopes of meeting the brigade were dashed when it became clear that they had already gone. Penned in now on all sides by massive enemy forces, Colonel Lee ordered his men to split into small groups and try to get over the hills to safety. Of the 689 men of the battalion who entered the battle only 200 were still under arms on 6 December. Their repeated bayonet charges and stalwart defence had allowed the rest of 11th Infantry Brigade to escape and had held up the German advance for four crucial days. In its bloody battle the battalion won one Victoria Cross, two Distinguished Service Orders, five Military Crosses, four Military Medals and numerous Mentions in Despatches. Colonel Lee was captured along with many of his men, but later escaped from a German POW camp and reached Switzerland.

General Nehring's offensive had bought valuable time for

the Germans to build up their defences, and by mid-December some 50,000 fresh German troops had arrived in Tunisia. The German 334th Infantry Division had taken up position in the Jebel Ang region to cover Tunis. Holding the vital feature known as 'Longstop' were the two infantry battalions and supporting units of *Kampfgruppe* Lang. On 22 December 1942 they moved out to occupy the summit of Longstop. They laid minefields in the passes below the summit and covered all the approach routes with mortars and heavy machine-guns. The hard rock on the summit meant it was impossible to dig in, so the German infantrymen had to construct rock sangars on the lower slopes.

In the early hours of the following night a white flare rocket alerted the Germans to the imminent arrival of British bayonets. Heavy tracer fire then slammed into the improvised sangars as the Germans watched hundreds of British infantry – men of the Coldstream Guards – struggling up the mountain. Machine-gun and mortar fire failed to halt the British, and rather than mix it in a bayonet fight the Germans withdrew from their positions on the lower slopes and took cover on the El Rhara summit. Thinking the Germans had been cleared off Longstop completely, the British went firm and prepared to hand over to a 'green' American infantry unit. When the Guardsmen had gone *Kampfgruppe* Lang made its move. Hurling grenades and pumping in machine-gun fire, the Germans raced down on the Americans. Totally surprised, the Americans could only flee in panic. By dawn *Kampfgruppe* Lang was back in command of Longstop. It had now started to rain, making all roads and tracks in the area impassable to vehicles.

Not knowing of the defeat, the Coldstream Guards were marching to the rear to celebrate Christmas when they were called back to retake the hill lost by the Americans. French colonial infantry were moved up to support the attack, which was launched in driving winter rain.

Attacking uphill is never easy, but fast-flowing torrents of rainwater were now rushing off Longstop down all the main approach routes used by the British and French. German machine-guns and mortars raked the attackers, who kept on pressing forward. The Guards managed to get small groups of men up to the summit and vicious bayonet fighting took place as they tried to clear a way through the German sangars. The hand-to-hand fighting continued through Christmas Eve and into Christmas Day. This time the Germans held the advantage and the British could not capitalize on their gains. They were pinned down on the slopes taking steady casualties for no gain.

Now the Germans decided to counter-attack to complete their victory. Elements of the *Kampfgruppe* and armoured cars of the 7th Panzer Division made a lightning attack on the village of Heidous at the bottom of Longstop. British troops put up determined resistance until the Germans charged forward to assault and clear each house with bayonets and grenades.

The weather continued to worsen and the battle for Longstop effectively closed down until the spring. British bayonets had met their match. To take it from the 334th Infantry Division the allies had eventually to employ flame-throwers.

The end was now getting near for the Axis forces in Tunisia, with heavy Allied attacks pushing them back into the extreme north-east corner of the country. During late April 1943, while the 334th Infantry Division provided the bedrock of the defence in front of the city of Tunis, all around them the German and Italian forces were collapsing.

Near Medjez-el-Bab on 28 April the US 1st Armored Division hit heavy resistance from dug-in German machine-guns. Company A of the 6th Armored Infantry Regiment was pinned down and taking casualties. Private First Class Nicholas Minue raced forward on a lone charge through withering enemy fire armed with nothing but his M1 Garand rifle and bayonet.

He made it into the enemy machine-gun post, bayoneting and shooting ten Germans. Still wild with battle rage he continued advancing, clearing enemy foxholes with his bayonet until he was hit by German fire and fatally wounded. His Congressional Medal of Honor citation said he faced 'inevitable death'. Inspired by their comrade's sacrifice, Company A soon cleared the rest of the German position and opened the way forward.

By 25 May 1943 the last remnants of the Axis forces in Tunisia had been defeated and resistance ceased. Some 238,000 Axis troops surrendered.

The US Rangers – Tunisia/Italy

The US Army Rangers were first formed in June 1942 to be an elite raiding force. This was initially intended only as a means to allow Americans to gain combat experience alongside the famous British Commandos on raids against Nazi-occupied Europe. Once 'blooded' in action the men would return to their parent units to pass on their new-found knowledge and skills.

Major-General Lucian K. Truscott, considered by many to be the 'father' of the Ranger idea, picked the name after Major-General Dwight D. Eisenhower, who was then working in the Pentagon, suggested that the new raiding force have an 'all American' name rather than adopt the British 'Commando' title. The name 'Rangers' was picked because of its association with groups of frontiersmen who operated long before even the American War of Independence. The new unit was designated the 1st Ranger Battalion.

The first intake of Rangers was drawn from US Army units based in Northern Ireland, and they were sent off to the British Commando Depot at Achnacarry, in Scotland, for their first taste of life in the special forces. Here the Rangers picked up the Commandos' use of knives and bayonets as silent killing tools. These skills were essential if the Rangers were to be able to penetrate deep behind enemy lines without being detected. A sharp blade was considered the best way to deal with an enemy sentry without alerting his comrades.

Under the command of their daring leader, Lieutenant Colonel William 'Bill' Darby, the Rangers learnt fast from the British instructors. A small group went ashore in Europe during the disastrous Anglo-Canadian raid at Dieppe in August 1942, so becoming the first US Army troops to set foot on Hitler's Fortress Europe.

The Rangers' first real combat operation took place in November 1942 when they spearheaded the Allied landings in French North Africa, code-named Operation Torch. In a surprise amphibious raid they stormed ashore and captured the docks at Arzew. After a brief firefight the French defenders surrendered to the Rangers, for the loss of only one American. They were later involved in mopping-up operations against a few pro-German Vichy French units, but were soon allowed to concentrate on recruiting and training new men.

A new Rangers training school was set up along the lines of the British Commando Depot, where budding Rangers were taught the basics of hand-to-hand combat. Knife and bayonet fighting skills were still a high priority, with Colonel Darby setting up the 'Bullet and Bayonet' course. This trained pairs of Rangers to fire and manoeuvre down a training range, shooting and bayoneting targets as they went. A 'buddy' was always covering a Ranger with rifle fire as he moved down the range or bayoneted an enemy.

Realism in training was considered very important by Colonel Darby, so training exercises such as the 'Bullet and Bayonet' course were conducted with live ammunition being fired over the heads of the participants and live grenades exploding nearby. Where possible captured enemy weapons and ammunition were used to allow Rangers to get to know their distinctive sounds. These exercises soon progressed and they then began to take place at night. It was recognized that Rangers would be killed or injured in these exercises and an 'acceptable' level of losses was built into the training programme.

In February 1943 the Rangers were sent to the front in Tunisia where they carried out hit-and-run raids against the German front line until Rommel's offensive drove back the Americans at Kesserine Pass. In response, Lieutenant General George Patton's II Corps was to spearhead the American counter-attack against the Germans and Italians in 'Operation Wop'.

The Rangers scouted ahead of the 1st Infantry Division, finding that the enemy had withdrawn into a strong, fortified defensive position in the Djebel el Ank Pass. Elements of the Italian Cenauro Armoured Division had dug in behind minefields, barbed wire and road blocks. Anti-tank guns, mortars and machine-guns covered the obstacles. The enemy commanders believed the high escarpments to the north and south of their position were impassable.

A frontal assault on Italian positions would have been suicidal, so Colonel Darby and his men were given the mission of infiltrating the northern escarpment and assaulting the Italians from behind, while the 26th Infantry Regiment made a diversionary attack in the front. The attack was set for first light of 20 March. Colonel Darby and his officers had two days to make their plans, and promptly set off on long reconnaissance missions to find a way through the escarpment.

They found a tortuous sixteen-kilometre route through fissures, rocks, cliffs and saddles to a position overlooking the Italians. These patrols confirmed that the Italians had indeed left their back door open. At 21.00 on 20 March the Rangers were ordered to begin their attack, with a 4.2-inch mortar company attached to provide heavy fire support. Colonel Darby's men, their faces blacked out with camouflage paint, were raring to go, and were soon led along the previously reconnoitred route by scout teams. Long before first light the Rangers were in position on a plateau overlooking the Italians. The mortars were struggling along with their heavy kit, and would not be in position before dawn. Colonel Darby decided to go ahead without them.

Dead on 06.00, Ranger machine-gun teams started to blast the Italian positions sending the unsuspecting troops scurrying for cover. The Rangers then charged forward with bayonets fixed, to the sound of a bugler standing amid the machine-gun positions.

Screaming insults in Italian the Rangers ran towards the enemy. They sprayed bullets and threw hand grenades on their way in. Once among the Italians the Rangers set to with the bayonet. Colonel Darby was at the front of this charge, repeatedly shouting to his troops, 'Give them some steel'.

In twenty minutes they had cleared the northern half of the Italian position, scores of enemy dead were sprawled around their gun pits and others had raised the white flag. The mortars now got into position and started to blast those small groups of Italians who were retreating. Colonel Darby sent one Ranger company to clear the southern half of the Italian position. They again charged across a section of open ground to get to the Italian trenches, but the fight had already gone from the enemy. The Rangers' Italian-speaking British chaplain was soon able to negotiate surrender terms with an enemy officer.

By 11.20 the 26th Infantry Regiment had been successfully guided through the now abandoned Italian defences by the Rangers, and the regiment started its advance eastwards. The Rangers alone took 200 prisoners, while the 26th Infantry mopped up a further 800 as they advanced through Colonel Darby's positions. Only one Ranger officer was slightly wounded during the daring charge.

Impressed by the performance of the Rangers in Tunisia, the US Army now expanded the force to three battalions, in time for the invasions of Sicily and Italy. Their daring was used to the full in these operations and they scored some notable successes. Promoted to full colonel, Darby was, however, very concerned that rapid expansion was diluting the quality of his elite force to unacceptable levels. The new 6615th Ranger Force (Provisional) was used as conventional infantry after the landings at Salerno in September 1943, before being pulled out of the line for retraining in amphibious warfare in preparation for the new landings planned for Anzio in January.

Allied advances up the Italian peninsula had been brought to a halt before Rome by the strong German defences of the Gustav Line. Repeated attempts to push through these defences had been halted with heavy casualties, so the Allies planned to outflank the Germans with an amphibious landing at Anzio and then go on to seize Rome. The Rangers were to spearhead this vital assault.

Only two German sentries opposed the Rangers when they waded ashore at Anzio on 22 January 1944. Both were killed and soon the rest of the American–British force came ashore in strength. The commander of the beachhead, US Army Major-General John P. Lucas, was too cautious, and he failed to capitalize on his early success, concentrating on building up supplies rather than aggressively pressing inland to unhinge the weak German defences. It was not until 30 January that General Lucas ordered his troops to break out of the bridge-head. The Germans had by then brought up the Hermann Goering Panzer Grenadier Division to bolster their defences.

Colonel Darby and his Rangers were given the mission of pushing three kilometres behind enemy lines in a night attack to seize the key town of Cisterna, which would allow the US 3rd Infantry Division to break through the main German defence lines. Good patrolling had discovered a three-kilometre-long drainage ditch, called the Fossa di Pantano, which would allow the Rangers to penetrate undetected through the Germans' lines.

Just after 02.00 on 31 January, the 1st and 3rd Ranger Battalions started to move forward into the ditch, while Colonel Darby set up his forward command post in a farm-house just inside Allied lines. The assault troops formed a long column as they hunched and crawled along the ditch. Now the inexperience of the Rangers began to affect the operation. Four of the 1st Battalion's radio operators got lost, and then the unit got split into two groups after three companies were left behind following a halt. The commander of the 3rd Battalion was also killed by a stray German tank shell.

In spite of these problems the Germans had not yet spotted the column, although enemy patrols had been seen moving nearby. Two groups of German sentries were killed with knives by Rangers to prevent the discovery of the column. Lieutenant James G. Fowler personally dispatched two Germans. An enemy artillery battery was bypassed successfully. Then, as dawn broke, the two battalions found themselves looking down on a large German tented camp outside Cisterna. Still undetected, the Rangers tried to radio Colonel Darby for orders but they could not establish contact. The men decided to attack regardless. They swept into the camp at bayonet point, silently killing scores of Germans, then moved on towards the town only 400 metres ahead. Now the Hermann Goering Division opened fire. Scores of Rangers were killed in the hail of machine-gun fire, tank shells and mortar rounds. Colonel Darby's 4th Ranger Battalion was due to attack up the main road to support the 1st and 3rd Battalions. It met heavy resistance from German tanks and got

THE SECOND WORLD WAR

nowhere near Cisterna. The veteran Ranger commander could only wait in his command post as his troops were being massacred just five kilometres away.

For two hours the trapped Rangers traded murderous fire with the Germans. Both sides tried to charge each other, only to be driven back with heavy losses. German tanks took up positions surrounding the Rangers, pouring fire into them. German paratroopers (*Fallschirmjaeger*) came up to complete the encirclement and *Nebelwerfer* rocket launchers blasted the Rangers, who were desperately trying to summon relief on their radios.

At midday the Germans ceased fire. The Rangers saw a couple of armoured half-tracks moving forward with a dozen American prisoners walking in front of them. The Germans were calling out to the Rangers to surrender. In response Ranger marksmen shot dead two of the German guards, who promptly bayoneted two Americans. Two more Germans were shot and two captured Rangers were bayoneted.

This bloody sequence of events was having a terrible effect on Ranger morale and some were starting to drift out of their trenches waving white flags. Pandemonium broke out when some of the more determined Americans opened up with rapid fire on the Germans and at a few Rangers who were trying to surrender.

Now the Germans moved in for the kill. Their *Fallschirmjaeger* surged forward, clearing out the remaining Rangers from their positions. Small groups made a run for it but only six of the 767 men who had infiltrated Cisterna the night before made it back to Colonel Darby's command post. The 500 or so who were captured were marched through the Italian capital like Roman slaves.

BAYONET BATTLE

Primosole Bridge

Allied troops gained their first foothold on Hitler's 'Fortress Europe' on 10 July 1943 with the start of Operation Husky. The invasion of Sicily, Italy's large southern island, began well enough with the British and American forces coming ashore to negligible opposition. This was not surprising as the dispirited Italian Army was in charge of the beach defences.

Inland, however, were four battle-hardened German divisions – which would prove to be no pushover. The German high command recognized the importance of Sicily to the Nazi war effort, and immediately ordered the movement of elite Waffen-SS panzer divisions and Wehrmacht units to Italy. If Sicily fell, Benito Mussolini's fascist regime could also fall, opening up the whole of Germany's southern flank to Allied attack. The Allies were equally determined to ensure that they cleared up Sicily before any German reinforcements could stabilise the situation and lock them into a bloody war of attrition. There was also personal prestige at stake. Lieutenant General George Patton and his British counterpart Lieutenant General Sir Bernard Montgomery were already great rivals. They both wanted the glory that would go with getting their tanks to the Straits of Messina first, thus blocking the escape of any Germans from the island.

On the east of Sicily, Patton's troops were pushing towards Palermo, while Montgomery's 8th Army had landed on the south-west corner of the island. Its route to Messina was shorter, but the Mount Etna volcano meant that there was only one road for the British Army to take, and that was up the western coast through Catania. To the south of the town was the Primosole Bridge. The fight for this bridge would be one of bloodiest of the whole war. It would also see the only time two rival airborne forces would parachute into battle against each other.

The normally plodding Montgomery decided on a daring dash to Messina, led by a parachute landing to seize the Primosole Bridge. The German Mediterranean theatre commander, Field Marshal Albert Kesselring, also recognized the importance of the bridge, and was rapidly building up his defences around Catania. He ordered his paratroopers (*Fallschirmjaeger*) to seize the Primosole Bridge before the British.

First to the draw was the German 3rd *Fallschirmjaeger* Regiment which jumped into the evening skies over Sicily on 13 July. They were unopposed because the drop was timed to coincide with the RAF's Spitfire pilots' tea break. However the Luftwaffe dropped them in the wrong place and they had to march northwards to the bridge. At almost exactly the same time, the British 1st Parachute Brigade was launching Operation Marston to seize the bridge. The 1st Battalion, The Parachute Regiment, dropped on the objective while two other battalions seized the high ground either side of the bridge. In a serious reverse, however, Allied ships offshore opened fire on the Allied Dakota transport aircraft carrying the British Paras, shooting down fourteen of them and scattering the rest of the force. Out of the 1800 men intended to drop that evening only 250 men made it anywhere near the intended target. British and German paratroopers were mingled together in the Italian olive groves – and it was a race to see who could get to the bridge first. The British won. There were enough of them to overpower the Italian guards and pull out the demolition charges planted all over the bridge's metal struts.

This was the only luck the British Paras were to have that day. Waiting until daybreak to allow time to organize and regroup their scattered troops, the *Fallschirmjaeger* attacked the British in overwhelming strength. First Luftwaffe fighters strafed the bridge, then mortars and 88mm flak guns pounded the Paras. Finally wave after wave of *Fallschirmjaeger* charged the bridge from the south. By 17.00 on 14 July only fifty Paras were left fit to fight, and they were ordered to withdraw to the north, leaving the bridge to the enemy. The remnants, under Lieutenant Colonel Alastair Pearson of the 1st Battalion, made their way southwards to link up with the troops of the Durham Light Infantry (DLI) Brigade. Recruited from the coal mines and shipyards of the north-east of England, the Durhams lacked the cocky arrogance of their airborne comrades, but they were to prove themselves just as tough over the next forty-eight hours. They were also to show how handy they were with the bayonet. After defeating the Italian Napoli Division and capturing its commander on 12 July, the DLI had been marching to link up with the Paras. When the advanced elements of the 9th Battalion, DLI, met Colonel Pearson's ragged group of survivors, most of the DLI Brigade were still some way behind. A counter-attack on the bridge was nevertheless scheduled for 07.30 the following morning. In the face of murderous machine-gun fire, a few platoons of the 9th Battalion were able to cross open ground and reach the river a few hundred metres upstream from the Germans.

In hand-to-hand fighting the DLI were driven back, leaving numerous dead and wounded. With daylight attacks looking suicidal, a night attack was planned with the help of Colonel Pearson for 02.00 on 16 July. The 8th Battalion, DLI, would have the honour of leading this effort. Using local knowledge gained during his brief occupation of the bridge, Colonel Pearson was able to lead the battalion's A and D Companies across a ford several hundred metres upstream of the bridge. It was planned that the rest of the battalion would join them once they had stormed the bridge from the rear.

For ninety minutes the bridge was pounded with artillery and machine-gun fire, then after 02.00 the two assault companies started to wade across the river. They began to hack their way through the thick vines and hedgerows between them and the bridge. Their daring paid off and they met almost no resistance before seizing the bridge. His objective secured, Lieutenant Colonel Bob Lidwill of the DLI now tried to call the remainder of his battalion forward. His radios had been damaged in the river crossing, his signal flares were missing and a Royal Engineers' Bren gun carrier with special radios had been knocked out. A civilian War Office observer on a bicycle saved the day when he took the message back to the follow-up force.

It was just getting light when B and C Companies managed to jog across the bridge and start fanning out to secure it from counter-attack. Someone shouted, 'Push on B Company! There's only a few Eyties [slang for Italians] up front!' This was a slightly optimistic assessment of the tactical situation.

As the two companies moved north from the bridge they were raked by fire from a couple of concealed German MG-42 machine-guns. The Durhams charged forward with bayonets fixed towards the enemy entrenchments that were in and around a sunken road. Lieutenant A. F. Jackson led his platoon towards a machine-gun post but was cut down, and most of his men killed or wounded. For twenty minutes a brutal struggle raged between the DLI and *Fallschirmjaeger*, as they traded bayonet strokes, hand grenades and pistol bullets. Company Sergeant-Major Brannigan bayoneted seven Germans in as many minutes. The bayonet soon became the preferred weapon in this confused battlefield because soldiers, on both sides, were worried about killing their comrades in the darkness if they used grenades or Sten guns. The trees in the forest were later found to be riddled with bullet holes, where soldiers had shot them by mistake thinking they were the enemy. This battle became a deadly game of hide and seek in the morning gloom.

B Company killed or wounded every German in their zone but had only about forty men unhurt. Both sides pulled back to regroup. Survivors described the battle as the 'hardest twenty minutes of the whole war for the 8th DLI'.

As B Company took shelter behind an embankment suddenly a swarm of *Fallschirmjaeger* surged towards them waving their bayonets, shouting and screaming. One platoon was overrun. Disaster threatened until Sergeant-Major Brannigan seized a Bren gun and firing from the hip cut down all the Germans before being killed himself.

As dawn finally broke Colonel Lidwill's men were busy securing their positions for the inevitable enemy counter-attack. A Company in the vineyard was now the target of a full *Fallschirmjaeger* battalion attack, with fixed bayonets. They crawled through the undergrowth and swarmed over the company's two forward platoons. Bayonet fighting and barrages of grenades overwhelmed the defenders, who had to dive into the river to escape. The remnants of A Company fell back on the bridge to seek protection by the rest of the battalion. Throughout the day the Germans tried to charge the 8th Battalion's precarious bridgehead, but they were beaten back with heavy losses. The battalion's mortar platoon alone fired 600 rounds to keep the enemy at bay, and helped stop the enemy putting their comrades to the bayonet.

At nightfall the 8th Battalion was holding firm – if only just. It needed help, and the DLI's 6th and 9th Battalions were ordered to use the same route as the previous night's river crossing and then push deep behind enemy lines, to ease the pressure on their comrades holding the bridge. Making their river crossing at 01.00 the two fresh battalions soon found the vineyard heavy going and the units quickly got split up. In the moonlight small groups of Durhams and *Fallschirmjaeger* fought it out in the thick undergrowth. Captain Reggie Atkinson's B Company, 6th Battalion, led the advance northwards until they met heavy German resistance. One of his platoons was virtually wiped out by machine-gun fire as it moved forward clearing *Fallschirmjaeger* positions with bayonets and grenades. The Germans stood and fought. Not one retreated. It was either kill or be killed. Scores of Germans were bayoneted but at heavy cost – Captain Atkinson lost two-thirds of his men.

The depleted company kept moving, using the same tactics, until they were in position astride the Catania road. The Germans fighting the 8th Battalion were now cut off from their natural line of retreat. Taking refuge in a large shell crater, the remnants of B Company prepared to make their last stand.

The 9th Battalion's night advance was less successful, with the lead company being scattered after suffering heavy casualties. At 06.00 the *Fallschirmjaeger* played their last card. They sent their handful of panzers down the road towards the bridge. British anti-tank gunners soon finished them off, and an hour later the first Shermans of the Royal Tank Regiment began to stream across the bridge. The British armour drove into the vineyard, blasting the German strong points holding up the 6th and 9th Battalions' advance.

A captured Durham was sent forward waving a white flag by the *Fallschirmjaeger* battalion still holding the vineyard. The remainder of the 3rd *Fallschirmjaeger* Regiment escaped by making a desperate march under the noses of the Durhams' blocking position. By midday the DLI Brigade had mopped up all resistance around Primosole Bridge. It was a scene of utter devastation, with British and German corpses, wrecked tanks, smashed rifles and shell craters everywhere. There were more than 300 dead Germans and some 160 were taken prisoner. The three DLI battalions had lost 500 killed, wounded and missing.

The Durhams were in awe of their opponents who had put

up such determined resistance, and their regimental history later said: 'There could have been few better German troops in Sicily than those who held the bridge. They were Nazi zealots to a man, but they fought superbly well.'

As the *Fallschirmjaeger* battalion commander was being led away over the hard-fought-for Primosole Bridge, Lieutenant Colonel Andrew Clarke, commanding officer of the 9th Battalion, reached out and shook his hand. It was just like the end of a toughly fought cricket match!

Italy – Mountain Warfare

They called Italy the 'soft underbelly' of Hitler's Europe; the Allied soldiers who fought there were nicknamed 'D-Day dodgers' because they missed the decisive battles with the Germans in France. For veterans of the Italian campaign, however, the Mediterranean theatre was far from a soft option. From the moment Allied troops set foot on the Italian mainland in September 1943 until the final surrender in 1945, they had to fight a brave and professional foe in some of the most demanding terrain in Europe.

Italy's mountainous 'spine' meant close-quarter fighting was inevitable, leading to a clash of bayonets in many battles. Combat in the Italian mountains was small-scale, involving desperate men fighting for survival against terrible odds. The German defenders always made excellent use of the terrain to delay and inflict casualties on the Allies. The Salerno landings near Naples on 8 September 1943 were almost driven back into the sea by a prompt German counter-attack that momentarily panicked the American 5th Army's commander, Lieutenant General Mark Clark. His subordinates were made of sterner stuff though, and one retorted, 'We are going to stay here.'

After much hard fighting the Allies broke out of the Salerno bridgehead and headed north for Rome. In retreat the Germans followed a deliberate plan to delay the Allies at every natural obstacle, to allow time to prepare their main Gustav Line defences some 112 kilometres south of the Italian capital.

This was in hilly terrain, with deep valleys and small villages. Olive groves and vineyards spread out from the villages. The hillsides were usually barren, giving the defenders on higher ground excellent fields of fire. As summer gave way to autumn, temperatures started to drop and the rains began.

As the American 45th Infantry Division, a National Guard unit from Oklahoma, Colorado and Arizona, moved out from the Salerno bridgehead, its soldiers were full of confidence that they had broken the back of enemy resistance. They were wrong. The Germans made a determined stand along the River Volturno in the final days of September.

On the 23rd the 157th Infantry Regiment was closing in on the German-held town of Olivieto. A machine-gun nest was pinning down two American platoons and inflicting heavy casualties. A squad was sent to find a way of outflanking the enemy. Corporal James Slatton, who was leading the squad, worked his way ahead to engage the enemy. He managed to sneak up on the machine-gun team and rushed them, bayoneting the gunner. The bayonet stuck fast in the corpse, so Corporal Slatton had to unclip his rifle and shoot the other German. He then knocked out another machine-gun post with a grenade and shot the crew of a third machine-gun. Thanks to this one man's charge the two platoons were able to withdraw out of danger and then continue the advance. For his efforts Corporal Slatton was awarded the Congressional Medal of Honor.

Operating in the same sector was a unique unit made up of American citizens of Japanese parentage. Known as the Nisei, they were determined to prove their loyalty in the face of great suspicion from most white Americans. The Nisei 100th Infantry Battalion arrived in Italy in September 1943 to join the 5th Army's 34th Division.

They first saw action on 4 November when they were ordered to seize a vital road junction on the far bank of the Volturno. The assault had to cross the steep-sided and fast-flowing river at night. Starting their assault at midnight, the Nisei advanced through intermittent mortar fire and easily crossed the river. One company, however, soon found itself inside a minefield and then was caught in the open by heavy German machine-gun fire.

At battalion headquarters, a few hundred metres behind, they heard a large number of screams and it seemed as if all was lost. Then American weapons were heard returning fire. Unsure what was happening, the battalion commander moved forward to investigate. There he saw a long column of Germans being led away by the Nisei.

It transpired that once the Germans had opened fire, the Nisei took cover behind a wall. In the darkness one platoon commander got lost and his men became despondent. The platoon sergeant discussed the situation and they concluded their officer had been captured. Urgent action was needed to get him back, so they decided to bayonet-charge the Germans. The sergeant ordered the platoon to fix bayonets, but the entire company heard the instruction and followed through. Screaming their battle cry, 'Go for broke!' the whole company surged forward and overwhelmed the startled Germans.

They achieved the distinction of conducting the first bayonet charge by an American unit during the Italian campaign. The following day they were ordered to clear the enemy from the heights above the crossroads. They spent the day using cover to move up close to the hill. As they were moving through the minefield in front of the German position, the enemy detected their presence. Without waiting for fire support the Nisei again charged forward to win the day.

The Nisei remained in Italy until August 1944, when they were transferred to southern France. During its time with the 5th Army the battalion became one of the most highly decorated units in the US Army. With the Volturno river barrier cleared, the American effort pressed on to their next objective, the so-called Reinhard Line. High in the mountains the 34th Division was ordered to storm Mount Pantano, which was held by a German battalion.

Colonel Frederick Butler's 168th Infantry Regiment was to lead this effort in a daring night attack on 29 December. Using a covered track, the colonel's troops were able to climb the mountain without attracting the attention of the defenders. By dawn they were at the summit, and after a brief artillery barrage the lead company formed a line. They raced forward and the few Germans on the summit were quickly overpowered. Captain Benjamin Butler's A Company was now in possession of the exposed summit, and set about preparing all-round defence until the rest of the regiment could join them. The Germans beat them to it and soon a reinforced company was executing its pre-rehearsed counter-attack plan. Methodically the Germans swept forward bayoneting and grenading as they went. A Company began to fall back under the weight of the attack, when Captain Butler decided to give them a taste of their own medicine. Rallying his small headquarters group and a rifle squad, he charged into the midst of the Germans. Shocked and confused they fled down the mountain, and resorted to mortaring the small group of Americans on the summit.

The clash of bayonets only set the scene for the six-day battle for Mount Pantano. It degenerated into a bloody stalemate after which only 62 Americans of the 173 who assaulted the summit walked off the mountain. Allied troops closed with the Gustav Line in December 1943, and in the first weeks of the new year set about breaching the defences of the main German strong point on the summit of Monte Cassino. The German defenders kept the Allies at bay all through January, inflicting brutal losses on the US 36th Division as it attempted to force a crossing over the River Rapido.

In February the 4th Indian Division and 2nd New Zealand Division took their turn in the Monte Cassino meat grinder. The 1st Battalion, The Royal Sussex Regiment made a rare breakthrough on the night of 15 February and got one of its companies on to the slope of Mount Calvary, just below the monastery that dominated the area.

At dawn the rest of the battalion charged forward and began clearing German positions with bayonets and grenades. Amazingly they managed to secure Mount Calvary. Then in a bizarre incident, the Germans fired three green flares to signal a counter-attack. This was also, however, the signal for the Royal Sussex to withdraw and they duly followed orders, leaving the German defences intact.

In May the Germans were still holding out. The answer was to breach the defences high in the mountains and drop down behind Monte Cassino. The US 383rd Infantry Regiment spearheaded the advance through the mountains. Its lead battalion ran into the Germans on 13 May and suffered a traumatic baptism of fire. In a night attack the troops suffered grievous losses, until a wounded lieutenant led his platoon in a mad bayonet charge at the Germans. Survivors said it was just like a drill, bayoneting the enemy as if they were dummies on a training field. After the fighting was over, the Americans regrouped and waited for the inevitable counter-attack. It did not come. The German defences were cracking open. On 5 June Rome fell.

Now the Germans withdrew to their Gothic Line near Florence and prepared for another round. The stage was set for a repeat of the Monte Cassino battles.

One bright spot amid the carnage was the daring attacks of the 4th Indian Division. It went into action on 26 August and battered its way through the Gothic Line, taking Monte della Croce and Montecalvo in a series of bloody battles. The last bastion of German resistance was the defence bastion of Tavoleto, which was defended by dug-in and interconnected machine-gun posts, along with numerous minefields.

In an unprecedented example of personal leadership a single British lieutenant managed to stir up the 2nd Battalion, 7th Gurkhas, into a fighting frenzy. One account says the Gurkhas refused numerous orders from higher command to advance because of the heavy defences around the German bastion. The lieutenant said he was going to advance anyway, with or without the Gurkhas, and started walking towards the German lines. Shamed by their behaviour, the Gurkhas swarmed after the officer brandishing bayonets, kukri knives and grenades. All through the night they stalked through Tavoleto killing Germans. At dawn the only Germans left alive were prisoners and only thirty Gurkhas were left unwounded.

Seeing action for the first time the 43rd Gurkha Brigade was determined to make a name for itself. In a daredevil assault on Passano Ridge on 13 September 1944 it certainly made an impression. The terrain was so broken by gullies and forests that conventional infantry tactics were discarded. Instead the Gurkhas moved forward in small parties, infiltrated German lines and overran their trenches with short charges. Bayonets and kukris were used to kill the King's enemies with terrible efficiency.

It was an engagement typical of the war in Italy, a bloody affair throughout, which reduced combat to a squalid level, where the bayonet was a highly suitable weapon.

BAYONET BATTLE

Waffen-SS Battles in Normandy

To throw back the coming Allied invasion of his 'Fortress Europe', Hitler ordered a massive build-up of forces in France during the final months of 1943. One of the units specially formed to counter the invasion was the 12th SS Panzer Division *Hitlerjugend* of the Waffen-SS, which was recruited almost exclusively from the ranks of the Nazi Party's youth movement. Stiffened by a cadre of veteran officers and non-commissioned officers from the 1st SS Panzer Division *Liebstandarte*, the division began training in October 1943.

Soon the division boasted a full complement of panzers, artillery, armoured troop carriers, mortars, machine-guns and other weapons. Crucially the veteran Waffen-SS instructors put great stress on teaching the teenage panzergrenadiers (armoured infantry) of the division's very high level of infantry combat skills. For months they drilled and drilled, with assault tactics, live firing and bayonet fighting. They were treated to a unique band of discipline, smoking was banned and soldiers under eighteen years old were not allowed to drink alcohol.

During their training, the youths' Nazi beliefs were further heightened by constant indoctrination with political propaganda. As the date of the Allied invasion approached, the *Hitlerjugend* considered themselves ready for anything the Americans and British could throw at them. They were eager to prove themselves in action and create new Waffen-SS legends.

The division was commanded by SS Brigadeführer Fritz Witt, but he was to die within ten days of D-Day, leaving SS Standartenführer Kurt Meyern, know universally as 'Panzer-meyer', to take over command for the remainder of the Normandy campaign. A veteran of all the Waffen-SS campaigns of the previous five years, he was totally fearless. However, he was also ruthless and would be later convicted of war crimes for murdering forty-five Canadians captured by his troops on 8 June 1944.

On 6 June the division was based to the east of Caen, just a few kilometres from the invasion beaches. It had to suffer a day of bombing before receiving orders to move against the Allied bridgehead. Naturally Panzermeyer was in command of the division's first *Kampfgruppe* (battle group) to see action, turning back the 3rd Canadian Division attacking the north-east corner of Caen.

Outside the town of Franqueville, he placed his panzers, 88mm flak guns and panzergrenadiers in ambush positions and waited for the Canadians to enter his trap. The Waffen-SS training and discipline paid off and Panzermeyer's troops held their fire until the Canadians were inside the 'killing zone'. When the Canadians were only eighty metres from his positions Panzermeyer gave the order to fire.

Reeling under the sudden barrage of well-aimed fire, the Canadians started to falter. The North Nova Scotia Highlanders, Cameron Highlanders of Ottawa, Sherbrooke Fusiliers, Regina Rifles, Royal Winnipeg Rifles, backed by the 27th Armoured Regiment, suffered grievous losses. They began to retreat and Panzermeyer launched his panzer-grenadiers in pursuit. By 05.00 the Canadians and Waffen-SS were fighting it out in the villages of St Contest and Buron. In the streets, back-alleys and courtyards, tanks and artillery were little use. Sub-machine-guns, grenades, bayonets and daggers were the weapons of choice. Said one participant, 'The strength of the Canadian Army was as close-in fighters. They went at it like hockey players.' That day the Canadians lost thirty tanks and 300 men, against 200 Waffen-SS casualties and six lost tanks.

At dawn the *Hitlerjugend* pressed their advantage against the Royal Winnipeg Rifles, seizing the villages of Norrey and Putot. By 17.30 the Canadians had reorganized and charged forward to turf them out. Panzergrenadiers were now loaded on the backs of a company of Panther tanks, which charged forward with guns blazing. They pressed deep into the Canadian lines, surprising the headquarters of the Regina Rifles at Bretteville-l'Orgueilleuse. The panzergrenadiers jumped off the tanks and with any weapon that could be found got stuck into a running brawl. They got the worst of it though. Six Panthers were knocked out and the *Hitlerjugend* beat a hasty retreat.

This pattern of combat was repeated for the next weeks, with the Canadians losing almost 3,000 casualties in the first six days of their engagements with the Waffen-SS. A month later half the soldiers of the *Hitlerjugend* would be dead.

On 17 June the British 49th Division was fed into the line as part of General Sir Bernard Montgomery's Operation Epsom. Two armoured and two infantry divisions were to smash into the *Hitlerjugend* and open the front to the west of Caen. Waves of British tanks and infantry struck against the beleaguered Waffen-SS outposts. Ten days later the British had pressed eight kilometres into German lines and were massing in Boislande woods ready to seize the village of Rauray. British tanks and a series of artillery barrages then knocked out the Waffen-SS tanks protecting the village.

At midday on 26 June the 11th Battalion, The Durham Light Infantry (DLI), formed up to take Rauray from the *Hitlerjugend*. Two companies fixed bayonets and started to walk towards the Germans in extended line. It was just like the Somme. Mortars and artillery peppered the village as the infantry advanced. Then the *Hitlerjugend* opened up with their MG-42 machine-guns and 81mm mortars.

Almost every officer in B Company was hit, the officer commanding D Company was killed, and scores of soldiers were cut down. The Durhams, though, kept going and reached Rauray in large numbers. They set about bayoneting and 'mopping-up' any *Hitlerjugend* they found. As they worked through the village the Durhams were plagued by snipers, who had come up with an ingenious way of avoiding the British bayonets – they tied themselves into trees. The DLI shot twenty snipers who were camouflaged in trees and left them hanging as an example to any others who were still thinking of resisting. Fanatical resistance was still the norm in the ranks of the *Hitlerjugend* . Only one sniper was captured. He was taken to Lieutenant Colonel Michael Hammer. The youth was weeping with rage at being captured alive and spat at the Durhams' colonel. A copy of *Mein Kampf*, the Nazi bible, was found in his pockets. The *Hitlerjugend* made the Durhams pay heavily for their success, inflicting 200 casualties that day.

By this stage in the campaign, Panzermeyer's division was so weakened that it could not muster the strength to mount a significant counter-attack against the Durhams. The writing was on the wall for the *Hitlerjugend*. Throughout July the Allies continued to grind down the German defences in Normandy in a series of short, sharp offences. The Germans eventually began to run out of reserves to plug the gaps. Lieutenant General George Patton's 3rd Army finally broke out, pushing south and then swinging east to trap the Germans in a huge pocket centred on the town of Falaise. To keep the pressure on, Montgomery then launched Operation Totalise to link up with Patton and seal the net around the 450,000 Germans still left in Normandy.

A 200-strong *Kampfgruppe* of the *Hitlerjugend* stood in the way of Operation Totalise at Falaise. It had only two Tiger I tanks to hold the 6th Canadian Brigade at bay, which was itself backed by tanks and artillery. The Canadians advanced at 03.00 on 16 August with strong tank support. After a duel between the Canadian and German tanks ended with the panzers withdrawing to avoid destruction, the South Saskatchewan Regiment moved forward, clearing

Hitlerjugend snipers from behind hedgerows and knocking out a number of anti-tank guns.

Inside the village the *Hitlerjugend* had created a number of strong-point houses, with barricaded doors and windows. To clear these out the Canadians brought up tanks and blasted an entry into the village. A runner brought the news to the *Kampfgruppe* commander SS Sturmbannführer Krause, warning him that the Canadians were moving towards the centre of the village.

The Sturmbannführer mustered twenty men – radio operators, drivers and clerks – from his small headquarters and headed out to deal with the incursion. He picked up a few panzergrenadiers as he advanced on the Canadians. They charged the Canadians up the street, fighting with entrenching tools and bayonets. In shock the Canadians retreated to the town walls and reorganized themselves. Next time they too came back with tanks. Not even daring bayonet charges could turn back scores of Shermans.

This was the beginning of the end for the Germans. They were soon trapped, and those troops that did escape from the Falaise pocket only carried away their rifles.

Defeating Germany

During August 1944 Allied armies surged across France meeting negligible resistance from the retreating Germans. It seemed as if the war was as good as over. The defeat of the Allied airborne forces at Arnhem in September shattered these illusions, however. German commanders were masters of improvisation and had reorganized their battered forces to establish a defence line along the Third Reich's western border. In October 1944 the Allies captured their first German city, Aachen, after a short but stiff fight. Hitler's infamous Westwall or Siegfried Line had been breached, so surely now, everyone thought, the Germans were finished. They were very wrong.

The scene was set for a series of bloody battles, as the Germans fought for every hill, wood, farmhouse, village, town and city west of the Rhine. Some of the bitterest fighting would take place in the wooded hills beyond Aachen. Known as the Hurtgen Forest, the region would take six months for the Americans to clear. It became known to the six infantry and two armoured divisions who fought there as the 'Death Factory'. Making use of the thick woods and deep valleys, the German defenders turned the forest into a fortress. Every two weeks the Americans rotated a new division into the front line to continue the futile effort to bludgeon a route through. The result was almost always the same – nearly 50 per cent casualties for no gain. Two American infantry regiments lost almost 100 per cent casualties. During the six-month battle 30,000 Americans were killed or wounded, plus 16,000 British and Canadians who were involved on the fringes of the battle.

More often than not the only way forward was to take on the enemy positions, with grenades, satchel charges or bayonet charges. It took exceptional bravery to get anywhere near the enemy bunkers.

The US 1st Infantry Division, 'The Big Red One', was considered one of the best infantry outfits in the European theatre, but even it hit the buffers in the Hurtgen Forest. Fighting in the northern section of the forest in November 1944, the division ran into fanatical German resistance. Its 16th Infantry Regiment successfully captured a German position near Hamich after taking heavy losses. Technical Sergeant Jake Lindsey's forty-strong platoon was reduced to only six men during the battle.

They began digging in by their objective when a German infantry company with five tanks mounted a counter-attack.

The sergeant moved forward out of his position, dodging enemy machine-gun and rifle fire to take out the enemy tanks with rifle grenades. He then started to get his anti-tank weapons on target, so the enemy panzers pulled back out of the action.

Although wounded, Lindsey now set up a one-man fire base, raking the German infantry with rifle fire and grenades until he ran out of ammunition. A German squad now set up a machine-gun fifty metres away from his platoon, so Sergeant Lindsey turned to the only option available to him. He fixed his bayonet on his M1 Garand rifle and single-handedly charged the eight enemy. Reaching the enemy position he set about bayoneting three of the Germans. Three others surrendered rather than share their comrades' fate, but two managed to escape.

His one-man charge had secured his platoon's position and driven back a massively superior force. For his superhuman efforts, Sergeant Lindsey was awarded the Congressional Medal of Honor.

Four days later, Lieutenant Colonel George Mabry was also to win the highest US award for valour leading a daredevil bayonet charge right into the heart of the German defences. The colonel commanded the 2nd Battalion, 8th Infantry Regiment, which was part of the 4th Infantry Division. Attacking near the small town of Schevenhutte, his unit was halted by a minefield and then pinned down by heavy enemy machine-gun fire.

Rushing to the edge of the minefield to join his troops, Colonel Mabry soon found a safe route through, then led the way with a small scout team. On the way through the minefield they found a booby-trapped obstacle of concertina barbed wire. He defused the booby trap and cut the wire. Up the track were three log bunkers housing machine-guns. Without waiting for his scouts, the colonel raced up to the first bunker only to find it empty. Moving to the next one, he found nine Germans inside who were at that very moment trying to get out of the door. Colonel Mabry butt-whipped the first German and then bayoneted a second. Now his scouts were on the scene and the remaining Germans were put to the bayonet.

The occupants of the third bunker were putting down fire on the small group of Americans, but this did not deter them. They charged into the remaining bunker, forced an entry and bayoneted the six defenders. With their defences breached, the Germans were not able to withstand the Americans' advance that day and the 2nd Battalion soon occupied a key piece of high ground. Unfortunately Colonel Mabry's success was a rare event in the otherwise uninspiring Hurtgen Forest campaign.

With the defeat of the German offensive into the Ardennes in December 1944, Allied forces now began the slow process of clearing the Germans from the west bank of the Rhine. This was a methodical and dangerous business with small groups of Germans establishing themselves in heavily fortified houses and defensive positions. Snap counter-attacks were always a constant danger.

Lieutenant General George Patton's US Third Army played a key role in defeating the Ardennes offensive, and was then tasked to clear up the remaining pockets of enemy resistance in Luxembourg. The US 319th Infantry Regiment of the 80th Infantry Division was holding the line near Dahl, when a German counter-attack struck its B Company. Sergeant Day G. Turner's squad took the brunt of the overwhelming attack, which was preceded by heavy artillery, mortar and rocket fire. Leading his nine comrades back into a large house, Sergeant Turner decided they had to fight to the last man.

The Germans started blasting the house with artillery, and eventually got into one of the rooms. Five of his men were wounded, but Turner still refused to give up. He drove back the first wave of Germans with a can of flaming oil. A hand grenade duel then broke out as both sides tried to gain the upper hand. At a crucial moment in the struggle, two Germans tried to kill Sergeant Turner when they charged through a doorway, but the sergeant was ready and bayoneted both of them. When his own ammunition was finally exhausted, the sergeant picked up German weapons and kept up his determined defence. Four hours later the Germans gave up the struggle. Twenty-five of them surrendered to the three unwounded Americans of Sergeant Turner's squad. Eleven Germans were dead and a large number wounded. For his amazing display of bravery, Sergeant Turner won the Congressional Medal of Honor.

In the final week of March 1945 Allied troops stormed across the River Rhine to begin their drive into the heart of Nazi Germany. With the last natural defence line breached, the German defences began to fracture. Huge Allied armoured columns raced deep into Germany. Only occasionally did the last remnants of the once mighty Wehrmacht put up serious resistance, but when fighting did occur it was short and brutal. The US 7th Armored Division was part of the Allied southern pincer that was racing to surround 500,000 German troops in the Ruhr industrial region. Some 300 metres outside the small town of Kirchain the division's lead task force of armoured infantry was halted by heavy small-arms and *panzerfaust* (hand-held anti-tank rocket) fire. The German defenders were trying to keep the Americans from two bridges that had been wired for demolition.

Staff Sergeant Robert Dietz and his infantry squad moved forward from their armoured half-tracks to protect combat engineers who were starting to clear a path through the mine-field. In a one-man effort Sergeant Dietz crawled forward under heavy fire to attack the *panzerfaust* teams holding the bridges.

He was able to shoot dead one of the teams and then moved on to take out the next team. Rushing in to surprise the enemy soldiers, he bayoneted the *panzerfaust* operator and shot the other two Germans. Despite being knocked to the ground by the back blast of another *panzerfaust* being fired, Sergeant Dietz was quickly able to locate and shoot the last enemy anti-tank team and kill them. His mission still not complete, the sergeant jumped into the waist-deep water under the bridges and started ripping and cutting the wiring of the demolition charges. As he stood up to signal to the stalled armoured column that the bridges were clear, a German sniper on the far bank shot him dead. For his lone charge Sergeant Dietz was awarded the Congressional Medal of Honor.

British troops were also in the thick of the action during the dying days of the Third Reich, clearing houses with bayonets and grenades all along the Rhine. One company of the 51st Highland Division even bayonet-charged their comrades by mistake. Seeing German bodies and helmets in their position the company commander thought it was an enemy strong point. He ordered 'fix bayonets!' The Highlanders braced themselves for death and set out at a terrible pace towards the enemy, who seemed to be waving white flags. Surrender was not on the agenda, so the Highlanders sprayed the 'enemy' trenches with Sten-gun fire as they ran in. As the Highlanders jumped down into the trench they were surrounded by scores of their comrades who were falling about laughing.

Banzai – Malaya and Singapore

Japan's surprise air attack on the US Pacific Fleet in Pearl Harbor on 7 December 1941 plunged the Far East into a four-year war. Within hours of the carrier-borne aircraft striking at the heart of US power in the Pacific, Japanese sailors and soldiers were beginning a series of coordinated offensives throughout South-east Asia. Hong Kong, Thailand, the Philippines and the Dutch East Indies would all fall within a few weeks. The most spectacular success would be in British-ruled Malaya and Singapore. Some 130,000 British and Dominion troops were captured and 9,000 killed in a 73-day campaign. This was the worst defeat of British arms in the twentieth century.

The key to the Japanese victory was aggressive tactics and fanatical determination to keep attacking no matter what the odds or losses. Under Japan's warrior code, or Bushido, death in battle was the ultimate honour for any of the emperor's subjects. Capture by the enemy on the other hand was the ulti-mate dishonour.

Japanese war minister General Hideki Tojo produced a booklet describing the moral code in which the warrior's duty was to die for the emperor. 'A sublime sense of self-sacrifice must guide you throughout life and death. Think not of death, as you push through, with every ounce of your effort, in fulfilling your duties. Make your joy to do everything with all your spiritual and physical strength. Fear not to die for the cause of everlasting justice.'

The caste of ancient warrior knights – the Samurai – had a powerful place in Japanese history. The Imperial Japanese Army of the 1930s and 1940s saw itself as heirs to the Samurai tradition. It literally believed in victory or death.

Swords and edged weapons have an important place in the Samurai tradition. Nothing was more honourable than for a Japanese officer to go into battle at the head of his soldiers with his Samurai sword in his hand. Many of these sword blades were handed down through generations, and some were over 400 years old. If he failed in battle then the only honourable course was ritual suicide – hara-kiri – using his Samurai sword to disembowel himself. For ordinary soldiers in the twentieth century, the bayonet was a sort of substitute weapon of honour. It was used to kill the emperor's enemies in battle and kill himself if he failed in his duty. A martial art was even developed in the 1930s around bayonet fighting. The Japanese believed their emperor was divine, and that the rising sun had special significance because the emperor was the son of the sun god. Before they went into battle Japanese soldiers would raise their swords and rifles, with bayonets attached, to the dawn sunrise, honouring the emperor's ancestors.

To this divinely inspired sense of self-belief, most senior Japanese officers added a very narrow view both of tactics and enemies. Modern types of weapons, such as tanks, were considered suspect because they were not true Samurai weapons, while all enemies were considered racially inferior and treated with utter contempt. The easy victories of 1941–42 reinforced these racial stereotypes and contributed to rampant overconfidence or 'victory disease'. One commentator summed up the basic tactical thinking of most Japanese commanders, circa 1941–45: 'A good bayonet charge was deemed the adequate response to most military problems.'

Hand-to-hand combat with edged weapons was seen as one area of military expertise where the Japanese were totally superior to their opponents. That inferior opponents would flee rather than fight the Japanese in close combat was a commonly held view among senior commanders throughout the Pacific War. According to the Japanese soldier's guide:

> You should engage in bayonet practice every day, with real weapons. Practice until the mind, the body and the weapon are all coordinated in a perfect forward thrust. Drive the bayonet to the hilt and immediately tackle a second and third enemy. Such practice is excellent for morale. Hand-to-hand combat is the deciding factor in an engagement and is most feared by the American and Australian forces.

Japanese bayonet charges were usually accompanied by blood-curdling shouts of the famous banzai war cry. It is difficult to translate into English but corresponds to, 'May the emperor's era or rule last for 10,000 years,' although the Japanese used it as a general celebration of success or victory. Those on the receiving end of banzai charges recorded that they were a fearsome sight, with hundreds of men running forward shouting, screaming officers waving Samurai swords, soldiers wielding bayonets and throwing grenades. It took strong discipline and nerves to hold position in the face of this torrent of fury.

All non-Japanese were considered inferior and therefore unable to put up any worthy resistance. The Japanese saw the bayonet as a symbol of moral superiority over their enemies – only true warriors, such as the Japanese, could succeed in hand-to-hand combat.

To enhance their prowess with the bayonet, Japanese soldiers had to conduct daily drills with the weapon, even when in the field. It was rare during combat operations for Japanese soldiers even to remove their bayonets. Few photographs show Japanese soldiers without their 15-inch bayonets attached to their Meiji 38 Arisaka rifles. The bayonet had a metal hook just above the hilt, which was designed to trap an opponent's bayonet during bayonet duels, and break it.

While much is made of the Japanese mythical attachment to the bayonet, their fondness for the weapon also had a practical rationale. Japanese strategy emphasized living off the land because they had minimal resupplies of food and ammunition. By restricting the use of scarce ammunition to the absolute minimum, the Japanese increased their tactical mobility and reduced their reliance on logistic support. For this reason the Japanese had a preference for the bayonet in situations where it could replace the bullet, such as close-quarter fighting, prisoner executions and ritual suicides. Hundreds of thousands of civilians and POWs were put to death by bayonet during the war, saving millions of bullets for the war with the Allied armies. Japanese logic?

Japan's Bushido code also meant that running out of ammunition was not an acceptable reason for stopping attacking or surrendering. If Japanese soldiers had no bullets left they just fought on with the bayonet. It was as simple as that.

Japanese regiments always went into battle with colours flying and their loss would dishonour all members of that unit. Once committed to battle they rarely desisted from an attack because of the implications for a unit's or its commander's honour.

Japanese officers were not all rigid automatons. There were small numbers of Japanese officers who recognized that brains rather than brawn could often win battles. Conservation of both troops and skilled officers was also important if the Japanese Empire was not to bleed to death in futile assaults on enemy defences.

The most successful Japanese field commander of the war, General Tomoyuki Yamashita, surrounded himself with open-minded staff officers, who planned and conducted the invasion of Malaya with a degree of flair that would not be witnessed again in a Japanese Army. His main assault force was made up of the 5th and 18th Divisions, which were the most experienced and best trained in the Japanese Army. The Imperial Guards Division was also attached to Yamashita's 25th Army, but it had not seen battle since 1905 and was not considered by the general to be fit for battle.

While Yamashita's subordinates fought according to the Samurai code, he was very careful to avoid unleashing them in situations where it might be to his disadvantage. He only had three infantry divisions to fight down to Singapore and he could not afford for them to be destroyed in futile attacks to satisfy the honour of his subordinates. Only 3,500 Japanese soldiers were killed in the Malaya campaign, testament to Yamashita's careful husbanding of his troops compared to the profligate waste of soldiers in Burma and elsewhere. Staff officers were also dispatched to dissuade subordinates who suffered set-backs from committing hara-kiri. Yamashita was an exponent of what is known in the West as infiltration tactics. He delighted in finding weak spots in the enemy's defences and then piling every soldier at his disposal against that decisive point. Nearly always he would send his troops through thick jungle to find the enemy's undefended flank or rear. Then a banzai charge would be unleashed, with terrible consequences for the enemy. The general was not averse to using banzai charges against the British front line, to distract attention while his troops worked their way round the flank. He usually sent one-third of a regiment to attack frontally while two-thirds were sent on flanking manoeuvres.

These tactics played havoc with the British and Dominion forces in Malaya, who had poor communications, low morale and defeatist commanders. In a crisis they panicked and looked for a quick way out. In any case, the British position in Malaya was a house of cards. Usually a surprise banzai bayonet charge out of the jungle was enough to spark a British collapse.

Japanese troop transports carrying elements of the 25th Army arrived off the Malay Peninsula within hours of the Japanese Navy's strike at Pearl Harbor. The first landing took place just across the border in Thailand and it was not until the early hours of 8 December that troops of Takumi Detachment's 56th Infantry Regiment began to load into launches for the short trip ashore to set foot in the British Empire, at Kota Bharu, on the north-east corner of Malaya.

The sea was rough, making the loading slow and dangerous. Then Australian bombers appeared and set fire to two of the transport ships. It was a do or die situation for the Takumi Detachment. They could not go back once their launches were heading towards the beach. Australian fighters then strafed the landing craft, adding to the carnage. When they finally got ashore a British-officered battalion of the 12th Indian Infantry Brigade was ready and waiting for them.

Field defences had been prepared along the shore line, which was a series of islands and sandbanks. Safe inside barbed wire and bunkers the Indians blasted the Japanese with a hail of point-blank fire. Hand grenades were traded across the barbed wire and the Japanese soldiers used their helmets to dig improvised trenches in the sand. Wire-cutters were brought up to open a path through but the Japanese then found themselves in a minefield.

A fanatically brave Japanese soldier crawled forward through the minefield and leaped up to cover the fire slit of a bunker with his body. With the weight of fire suddenly reduced, a squad of Japanese charged forward to break into the defence system. They gained entry with a barrage of grenades and set about bayoneting the defenders. Shouts of banzai were drowned out by the screams of dying Indians. Every Indian soldier in the front-line trenches was put to the bayonet.

Flushed with their success the Takumi Detachment then charged forward through the surf to assault the second line of defence on the islands further up stream. The Japanese had their tails up. Within minutes they were among the Indians bayoneting like mad.

It took two days for the Japanese to clear the Indian brigade from the town of Kota Bharu and capture its two strategic airfields. After their initial stand on the beaches, the fight had gone out of the Indians and they were soon heading southwards. They gave the Japanese their toughest fight of the campaign, with the invaders losing 320 dead and 538 wounded.

Further east the Japanese 5th Division was crossing the

border into Malaya from Thailand. Its advance was halted by a demolished bridge, so Lieutenant Colonel Saeki sent 200 of his infantry across the ruins of the structure to press southwards.

Mortar shells and machine-gun fire from the Indian rearguard in a rubber plantation raked the Japanese troops, who dived for cover. Green flares were fired in the air ordering the rearguard to withdraw, then the Japanese heard large numbers of vehicle engines starting up. A platoon of Japanese charged forward into the rubber plantation to catch the Indians. Rifle shots and the screams of Indians on the receiving end of the bayonets could be heard. The rest of the Indians did not wait to help their comrades, fleeing at high speed in their trucks.

The systematic destruction of bridges and other items of communication infrastructure threatened to disrupt the Japanese advance, so unorthodox methods were required to seize these vital targets. In the early evening of 11 December, under cover of a heavy tropical rainstorm, a truck column led by a few Japanese tanks drove towards the Changlun bridge. Its defenders, a Gurkha battalion, were sheltering in the plantation on either side of the road when the Japanese suddenly appeared among them. A fierce mêlée developed as the Saeki Detachment and the Gurkhas fought bayonet to kukri in the rain. The road was awash with blood.

As the infantry fought it out, the Japanese tanks drove on, overrunning several bridges and removing demolition charges until they were halted by the main British defensive position in North Malaya, the so-called Jitra Line. Again the Japanese were quick to follow up their success, and within a few hours the Saeki Detachment's infantry were probing the Jitra Line position in the darkness. A young Japanese second lieutenant came back from patrol, reporting the defences were thinly held. So the detachment reserve company was sent forward. With no reconnaissance or artillery support the company charged forward to be cut down almost to a man by the Indian defenders.

Their company commander was killed and the only man to survive came back to report to the detachment commander on their 'success', before collapsing seriously wounded. In Japanese terms death in battle was considered a success.

Downcast, the lieutenant and Colonel Saeki were contemplating hara-kiri but were talked out of it by one of General Yamashita's staff officers. The furious bayonet charge, however, had terrorized the Indians who, seeing the Japanese bringing up reinforcements, fled southwards. Only 150 Japanese had scared away a full Indian brigade. The chase was now on. To maintain the momentum of the advance more bridges had to be seized before the British could blow them. The Japanese 5th Division's advance was led by the Asai Pursuit Troops of the 11th Infantry Regiment. It captured Alor Star on 13 December and began pressing southwards to take two key bridges to the south of the town. An eleven-man squad under Lieutenant Hajime Asai found the main road undefended on the northern bank. He led his men across the bridge under heavy fire to try to disable the demolition charges. The lieutenant jumped down under the bridge to rip out the wiring of the charges when the British blew the bridge, taking the Japanese officer with it. Two corporals guarding the officer survived and were immediately set upon by Indian soldiers. They fought them off with their bayonets, killing several before being wounded themselves. Taking advantage of the confusion, the remaining Japanese soldiers bayonet-charged the nearby railway bridge, putting its defenders to flight. This successful charge won the 5th Division control of a valuable bridge, while the Asai Pursuit Unit was awarded a rare citation for valour by General Yamashita.

For the next two weeks the British and Indians retreated as fast as they could. The 28th Indian Brigade made a determined stand in prepared positions at Kampar in central Malaya, inflicting heavy losses on the Okabe Infantry Regiment in the final days of December.

Now the Japanese employed their infiltration tactics on a massive scale. For two days the Ando Infantry Regiment hacked its way through the thick jungle surrounding the Kampar position. Surviving on cold rice and covered in blood-sucking leeches, the men of the Ando Regiment surged out of the jungle to take the Indians by surprise.

A furious fight developed as the Okabe Regiment again surged forward on the Indians' front. Only a handful escaped the bayonet charge. Hundreds surrendered. The brigade ceased to exist as a fighting unit. For the rest of the month the Japanese kept the British on the run down the length of the Malay Peninsula. The Japanese outflanking tactics nearly always sent the British fleeing. Sometimes the British, Australian and Indian troops stood and fought, but the resistance did not last long. Japanese bayonets usually turned the battle in favour of the Rising Sun. On 26 January a British unit in a fortified section of Mengki Bahru put up a determined last stand against the Japanese Watanabe Regiment. In a massive scrap the British held the attack, until the Japanese managed to sneak a small platoon of twenty-three men through the jungle behind them. Lieutenant Itabana immediately got to the edge of the jungle and opened fire on the British, causing huge panic. The British and Japanese traded furious rifle and machine-gun fire until Itabana's platoon was out of ammunition. The lieutenant then pulled out his sword and led his men in a suicide charge against the British lines. Slashing and stabbing furiously they inflicted grievous losses on the British but at the cost of the entire platoon.

General Yamashita's citation for gallantry said: 'The whole platoon met a heroic death in battle. Their valiant attack was responsible for the destruction of a large number of the enemy, and it must be said, serves as an example for the future conduct of troops in battle. It is acknowledged as a permanently great achievement.'

By the end of January the British had given up trying to hold Malaya and withdrew across the Straits of Johore.

On 8 February the Japanese made their move, storming across on to Singapore Island and scattering all before them. On 10 February the 12th Indian Brigade – the last British reserve – was put into the line to hold the village of Bukit Timah, which controlled Singapore's vital water reservoirs. Realizing the importance of the village the commander of the Japanese 18th Division wanted to take it at all costs.

His advance had outstripped his artillery support and no tanks had yet been ferried across the Straits. Lieutenant General Mutaguchi ordered his troops to take the village at bayonet point in a night attack. Troops from the 5th Division joined the effort. In a brutal night of fighting the defenders of Bukit Timah were put to the bayonet.

The game was up. Singapore was defenceless. British counter-attacks got nowhere. Four days later the garrison surrendered. Japanese bayonets had defeated the might of the British Empire.

Guadalcanal – 1942

Flushed with victory at Pearl Harbor, Hong Kong, Thailand, Malaya, Singapore, the Philippines, the Dutch East Indies, Burma and Wake Island, the Japanese Empire, for the first six months of the war in the Pacific, seemed invincible.

The Rising Sun, however, suffered its first set-back at Midway in June 1942 at the hands of the United States Navy, losing four irreplaceable fleet carriers and 332 naval aircraft. As yet the Imperial Japanese Army had not been defeated in

battle. Its fanatical banzai bayonet charges had carried all
before them, defeating Australian, British, Chinese, Dutch,
Indian, Philippino and United States troops with ease. They
had yet to cross bayonets with the United States Marine
Corps, though.

By the summer of 1942 the Japanese were in control of all
South-east Asia. After the rebuff at Midway, they switched
their line of advance to the Solomon Islands to cut Australia
and New Zealand's vital supply lines to the USA. The
Americans were equally determined to keep this lifeline open
and massed an amphibious task force to turn back the Japanese
advance. Leading this effort was the US 1st Marine Division
under Major-General Alexander Archer Vandegrift. They
were to inflict on Japan their first land defeat of the Pacific
War.

The target for the 1st Marine Division was the Japanese
base on the island of Guadalcanal. Covered in tropical jungle
and with hardly any population, apart from native tribesmen,
the island was a neglected outpost of the British Empire when
the Japanese occupied it in May 1942. The only thing of any
value on the island was its small airfield, which the Japanese
started to build soon after their arrival. Control of the airfield
would bring aerial and naval supremacy over the South Pacific,
and it was to be the Marines' objective.

Dodging Japanese torpedo bombers, cruisers and submarines, the Marines landed on Guadalcanal on 7 August.
Their landing was virtually unopposed by the poorly trained and
equipped Japanese construction troops. When the Marines
advanced on the airfield the following day, the defenders fled
into the jungle. Now the Marines set about building up their
bridgehead and getting the airfield ready to receive fighters.
This build-up suffered a major set-back on 9 August when news
reached the US Navy of the approach of a large Japanese naval
task force. In the space of a few hours the flotilla of US

warships and supply ships off Guadalcanal had upped anchor and put to sea, leaving the Marines to their fate. General Vandegrift, however, was made of sterner stuff than the defenders of Bataan, Corregidor or Singapore. Surrender was the last thing on his mind.

The airfield had been cut out of the tropical rain forest and a large area around it cleared of vegetation. The Marines and Navy Seabee, mobile construction units which were trained and equipped to build airfields and ports in combat zones, continued to improve the airfield and spread their defences around the vital area of open ground. Their perimeter included a large area of beach at the mouth of the River Lunga, which overlooked large sandbars. By 20 August the airfield, newly christened Henderson Field, was ready to receive the first of a continuous stream of US fighters, which would be the saviour of the small American outpost.

The American landing was seen as a major insult to the honour of the Japanese Army. Orders were issued by Tokyo to 'eliminate' immediately the 2,000 Americans believed to be ashore. The Japanese regarded the Marines with total contempt. They would fight no better than the hundreds of thousands of other white troops who had surrendered to the Japanese over the past six months. One good banzai bayonet charge and it would be all over.

Lieutenant General Harukichi Hyakutake's 17th Army was given the task of swatting this stain on the emperor's honour. He ordered the 35th Infantry Brigade to go to Guadalcanal to destroy the Americans. Its first echelon landed on 18 August thirty kilometres down the coast from the Marines. In the mythology of the battle, the Japanese general is reported to have asked 'What is a Marine?' when being briefed on the American landings.

The first troops ashore were under the command of Colonel Ichiki, a distinguished veteran of the China campaign who was convinced that the Americans would put up no serious resistance to his 1000-man force. He decided on a plan of campaign which comprised one day of advancing, one day of battle and then a period enjoying 'the fruits of victory'. So without waiting for the rest of 35th Brigade he set off at the head of his men towards the Marines' lines. The advance was a nightmare and it took twice as long as he expected, but on 21 August Colonel Ichiki was ready to attack.

Listening posts on the western flank of the Marine position heard the Japanese hacking their way through the jungle as they approached. It was as if they wanted to advertise their arrival.

In spite of the warning it was still a shock to the Marines when at just after 03.00 they saw 900 men wading through the surf along the coast, screaming and shouting. Colonel Ichiki, his sword drawn, led his men in a banzai bayonet charge across the sandbar towards the Marines. Many of the Japanese did not even have bullets in their rifles. It was a massacre. Hundreds of Japanese were cut down by the Marines' machine-guns and anti-tank guns, which were firing canister shells. A handful of Japanese got into the American foxholes, bayoneting the defenders before the Marines' reserve battalion could arrive and evict them. Colonel Ichiki rallied his men and led them forward again at dawn. This time they did not even get near the American wire.

At dawn the Marines brought up their Stuart light tanks and a fresh battalion to sweep around behind the Japanese, trapping them in a small pocket at the mouth of the River Tenaru. Marine fighter-bombers joined the battle and began strafing the enemy. Now the mopping-up started in the face of fanatical resistance. Japanese soldiers even faked injury, only to explode grenades when Marine medics tried to administer first aid. When the afternoon's slaughter was complete more than 800 Japanese bodies were piled up in front of the Marine positions. Colonel Ichiki was not among the dead. He and a small group of acolytes managed to evade the Marine cordon. Overcome with grief at his dishonour, the colonel tore up his regimental flag, poured oil on its shreds and set them on fire. He committed ritual suicide with his Samurai sword.

In the face of heroic resistance from Guadalcanal's fighter pilots – the famous Cactus Air Force – the Japanese Navy succeeded in setting up a shuttle service, known to the Americans as the Tokyo Express, to bring in the remainder of the 35th Brigade under Major-General Kawaguchi to complete Colonel Ichiki's unfinished business.

More than 3,000 men were brought ashore by the end of August, and they soon set off on the long slow march towards the Americans to 'avenge the spirits of the Ichiki detachment'. Realizing that the Japanese would attack again the Marines had continued to build up their defences. They worked on the principle that to stop night infiltration by the Japanese, no Marine's foxhole should be more than four and a half metres from his comrade's. The defences around Henderson Field as a result were tight and strong. To complete the ring of steel the Marines' Raider and Parachute Battalions had been allocated the defence of the ridge overlooking the airfield. It was soon known as Edson Ridge after the commander of the Raiders, Lieutenant-Colonel Merritt 'Red Mike' Edson. In the days to come it would also become known as Bloody Ridge.

Like Colonel Ichiki before him, General Kawaguchi was not willing to wait for all his force to hack its way through the jungle or for diversionary attacks to be launched on the rest of the Marine perimeter. As soon as his first troops were close to Edson Ridge, on 12 September, he ordered them into action. A flare was the signal for the attack. Machine-guns softened up the Marines' positions, and then the banzai bayonet charge began. In most places along the line the Japanese attacks were cut down in droves. General Kawaguchi's impetuousness meant there were never enough Japanese soldiers to break through decisively. In a lull in the fighting, the Americans brought up reserves and laid more wire.

At 21.00 General Kawaguchi launched 2,000 of his men in a massive charge. The screaming wave broke over the American lines six times during the night. For nine hours 400 Americans battled the superior numbers in vicious hand-to-hand combat using knives, swords and bayonets. The pressure was too great for the Raiders and they pulled back into a horseshoe-shaped position near the summit to hold the Japanese during daylight. Two bayonet charges before dawn were repulsed when Marine artillery got the range and sliced the attackers to bits. Small groups of Japanese swarmed past the American lines, heading for General Vandegrift's headquarters 1600 metres behind the Raiders' positions.

One Japanese officer tried to break into the command post by hurling his sword 'like a spear' at the Marine gunnery sergeant guarding the entrance. The Marine died but his comrade shot the Japanese officer. On the ridge, Colonel Edson rallied his men for a last stand on the summit, shouting to groups of Marines separated from their units in the confusion of battle, 'Raiders, parachuters, engineers, artillerymen, I don't give a damn who you are. You're all Marines. Come up this hill and fight!' They held out until dawn, when Marine fighter aircraft took off from Henderson Field to strafe the Japanese who remained. Colonel Edson won the Congressional Medal of Honor for his successful defence of Bloody Ridge.

The two days of fighting had left 1200 Japanese dead littered around Bloody Ridge, and more than 500 Marines killed or wounded.

Later that day 4,000 more Marines arrived on transports after slipping past the enemy blockade. General Kawaguchi pulled his wretched survivors back into the jungle, carrying more than 400 wounded with them. He chose not to emulate

Colonel Ichiki's suicide and commented, 'Guadalcanal is not the name of an island: it is the name of the graveyard of the Japanese Army.'

Lieutenant General Masso Maruyama's 2nd Sendai Division was now ordered to Guadalcanal to put paid to the American bridgehead once and for all. The Japanese overall commander, General Hyakutake, had been enraged by the defeats inflicted on the Imperial Army by General Vandegrift and his Marines. He even composed a special set of orders setting out how the Marine general was to be captured and brought before him barefoot. Great honour was now at stake, so the Japanese were committing their best troops. The Sendai Division was spearheaded by the 29th Infantry Regiment, the elite of the Imperial Army, which every December climbed to the summit of Mount Fujiyama in its underwear to prove its physical prowess! To complete his force and close the American airfield for good, General Hyakutake ordered in heavy artillery, and the 38th Division, which was to move to Guadalcanal from Borneo.

To try to disrupt the Japanese preparations, General Vandegrift started to send out Marine battalions on sweeps through the jungle around Henderson Field. On 8 October, during one of these sweeps, they trapped the Japanese 4th Battalion in a gully near Matanibu. In a futile attempt to break out, hundreds of Japanese banzai bayonet-charged the American lines. The whole unit was annihilated and later 600 bodies were found on the battlefield.

General Maruyama was having just as much trouble moving his troops through the jungle as his predecessors, in spite of setting his engineers the task of cutting a road. Still the Japanese commanders were keen to attack before they were ready. Honour was at stake.

On 21 and 22 October Japanese tanks, with hordes of charging infantry behind them, tried to push along the sandbar into Marine lines. Anti-tank guns knocked out the armour and the infantry were slaughtered by machine-guns and artillery before they got near the American wire. Some 22,000 men from the Sendai Division were now massing ready to launch a three-pronged attack. Unknown to the Americans, General Hyakutake kept having to delay the attack because his troops were still struggling to get into position. By the evening of 24 October American patrols was bringing in reports of Japanese troops massing all around the perimeter. Just after dark the glow of the enemy's rice fires were spotted and the Marines went on alert. Then a tropical thunderstorm struck, delaying the Japanese attack again. At 17.30 the Sendai troops moved forward. A small outpost of the 7th Marine Regiment spotted them coming and opened fire, giving a valuable warning to defenders before they slipped into the night to escape. Around midnight the Japanese force of nine battalions screaming banzai reached the edge of the jungle near Bloody Ridge. The Marines held their fire until the Japanese were on their wire and opened up with every machine-gun they had. Every Japanese in the first wave was cut down. Colonel Furumiya then led a second wave over the pile of corpses into the American lines. His men breached the wire, slashing and stabbing with their swords and bayonets. A Marine counter-attack snapped shut the breach. The Japanese officer and his small band reacted in the only way they knew. Banzai! They charged an American machine-gun post, bayoneting its occupants before being cut down by Marine reinforcements.

Throughout the night the Sendai warriors kept charging until they punched hole after hole in the American lines, over-running and bayoneting isolated Marines in their foxholes. With dawn a battalion of US Army troops was sent in and mopped up the Japanese incursions. The surviving Japanese melted back into the jungle. General Hyakutake then mustered his strength for his final death-defying attack.

After dusk the Sendai troops began massing in the jungle opposite Hill 67. In the build-up to the attack they shouted insults at their intended victims, 'Marines you die tonight!' Then came the cry, 'Banzai!' Thousands of Japanese surged out of the jungle to be met by a hail of machine-gun fire. They swarmed over the defenders, slashing and stabbing until reinforcements drove them off. Some 2,500 Japanese were left dead in front of the position.

Marine Sergeant 'Manila' John Basilone won the Congressional Medal of Honor commanding a machine-gun section, which mowed down hundreds of Japanese, securing a vital section of line.

The Japanese, though, were still not finished. General Kawaguchi now had the chance to redeem himself. The battered and half-starved remnants of his brigade (the Japanese restricted rations and medical support to dishonoured units) threw themselves against Bloody Ridge once again. They were repulsed without even getting near the American lines. Again the general refused to commit hara-kiri. He would be later drummed out of the army in disgrace.

Another disgraced officer, Colonel Oka, led the third attempt against Marine lines that night. His troops charged the thinly spread 2nd Battalion, 7th Marines, and overran several positions. Only the platoon of Sergeant Mitchell Paige held out. Hundreds of Japanese charged his small outpost. Eventually all his men were cut down by Japanese fire. Alone, he kept firing until his machine-gun was knocked out. He picked up a weapon from a dead comrade to keep up the withering barrage on the still-advancing enemy. Just as it seemed as if the Japanese would overwhelm his position, reinforcements from the regimental band arrived to help him. Not content to hold the line, Sergeant Paige led his men in a daredevil bayonet charge into the Japanese huddling down the hill. They fled and the brave sergeant was awarded the Congressional Medal of Honor.

To complete the Japanese defeat, the US Navy intercepted a convoy carrying reinforcements to General Hyakutake in the middle of November. It took just over two months for the Marines and newly arrived US Army units to clear the remnants of the Sendai Division from around Henderson Field. In January 1943 the Japanese Army asked to be evacuated from Guadalcanal, its honour for ever tarnished. The Japanese banzai bayonet charge had at last found its equal. In light of the defeat, one Japanese officer wrote, 'The Imperial Staff must reconsider the matter of firepower.'

Aussie Bayonets at Buna

Australia took a very keen interest in the Japanese surge across the Pacific in the spring of 1942. When Singapore and the Dutch East Indies fell, alarm bells started ringing in Sydney. The last line of resistance was New Guinea but it was defenceless. Almost all of Australia's regular troops were fighting in the Middle East with the British 8th Army. In desperation, the Australian Government recalled its troops and hoped the Japanese would not seize Port Moresby, the capital of the Australian territory of Papua, before then. In the meantime the Australians shipped over to Port Moresby as many Citizens Military Force (CMF) Militiamen as could be found. The reservists of the CMF were poorly equipped and few had heard a shot fired in anger.

In the space of a few months the Australian Regulars and Militiamen had turned back the Japanese tide. Then with the help of General MacArthur's Americans they drove the Japanese out of a prepared defensive position for the first time. Just like their forefathers at Gallipoli, the 'Diggers' in the jungles of New Guinea would develop a liking for the bayonet.

Unlike the British who adopted the spike or 'pig sticker'

bayonet for their SMLE rifles, the Australian Small Arms Factory at Lithgow continued to produce the original 17-inch long sword bayonet. This design was closely based on the Japanese Arisaka bayonet, so when the two sides met in New Guinea they both fielded long blades. There would be some vicious bayonet fighting.

Japanese troops landed on the northern coast of New Guinea on 21 July and then began to march over the Owen Stanley range of mountains to attack Port Moresby. The Militiamen of the 39th Battalion made a stand in the mountains but it was a hopeless struggle. Lacking food and ammunition they were not in good condition to stand up to the Japanese banzai charge. They fell back and only just managed to escape Japanese outflanking moves. It only seemed a matter of time before the Japanese reached their objective.

Help was on hand in mid-August when the veterans of the Australian 7th Division began landing at Port Moresby. The first thing they did before marching up tropical jungle-covered mountains was to sharpen their bayonets on rubber plantation grindstones.

A more immediate danger was the threat to the airfield and port at Milne Bay, on the extreme eastern landfall of New Guinea. A large Japanese force with tanks had landed by ship and had pressed on to destroy the militia unit defending the strategic location. They swept everything before them until they tried to storm Airfield No.3. Here the Militiamen held firm and inflicted heavy losses on the banzai charge. The Japanese were caught in the open on the airfield and pulled back when they could not get into bayonet range. A freshly arrived battalion of Regulars then landed and drove off the Japanese, thwarting their offensive in this area for good.

Up in the mountains the Militiamen were at last being reinforced by the newly arrived Regulars. The 39th Battalion received its first reinforcements on 27 August. It was just in time.

BAYONET BATTLE

Late in the morning the Militiamen and a company of Regulars heard a chorus of banzai cries from the jungle, then mortar bombs and artillery bombs rained down on their positions. While the 'Diggers' were still recovering, hundreds of Japanese charged out of the jungle. They were all over the Australian lines, fighting with grenades and bayonets. The fighting turned into a running battle as small groups stalked each other in the undergrowth. Fortunately a fresh company of Regulars arrived. Then the Japanese commander ordered a retreat and a bugle sounded. As if by magic the Japanese disappeared.

Next morning fog descended on the battlefield. Using this as cover the Japanese swarmed out of the jungle again. Observers said they 'screamed wildly' as they charged. Again the Diggers chased them off.

The Australians could only hold their positions at most for another day, until the Japanese found a way to outflank them. Retreat was the only option, and it continued until the middle of September. Disease and lack of food weakened both armies as they struggled across the Owen Stanley Range. The Japanese started to retreat on orders from Tokyo. American victories on Guadalcanal had forced a major rethink.

It was now the turn of the Japanese to suffer in retreat. By the end of November they were besieged in their bridgehead at Buna on New Guinea's northern coast. Now began a month-long battle to batter through the Japanese defences. American troops joined the Australians for this bloody battle.

On 29 November the Americans made a successful attack with fixed bayonets to take a hamlet on the edge of the Japanese positions. It was to be the first of many victories.

As the Allies advanced the Japanese reacted with equal fury. At first the Americans were shaken by the banzai charges. When the Japanese tried to sneak along the beach and take the Americans by surprise on 7 December they made so much noise that the defenders were ready for them. Machine-guns and grenades were turned on them and then a bayonet charge finished off the survivors.

Further up the coast from Buna, the Australians made a surprise attack and trapped 600 Japanese troops in the remote settlement of Gona. The trapped Japanese frantically tried to break out, charging time and again at the Australian lines. Flares lit the night so the machine-gunners could see the enemy. All through the night the isolated shots and screams could be heard. Throughout the following morning the Diggers swept through the Japanese positions, checking the enemy dead and collecting their own wounded. Nine Japanese wounded were found but even they opened fire with rifles and threw grenades at the Australians from their stretchers.

Then suddenly a Japanese officer charged out of the jungle waving his sword and shouting curses. He was shot dead.

After almost three weeks of stiff resistance, the Japanese were beginning to crack. On 18 December the Australians moved up seven Stuart light tanks to the front and massed 500 troops to clear out Japanese positions on Cape Endaiadere, close to Buna.

The attack went in at a walking pace, with the infantry spread out between the tanks for mutual protection. If a bunker opened fire on the infantry the tanks would reply with their 37mm guns. The infantry would then dash forward to bayonet any occupant who might have survived. This was a methodical operation, which was soon cutting deep into the 1,000-strong Japanese garrison. They reacted furiously, charging forward to fire rifles into the driver's slits of the tanks or dropping incendiary bombs on their engines. Only two tanks were knocked out, and the Diggers made sure no more Japanese got close. The advance continued. To help identify the targets, infantrymen fired flares into bunkers. This also set the bunkers on fire and forced more Japanese out into the open to be bayoneted or machine-gunned.

On 2 January 1943 the Americans and Australians launched their final push to clear the remaining Japanese positions around Buna. Using their proven infantry-tank tactics the Allies sliced through the Japanese defences.

The Japanese had already been ordered by Tokyo to evacuate the garrison, but only a few hundred managed to escape on small boats or swim along the coast. The Japanese commander, Colonel Hiroshi Yamamoto and his aide were determined to go down fighting. Their bunker was surrounded by Australian tanks and they were seen coming out. An Australian officer sportingly gave them to the 'count of ten to surrender'. Colonel Yamamoto just tied a Japanese flag to his Samurai sword and held it over his chest. Their count to ten ignored, the Australians riddled him with machine-gun fire. The other Japanese hanged himself from a tree. Some 1400 Japanese bodies were found amid the ruins of Buna. Three weeks later Japanese ships evacuated what remained of their invasion force from New Guinea. Australian and US Army bayonets, like those of the US Marine Corps, had proved themselves against the feared Japanese.

Bayonets in Burma

Fresh from victory in Malaya, the Japanese immediately pressed their advantage against the weak British garrison in Burma. One disaster after another befell the undermanned and poorly equipped British Army, which retreated as fast as it could for the safety of India. Only a miracle prevented the total destruction of the British force.

For two years see-saw battles raged in the thick jungles along the Burma–India border region, in which close-quarter combat with the bayonet played a significant part. The Japanese fixation with bayonet charges continued and was ultimately to be their downfall. However, the British were equally keen on the bayonet when it came to close-quarter combat. One observer described the clash of British and Japanese units in the Burmese jungle as a 'medieval mêlée', as both sides slashed and stabbed at each other. The bayonet was quick and efficient. Too often fanatical Japanese soldiers just kept fighting after being shot or 'winged'. A good jab with a bayonet to the heart or brain ensured they were definitely out of action for the duration. Bayonets were also very useful for ensuring that Japanese corpses were really 'dead' and not just faking it, ready when no one was looking to get up and kill British soldiers from behind. Silent killing was also an essential tactic in jungle warfare, where visibility only measured a few metres. Soldiers fought battles by sounds, listening for the distinctive sound of vegetation breaking underfoot or animals being spooked. Killing with the bayonet allowed positions to be taken in silence and the attack advanced, without alerting the enemy until it was too late.

The thick jungle also to a degree neutralized British fire-power, because it was often impossible to locate the Japanese until they were a few metres away. Then it was too late, and hordes of Japanese would be on top of the defenders, slashing and stabbing with bayonets and Samurai swords. If a Japanese soldier got anywhere close, shooting him became very difficult. British soldiers had to use their own rifles instantly to parry the Japanese bayonet thrusts or risk getting stabbed, before having the chance to get off any aimed shots. Early experience in jungle bayonet fighting led the British to find that their 8-inch spike or 'pig sticker' bayonet for their Short Magazine Lee Enfield (SMLE) left them at a disadvantage against Japanese wielding the 15-inch Arisaka blades. The

Japanese had an immediate length advantage that could prove decisive.

While the British spike bayonet was ideal for stabbing a victim, it was not a slashing weapon, and often a slashing stroke was needed to get an early advantage over the Japanese.

To rectify this deficiency and provide an additional 'machete' capability to help soldiers hack through jungles, the rifle factory at Ishapore, India, began to produce a series of 11–17-inch-long sword bayonets for troops serving in the South-east Asia theatre of operations.

Soldiers armed with sub-machine-guns also demanded bayonets to provide them with some degree of self-protection while changing magazines or if they ran out of ammunition, so a series of bayonets were also made to fit the Sten gun.

During 1942 and 1943, the British and their new 14th Army tried to regain the initiative in Burma, but they soon found the Japanese tenacious in defence as well as attack. The British offensives along the Arakan coast were repulsed with heavy losses. The only bright spot in the disaster-ridden Burma campaign was the daring raiding force of Brigadier Orde Wingate – the legendary Chindits. Roving behind Japanese lines, they spread confusion and chaos but suffered heavy losses. The Japanese learnt to fear them and gave no quarter. Captured Chindits could expect to be tied to trees and used for bayonet practice by the Japanese.

The tide did not turn for the British until the spring of 1944, when another Arakan offensive had ended in bloody failure and the Japanese had broken through the British lines. Now an isolated group of British and Indian soldiers fought an epic engagement that raised the morale of the 14th Army by breaking the jinx of defeat. Bayonet fighting played a major part in the successful defence of the so-called 'Admin Box'.

Marching through the dense jungle, the crack Japanese 55th Division dodged past the British front line to surround the 7th Division headquarters and logistic support base. The success of their 'Ha-Go' offensive depended on the quick capture of the British supplies stockpiled there for the next phase of the operation aimed at capturing the port of Chittagong.

The defenders of the 'Admin Box' – as the base became known – were almost all rear-echelon administrative troops except for a few companies of infantry from the 2nd Battalion, The West Yorkshire Regiment, and 3/14th Punjabis, along with M3 Lee tanks of the 25th Dragoons.

First blood went to the Japanese on 7 February 1944 when they infiltrated the perimeter and overran the main dressing station or hospital, bayoneting its guards and scores of patients. At first light the West Yorkshires retook the hospital at bayonet point because of the danger of grenades or bullets injuring any wounded still alive inside. All the Japanese were killed and the surviving British wounded evacuated. Another Japanese column tried to infiltrate the garrison near the head-quarters of the West Yorkshires, but were spotted, and in a few minutes of gunfire 45 of their 110-strong detachment were shot down. The survivors charged up a hill at the British. A Japanese officer reached the British lines and tried to slash his way past a British sergeant with his Samurai sword. The sergeant parried the blow with his rifle and then dispatched the officer to his ancestors with a well-aimed bayonet thrust. The rest of the Japanese fled.

Japanese attacks now settled into a pattern. Sniping and artillery fire were used to harass the defenders and deny them sleep. Japanese soldiers would constantly shout insults from the jungle at the defenders a few metres away. Then a horde of screaming Japanese would rush forward. If the defenders were ready the Japanese would be gunned down before they got close. Many times the enemy made it into the British trenches and bayoneted the occupants. It was then the job of the West Yorkshires, with fire support from the tanks, to clear them out at bayonet point. On 15 February, for example, the Japanese succeeded in overrunning C Company of the West Yorkshires. A Company moved forward to counter-attack only to be met by a shower of Japanese grenades. Tank fire took out the offending bunker and the infantry then rushed forward to clear out the remaining enemy. Some seventeen Japanese were bayoneted and the position retaken.

In the early hours of the following morning the first troops of a relief column fought their way into the Admin Box, but five days of bloody fighting still remained before the enemy gave up the unequal fight. On the night of 21/22 February the seventy-six survivors of the Japanese 2nd Battalion, 122nd Infantry Regiment, made the final bayonet charge to capture a British food depot – they had not been resupplied for ten days and had been living off roots while the besieged British had been sustained by parachute drops. With cries of 'banzai' the remnants of the once 1,000-strong battalion charged the British lines. Machine-gun fire cut down twenty-seven and the remainder melted away into the jungle. Ha-Go had failed and 5,000 Japanese lay dead around the British position.

Lieutenant General Bill Slim, veteran commander of the 14th Army, now launched newly-promoted Major-General Wingate's Chindits on their most daring campaign to date. In cooperation with American and Chinese Nationalist forces advancing from the north, six Chindit bases would be set up behind Japanese lines to disrupt their communications. The bases were to be supplied almost exclusively by air, so the Chindits would have to fight without heavy weapons or equipment.

Once behind the lines, the Chindits fought running battles with the Japanese, trying to dodge conventional fighting to slip away and harass poorly defended enemy garrisons. For five months the Chindit campaign tied down tens of thousands of

Japanese troops who could have been helping in their ill-fated advance on India. Chindit columns got into some major scraps with isolated Japanese units, which put up ferocious resistance. When the 77th Chindit Brigade found itself up against an entrenched Japanese unit on 13 March, the 1st Battalion, South Staffordshire Regiment, and 3rd Battalion, 6th Gurkha Rifles, charged forward to clear the fortified hill at bayonet point. The Japanese rose out of their trenches to fight their attackers on even terms. Lieutenant George Cairns was leading a platoon of Staffords when a Japanese officer attacked him with his Samurai sword and hacked off the British officer's left arm. After killing the Japanese, Lieutenant Cairns seized his dead opponent's sword and led his men forward again, killing a number of enemy soldiers with the blade. The Chindits were able to capitalize on this success and evict the Japanese from their positions. Unfortunately the gallant officer soon expired through loss of blood but was posthumously awarded the Victoria Cross.

Despite some early successes, quick Japanese countermeasures pinned a number of the Chindit columns in landing zones, which then developed into protracted sieges. Some people have suggested the Chindit bases were the inspiration for the French base at Dien Bien Phu, Indo-China, in 1953.

The Japanese 2/29th Battalion staged a major effort to capture the Chindit base and airstrip codenamed 'White City' in April. They repeatedly banzai-charged the base's barbed-wire perimeter and gained a foothold on 10 April after blowing a hole in the wire.

A bayonet charge by the Chindits threw them out after a bloody fight. More than 700 dead enemy troops were found around the wire. 'White City' was abandoned before the Chindits became surrounded by overwhelming Japanese forces, a fate that was soon to befall the new Chindit base at 'Blackpool'.

Four Chindit columns were penned-in by aggressive and well-armed Japanese troops who slowly ground them down. Enemy artillery closed the airstrip to resupply flights, and then nightly banzai charges began which broke into the perimeter on a regular basis. By 14 May they could no longer be expelled by bayonet charges, so the Chindits were ordered to break out. The wounded who could not be carried were drugged with morphine and then shot, rather than leave them to be bayoneted by the Japanese.

Driving down from China to help the Chindits, US Army and Chinese Nationalist troops inflicted heavy casualties on the Japanese. On 16 June, the 149th US Infantry Regiment and Chinese 22nd Division made a daring attack on the Japanese garrison at Kamaing. A tropical rainstorm covered the sound of their advance so they were able to launch a dramatic bayonet charge into the town, which routed the defenders.

By the late summer of 1944, the fortunes of war had shifted irrevocably against the Japanese, and Allied raiding forces were withdrawn from behind enemy lines, their mission accomplished.

In spite of their setback in the Arakan, by March the Japanese were ready to try again to break through into India. Some 100,000 men were mustered for the offensive with the key British supply bases at Imphal and Kohima as their objectives. Only by capturing the British supplies would the Japanese be able to sustain operations for longer than a few weeks. Realizing the weakness in their concept of operations, General Slim had turned the two bases into fortified 'boxes', surrounded by barbed wire and protected by field defences. He proposed to pull his troops in to defend the boxes and allow the Japanese to smash themselves against the defences in hopeless banzai charges. Air drops would sustain the defenders with essential supplies.

To the south of the main Imphal base, the 20th Indian Division was to hold its own box to prevent a key road falling to the Japanese.

It bore the brunt of the first enemy drive, a key feature in its defensive lines, Nippon Hill, falling to the Japanese at the beginning of April. The 1st Battalion, The Devonshire Regiment, was sent to retake the hill, which they did after chasing the enemy out of a warren of tunnels and trenches. During the night the Japanese massed on their new perimeter, firing wildly and taunting the Devons. Then they charged.

The first and second charges were beaten off with heavy losses, but by then the Devons were running short of ammunition and the enemy succeeded in taking two bunkers. Now was the time to commit the reserves which pushed into the enemy positions, bayoneting the few Japanese who were inside the wire. Along the perimeter were sixty-eight dead enemy soldiers.

For two months, the 20th Division, and later the 23rd Indian Division, held the Nippon Hill and a series of nearby hills against repeated Japanese banzai charges. The defensive fire stripped the jungle of vegetation and Japanese dead were piled high in front of the British and Indian wire. The line held.

Attempts by the Japanese 15th Division to take the high ground at Nungshigum overlooking Imphal were defeated by the Indian 17th Dogra Regiment and British M3 Lee tanks from B Squadron, The 3rd Carabiniers. In mutual support the two famous regiments charged up the hill, with the tanks blasting bunkers and the infantry bayoneting any remaining Japanese.

Now it was the turn of the Indian 50th Parachute Brigade to feel the weight of 'U-GO'. On 22 March, its two battalions were surrounded by four times as many Japanese, but supply problems meant they were not able to dig in and form a proper defensive position. The brigade went down fighting. Its rear-guard company was wiped out to a man making a last-ditch bayonet charge at the Japanese. The last British officer of the company still alive shot himself rather than surrender. This really impressed the Japanese who later spared the brigade's captured wounded from ritual bayoneting.

Under their brave commander, Brigadier Tim Hope Thompson, the Indian Paratroopers formed a close perimeter to hold off the Japanese banzai charges. Small mountain howitzers, firing over open sights directly at the charging Japanese, slaughtered hundreds of enemy soldiers with 'canister' shells. The remaining 500 men of the brigade eventually managed to break out to safety.

To the south of Imphal, the Japanese surrounded the 17th Indian Division before it could retreat into the main defensive position. But the Division successfully withdrew with its equipment to set up a defensive position around Bishenpur. Here it held out against repeated attacks by the Japanese 33rd Division. Enemy penetrations were quickly destroyed by Indian or Gurkha troops wielding bayonets or kukris.

Moving rapidly through the dense Burmese jungle in a move that surprised the British, Major-General Sato's 31st Division was positioned above Kohima: on 4 April it cut the roadlink to Imphal. The administrative base of the British 2nd Division was prepared for defence but only rear-echelon troops were present. Fortunately, the 4th Battalion, The Royal West Kent Regiment, had been able to get into the base before the road was shut.

Two nights later the Japanese 58th Regiment put in the first determined attack of the siege. After the traditional Japanese psychological warfare efforts against the defenders at the Dental Issue Store (DIS) hill, including English-speaking Japanese pretending to be lost Tommies, the cry of 'banzai' went up. Two hundred Japanese charged the hill held by C

Company of the West Kents. Scores of Japanese were mown down by machine-gun fire and supporting artillery. The enemy kept coming and were soon on top of the British wire. C Company charged out of their trenches and got stuck into the Japanese with their bayonets. The enemy fled. Ignoring their losses, the 58th Regiment put in three more attacks against the hill and all were beaten back with huge losses. Time and again during the battle, the Japanese would simply repeat such futile attacks for no gain.

The West Kents' D Company, sent over at first light to help their tired comrades, found some hundred enemy soldiers had gone to ground in and around their position. It took a whole day to winkle them out. During this messy business a Japanese machine-gunner started to harass the West Kents. Lance Corporal John Harman calmly crawled up to the bunker and posted a grenade into the firing slit before picking up the weapon and bringing it back to his company's line. With the machine-gun nest out of action, Indian sappers rushed forward to blast holes in the walls of houses occupied by the Japanese. In seconds, the walls were open and the West Kents were inside, shooting and bayoneting any enemy they found. The victorious attackers withdrew back to their lines covered in Japanese blood.

The next day the Japanese 138th Regiment swarmed over DIS hill in such large numbers that the West Kents could not stop them bursting into their positions. Corporal Harman was outraged when five Japanese soldiers turned a nearby trench into a fire base. To cheers from his comrades, the corporal charged down the hill with his bayonet fixed. He shot his way into the trench and then could be seen bayoneting the occupants. The enemy were screaming in agony as he worked his way along the trench. Observers describe him as a 'Norse berserker'. Again he grabbed the Japanese weapons and nonchalantly walked back to British lines with them over his shoulder. A Japanese sniper then shot him in the back. The fearless corporal was awarded with the Victoria Cross for his one-man charge which turned back the Japanese advance. His dying words were, 'It was worth it – I got the lot.'

For another week the Japanese just kept coming. Each time the British artillery and machine-gun fire turned them back with heavy losses, but with 600 British dead in the small garrison, it was becoming increasingly difficult to find the men to launch counter-attacks. Three of the defended boxes now fell to the Japanese. It only seemed a matter of time before the enemy advanced the last 100 metres to take the British head-quarters. No quarter was shown by either side in this battle. A West Kents' patrol found one of their own men tied to a tree where he had been used for bayonet practice by the Japanese.

While the Japanese increased their grip on the Kohima garrison, a relief force tried to punch a corridor through to them. The Japanese 138th Regiment set up a roadblock based on a series of timber-reinforced bunkers. British M3 Lee tanks blasted the bunkers, then the 1st Battalion, The Queen's Own Cameron Highlanders, moved in to bayonet every defender left alive.

The relief force arrived just in time. General Sato, however, was not done yet. His troops held on to their dearly won position around Kohima for another month. Fresh British troops, from the 2nd Battalion, The Durham Light Infantry (DLI), and 1st Battalion, The Royal Berkshire Regiment, took up where the West Kents had left off. On their first night defending Kuki Piquet hill, the Japanese 124th Regiment swarmed towards the Durhams' lines. This first attack was beaten back, but then at 03.00 they attacked again. This time they were all over the trenches. Bayonets, grenades, Sten guns, rifles, Bren guns and knives were all traded in the massive mêlée.

A bayonet charge at 04.00 succeeded in driving away some

of the enemy, but it was not until dawn that the Durhams could take stock. Some 200 DLI soldiers were dead or wounded. The Japanese suffered even more grievously.

The Japanese kept charging the British nightly until the end of April. Then General Sato called off the attacks because he was losing too many men. It was now the turn of the British to attack. Every Japanese position had to be blasted by artillery, tanks, grenades and then cleared at bayonet-point before Kohima was finally free.

As General Slim had planned, the Japanese bled to death trying to charge his defences surrounding Imphal. Some 53,000 Japanese soldiers died during the three-month U-GO offensive, either in battle or from starvation, because of their failure to capture the British supply dumps.

The Japanese lost the battle because of their slavish adherence to frontal banzai bayonet charges. Even fanatical Japanese officers, such as General Sato, were exasperated at the stupidity of U-GO's strategy and tactics. He reportedly signalled his superior officer: 'The tactical ability of XV Army staff lies below cadets,' before switching off his radios to prevent further mad orders being received.

'I have returned'

On 20 October 1944 General Douglas MacArthur waded ashore from a landing craft on the island of Leyte, just hours after the first US Army troops had hit the same beach. It was still 'hot', with Japanese soldiers putting up fanatical resistance only a few kilometres inland.

'People of the Philippines. I have returned. By the grace of Almighty God our forces stand once again on Philippine soil,' declared General MacArthur. He made it sound so easy. The Japanese on the other hand would fight tenaciously for every metre of the Philippines, and by the time Tokyo surrendered in August the following year some 65,000 of them would still be fighting it out. To make progress in the Philippines the Americans would have to fight a series of vicious small-scale battles. The Japanese garrison in Leyte fought tenaciously to stop the Americans gaining control of the island's strategic airfields. Rings of concrete pillboxes, reinforced artillery positions, deep trenches with overhead cover and other field defences held up the American advance. Superb camouflage meant that the advancing GIs could only locate Japanese positions when the defenders opened fire.

Company F of the 17th Infantry was clearing the town of Dagami when the lead platoon came under heavy fire from hidden Japanese machine-guns. Private First Class (Pfc) Leonard Brostrom, on his own initiative, decided to take out the pillbox at the centre of the defence complex. He dashed forward and immediately became the prime target for all the enemy fire. Miraculously he reached the pillbox and was starting to throw grenades into its rear entrance when six enemy soldiers bayonet-charged him from a nearby trench. Before they could get within stabbing distance Pfc Brostrom was able to shoot one dead and then drive off the others with rifle fire.

He returned to grenading the pillbox but was cut down by Japanese fire. In spite of his wounds he rose to his feet and threw more grenades inside. The enemy now fled the defence works and were gunned down by Pfc Brostrom's comrades. The brave soldier who defied Japanese bayonets to destroy their defences died soon afterwards of his wounds and was posthumously awarded the Congressional Medal of Honor.

The Japanese were determined to put Leyte's American-controlled airfields out of action. On 27 November they sent transport aircraft loaded with commandos to destroy them. Most were killed as the aircraft crash-landed, but one group survived and put in a bayonet and grenade attack on the head-quarters of the US 728th Amphibious Battalion. In bitter hand-to-hand combat all the Japanese were killed. A week later 150 Japanese infiltrated through the jungle and surprised the American-held Buri airfield. They were driven off after a banzai charge.

Nothing could halt the American advance as it ground through the towns and jungles of Leyte. For two days a Japanese contingent held out in a three-storey concrete building in the middle of Cognon. Tanks were provided to cover Company E of the 305th Infantry as it moved in for the kill. Still the Japanese put up ferocious resistance as Lieutenant Robert Nett led his men into the building. To gain entry, the lieutenant had to kill seven Japanese who blocked his path. In spite of a serious wound suffered during the bayonet fighting, he remained at the head of his men and led them deep into the building to clear it of enemy soldiers. Wounded again he only went for medical attention after he had turned over his command to another officer. He then walked away unaided for treatment. This cool-headed officer was rewarded with the Congressional Medal of Honor.

With Leyte secure, General MacArthur now sent his forces to invade Luzon, the largest island in the Philippines archipelago, which was defended by 250,000 fanatical Japanese soldiers, sailors and airmen. Japan's most successful senior commander, Lieutenant General Tomoyuki Yamashita – the victor of Malaya – chose not to oppose the main American landings but draw them inland to bleed them to death in a series of small engagements. He wanted to tie down US troops in the hope of delaying the final invasion of Japanese Home Islands.

Four days after coming ashore the 169th Infantry Regiment found its line of advance blocked by an enemy company dug in on a hill, and amply supplied with machine-guns, ammunition, hand grenades and TNT satchel charges. The only way up the hill was via a narrow sixty-five-metre-long bridge, which was defended by a concrete pillbox.

Company G was ordered to lead the advance across the bridge, so heavy covering fire was laid on to allow Staff Sergeant Robert Laws to race forward. Under heavy enemy fire he managed to reach the pillbox and started to throw grenades at it. The Japanese replied with their own barrage of grenades but eventually the sergeant's ordnance found its mark and knocked out the pillbox. Sergeant Laws' squad now joined him across the bridge and they moved off to take out enemy trenches further up the hill.

Three Japanese soldiers now charged down the hill, attempting to bayonet the sergeant. Before they could get close, Sergeant Laws emptied the thirty-round magazine of his M3 sub-machine-gun into two of his assailants. The surviving Japanese kept coming, and finding himself temporarily defenceless, the sergeant had to seize his opponent's rifle and the two men ended up rolling together down a fifteen-metre bank. At the bottom of the hill, the Japanese was dead and the American had a badly gashed head, along with a Congressional Medal of Honor. The hill was now cleared with minimal losses to the Americans.

To block any Japanese escaping southwards, the US 11th Airborne Division parachuted into drop zones near Manila, the capital of the Philippines. The American forces advanced on the city, trapping some 17,000 Japanese naval personnel who were going to ignore their commander's guerrilla warfare strategy. The naval commander signalled the high command in Tokyo, 'Banzai to the Emperor! We will fight to the last man.' Just under 2,000 men held the old citadel, Fort McKinlay, against the American paratroopers. A ring of concrete pillboxes outside the old fort raked the Americans with machine-gun fire.

Pfc Manuel Perez of the 511th Airborne Regiment was part of an assault squad, which was methodically clearing out the pillboxes with grenades. At the centre of the defence line was a pillbox with a twin-mounted .50 machine-gun, which was proving particularly difficult to take out. Crawling forward, Pfc Perez managed to get behind the pillbox and from twenty metres threw a grenade inside. The occupants started to withdraw through a tunnel at the rear of the pillbox. Pfc Perez killed four of the Japanese but emptied his M1 Garand rifle magazine.

As he was reloading one of the Japanese soldiers threw his rifle, with bayonet attached, at the paratrooper. He parried the improvised spear with his own rifle but the impact knocked the weapon to the ground. Picking up the Japanese weapon, Pfc Perez continued firing on the escaping enemy as he charged towards them. Killing three Japanese in the tunnel with his rifle butt, he then charged into the pillbox. The only occupant was then dispatched with an Arisaka bayonet. All told, Pfc Perez killed eighteen Japanese in his single-handed battle. He was awarded the Congressional Medal of Honor.

As the Americans closed in on the downtown districts of Manila in February the Japanese trapped inside started an organized murder campaign against civilians. To avoid using bullets the Japanese soldiers were ordered to bayonet their victims.

In one of the bloodiest battles of the war, the Japanese garrison in Manila was exterminated. General Yamashita withdrew his surviving troops into the Sierra Madre mountains to sit out the war.

Out in Manila Bay, some 6,000 Japanese naval personnel were still holding out on the fortress island of Corregidor. On 16 February 1945 US Army paratroopers of the 11th Airborne Division jumped on to the island to begin its liberation. The Japanese were soon trapped inside the island's deep bunkers, which the Americans began dynamiting shut, sealing them inside. Then in desperation they started to stage suicide banzai attacks. On the evening of 17 February some fifty Japanese came screaming out of a tunnel at a group of Americans. They were described as 'rampant baboons, screaming and squealing'. All of them were gunned down. A few hours later more Japanese attacked. As the US 34th Infantry Regiment history recalls: 'It was a monstrous, bloody, twisting turmoil of flesh and sweat and shells and hot lead and cold steel. They kept coming until 04.00. K Company counted them off again. Thirty-three men – three officers fit for duty. Before them and below them on the churned-up limestone of Malinta Hill 150 Jap cadavers stared unblinking into the dawn.'

This scene would be repeated time and again as US forces closed the noose on the Japanese Home Islands.

Iwo Jima and Okinawa – 1945

Overwhelming Allied manpower and material superiority turned the tide in the Pacific from 1943 onwards. Over the next two years Japanese air, sea and ground forces were driven back on all fronts.

The Americans' 'island hopping' campaign to seize bases for the invasion of Japan culminated in the operations to occupy Iwo Jima and Okinawa in 1945. In these two battles, the Japanese made the Americans and their allies pay grievously, employing in large numbers 'kamikaze' or suicide aircraft, ships and submarines. Kamikaze was the 'divine' wind that saved Japan from invasion in the middle ages by scattering a Mongol fleet as it approached the country's shores. The ultimate kamikaze attack was the foray by the monster battleship *Yamato* on 7 April 1945. Its one-way cruise to attack Allied shipping off Okinawa ended in the world's largest battleship, displacing 65,000 tonnes, going to the bottom with 3,000 crewmen. Only ten American aircraft were lost in the air attack that sank the battleship.

The defenders of Iwo Jima and Okinawa were equally determined to uphold the honour of the Imperial Japanese Army. So Japanese defenders fought fanatically to fulfil their orders to kill ten Allied soldiers before dying themselves. In these island battles the banzai charge took on a new significance. No longer were the Japanese hoping to defeat their enemies but just to die gloriously in battle. Charging into the enemy with sword or fixed bayonet was the ultimate act of sacrifice for the emperor. Senior Japanese officers, however, chose hara-kiri.

Located 1100 kilometres south of Tokyo, Iwo Jima was a key island bastion for the Japanese. They garrisoned it with 22,000 troops who turned the island into the most heavily defended location on earth. Three US Marine Corps divisions were committed to taking the island, which was just nineteen square kilometres in size. The Japanese commander Lieutenant-General Tadamichi Kuribayashi filled the island with bunkers, trenches and tunnels and vowed to make the Americans pay in blood for every bit of ground they took. Eight battleships, nineteen cruisers, forty-four destroyers and aircraft from twelve aircraft carriers blasted the island before the Marines went ashore on 19 February 1945. Emerging from their subterranean cover, the Japanese raked the Americans with a hail of fire.

Every bunker, trench and tunnel had to be cleared individually. Banzai charges were not attempted on a large scale, the defenders preferring to infiltrate in small groups and bayonet or knife unsuspecting Marines. By keeping as close as possible to the American lines the Japanese hoped to avoid the full weight of the enemy's firepower.

To cover their advance the Americans deployed large

numbers of tanks and armoured amphibious troop carriers, called Buffalo LVTs. On 23 February the 21st Marine Regiment was ordered to take Iwo Jima's No. 2 Airfield which was ringed by hundreds of concrete pillboxes and trench complexes. The volcanic terrain made it impossible for the tanks to give their usual close support, so the Marines had to rely on bayonets, grenades, flame-throwers and demolition charges to clear the enemy positions. It was not unusual for individual Japanese soldiers to engage the Marines in bayonet duels to stop them planting demolition charges or using flame-throwers.

Corporal Hershel Williams, of the 21st Marines, was part of a demolition team that was clearing a path through the Japanese defences. He went forward repeatedly to destroy bunkers, covered only by a four-man fire team of riflemen. On one occasion as he climbed on to a bunker before inserting the nozzle of his flame-thrower through its air vent, the occupants charged out trying to stab him with their bayonets. Corporal Williams calmly turned his flame-thrower on them. Resistance ceased. For his bravery the corporal was awarded the Congressional Medal of Honor.

The Americans advanced, and organized resistance soon began to crumble as the Japanese became hemmed in along the northern coast of the island. Individual Japanese now sought to redeem their honour by going down fighting. On the night of 8/9 March the remaining 1,000 Japanese naval personnel emerged from their dugouts and charged the US 4th Marine Division. It was hopeless. More than 800 men were cut down in a few minutes. The next day the headquarters staff of the Japanese II Mixed Brigade were all killed in another suicide charge.

General Kuribayashi now told his few surviving troops that (the) 'battle situation has come to the last moment. I want surviving officers and men to go out and attack the enemy

Above: When the US fight back gathered momentum in the Solomons in 1943, bayonets proved the only way to clear out determined Japanese defenders from deep bunkers. (TRH Pictures)

Below: US Marines often had to resort to the bayonet to clear out Red Chinese troops from houses and bunkers in the Korean War. The Marines were always involved in tough hand-to-hand combat. (TRH Pictures)

Red Chinese troops in Korea used human-wave attacks to overrun United Nations positions. Bugles sounded the advance and then a huge cheer would go up. Thousands of Chinese troops would then surge forward. (TRH Pictures)

A Royal Marine prepares his kit during the 1982 Falklands War. Note the bayonet in the bottom right-hand corner. The Marines used bayonets to good effect during the conflict. (TRH Pictures)

Previous page, above and below: US Army recruits of the 7th Infantry Division are put through the basics of bayonet practice. The essentials of bayonet fighting, as taught by the US Army, have not changed much since 1914. (TRH Pictures)

Right: A US Marine Corps recruit finishes off an 'enemy' during basic training. Bayonet training is still used to instil aggression in new recruits in the Corps. (TRH Pictures)

Below: French Foreign Legionnaires on parade, with bayonets fixed to their FAMAS assault rifles. Short 'bullpup' weapons are actually very good for bayonet fighting in confined spaces, such as trenches and buildings. (TRH Pictures)

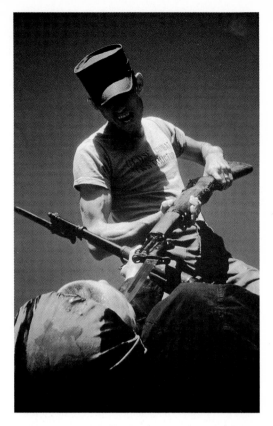

Above: The modern British bayonet for the L85A1 Rifle (SA-80) reverts to the tried and tested 'socket' design from the eighteenth century. It can also be used as a wire cutter when combined with the scabbard. (TRH Pictures)

Below: 'Fix bayonets'. British troops prepare to cross the start line during a live firing exercise in the 1980s. The weapons are 7.62mm SLRs. (Tim Ripley)

Above: British troops during a trench clearing exercise, this 'Squaddie' is carrying an M72 light anti-tank weapon (LAW), which is used to blast enemy bunkers before they are cleared out with the bayonet. (Tim Ripley)

Below: Winning the firefight. Before going in for the kill, British soldiers put down heavy fire to allow their comrades to close to bayonet-fighting range. (Tim Ripley)

Above: British troops regularly train with bayonets fixed to get soldiers used to having them on their weapons. The additional weight of the bayonet can effect the position a soldier needs to adopt to fire his weapon accurately. (Tim Ripley)

Below: Trench clear! A British soldier of the Worcestershire and Sherwood Foresters Regiment practices trench clearing, with bayonet fixed, during a training exercise in Bosnia. Such high-profile exercise are used to send messages to potential opponents that the British Army means business. (Tim Ripley)

until the last. You have devoted yourself to the emperor. Do not think of yourself. I am always at the head of you all.'

When the Americans closed in on the cave, which was the general's command post, and called for the occupants to surrender, the request was dismissed as a 'childish trick'.

The end came on 26 March when a 350-strong band of Japanese banzai-charged an American construction camp. Navy Seabees and Marine pioneers formed an improvised firing line that checked the charge. For the rest of the day the Americans hunted down and killed all the Japanese, who had gone to ground in the area. Individual Japanese fought ferociously, hurling themselves at the Americans with grenades, bayonets or Samurai swords. The Japanese general committed hara-kiri according to tradition.

In the 36-day battle more than 20,000 Japanese were killed and some 1,000 were captured – most of whom were wounded. Of the Marines, 6,821 were killed and 17,000 wounded in the Corps's toughest fight in its 168-year history.

The final island fortress of Okinawa, only some 400 kilometres from Japan, was garrisoned by more than 80,000 Japanese troops of the 32nd Army, under Lieutenant-General Mitsuru Ushijima. Like his counterpart on Iwo Jima, General Ushijima did not deploy his troops to defend the beaches against the American invasion. He wanted to protect his troops from the impact of the American naval bombardment, so the initial landings on 1 April 1945 by the US 10th Army were largely unopposed. The bulk of the Japanese forces instead were concentrated in underground defences on the southern end of Okinawa, below the ancient Shuri Castle. Here they would wait for the Americans, ready to inflict grievous casualties. The battle slogan of the 32nd Army was, 'One plane for one warship, one boat for one ship, one man for ten enemy, one man for one tank.'

US Army soldiers and Marines had to resort to the same

tactics used on Iwo Jima to dislodge the Japanese from the defences. Where possible tanks and armoured vehicles protected the assault parties. On Cactus Ridge on 5 April, the Japanese had dug an anti-tank moat, so the 2nd Battalion, 383rd Infantry Regiment, had to charge the hill and clear it out with bayonets and grenades. The 184th Infantry Regiment ran into more trouble two days later when carefully hidden Japanese artillery pieces were able to drive off American infantry protecting a tank force. Japanese infantry then swarmed out of their underground trenches, jumping on top of the tanks and bayoneting their crews.

The 383rd Regiment continued its advance against Kakazu Hill, only to find its way blocked by a massive bunker complex. Lieutenant Willard Mitchell led Company L of the regiment's 1st Battalion up the hill, bayoneting its way past a series of Japanese trenches before it reached the summit. Unfortunately the rest of the battalion was held up by determined resistance and Lieutenant Mitchell's men were cut off. More than 120 Japanese soldiers emerged from their cave to charge the surrounded Americans, who held them off. By the time Lieutenant Mitchell had worked his way off the hill, only thirty-eight men of the company were left alive. Hand-to-hand fighting on the hill continued for three days, with Sergeant Alfred Robertson alone killing twenty-eight Japanese with his bare hands, knife, bayonet and rifle.

The American advance had been temporarily halted by the Shuri Castle defence line. Now the hotheads on General Ushijima's staff decided the time was ripe to counter-attack and drive back the Americans. They wanted to 'restore' the morale of their troops and were unhappy at the 'unnatural' defensive tactics being followed.

Elements of the Japanese 22nd Regiment and 62nd Division made their attacks on the early morning of 12 April, to coincide with a major kamikaze attack on the Allied fleet offshore. The Japanese troops could only advance 450 metres before being stopped by American firepower. They were still out in the open at dawn and were then cut to bits by artillery fire.

This bloody nose did nothing to dampen the Japanese Army's aggressive instincts. Lieutenant General Isamu Cho, the 32nd Army's Chief of Staff, persuaded his general that an even bigger attack was needed to turn back the Americans. Under the influence of a heavy session on his favourite Scotch whisky, General Cho ordered the attack for 4 May. Kamikaze planes and boats, along with commando raids behind enemy lines, were to join the attack by 15,000 fresh troops.

A thirty-minute barrage fired off 5,000 shells before the Japanese infantry advanced at dawn, 'with orders to kill one American devil for every Japanese'. The Americans were amazed that the Japanese infantry attacked even before the barrage had lifted, achieving tactical surprise. The initial banzai charge made some local gains but by late morning the Japanese infantry were rebuffed. Out in the open along the American wire, the Japanese were massacred by artillery and machine-gun fire. More than 5,000 Japanese died in the futile offensive.

With many of their best troops killed in the offensive, the Japanese defences started to crack. US troops started to clear out Japanese bunkers with flame-throwers, tanks, demolition charges, grenades and bayonets. By early June the Americans had pushed the Japanese back to a narrow peninsula, where resistance began to fragment. The kill rate was nearing 4,000 Japanese a day as the Americans got into their stride. Whole Japanese regiments and brigades just ceased to exist. Increasing numbers of Japanese, mainly natives of Okinawa, began to surrender, but the officers still fought on according to their Samurai warrior code. Groups of Japanese began to attempt suicidal banzai charges, emerging from hidden cave entrances to surprise the Americans. They nearly always ended in mass slaughter.

In his command post in a cave General Ushijima saw the end coming. During the evening of 22 June his staff officers made their way up to the top of the cave to do or die against the Americans outside. Shouting 'banzai', while brandishing Samurai swords and bayonets, they plunged out into the darkness. It took the waiting Americans several minutes to kill all the Japanese as they sprinted towards them through the low rocks.

Generals Ushijima and Cho put on their full-dress uniforms, drank some whisky and then committed hara-kiri. First they disembowelled themselves with a traditional dagger and then a trusted adjutant beheaded them with a Samurai sword.

During the three-month campaign more than 110,000 Japanese soldiers died, but unlike previous battles with the Americans and British some 7,400 unwounded Japanese surrendered. More than 60,000 Americans died. The scene was now set for the Allied invasion of Japan. Rather than face more banzai charges and kamikaze attacks, US President Harry Truman ordered the dropping of the atomic bombs. Still the Japanese military wanted to keep fighting and only the personal intervention of Emperor Hirohito brought the slaughter to an end.

THREE

HUMAN WAVE –
EAST ASIA

Introduction

In June 1950 the Cold War confrontation between the communist East and the capitalist West sprang to life on the Korean peninsula. Communist North Korean troops poured across the 38th Parallel into the pro-American South, quickly routing the poorly trained defenders in a matter of days. For the next year all-out war raged up and down the peninsula between mainly American United Nations forces and communist Chinese and Korean troops. The war then settled down into a bloody stalemate astride the 38th Parallel. For almost two years two giant armies struggled for advantage in battles that resembled the trench warfare of the First World War.

The bayonet played an important part in the fighting in Korea. For the Chinese it was an essential part of their surprise night-attack tactics. It enabled the Chinese to advance silently and push deep behind American lines, spreading panic and confusion. The Americans and their Free World allies used the bayonet in much the same way as they did in the Second World War, notably during the final phase of deliberate assaults, to clear out trenches or hold positions in danger of being overrun.

Just as the Korean War was winding down, in November

1953, the French Colonial authorities in Indo-China were embarking on a six-month-long battle at Dien Bien Phu to defeat communist-backed Viet Minh guerrillas. The French strategy was flawed and its garrison at the base soon succumbed to non-stop human-wave charges by the Viet Minh. It was fitting that the siege ended with the last remaining Foreign Legionnaires being mown down while making a hopeless bayonet charge *à la* Camerone, as the enemy closed in to finish them off.

While American and Allied forces had to make do with Second World War-vintage small arms and bayonets, communist forces were using large quantities of new equipment. The need to provide simple and robust weapons for the millions of peasants serving in Russian, Chinese, North Korean and Vietnamese armies meant that the new generations of communist weapons followed the KISS principle – 'Keep It Simple Stupid' – in every feature, including the design of their bayonets. The Russians even took the brainpower out of fixing bayonets by fitting folding bayonets to their most popular weapons – namely the M1944 Mosin Nagent rifle and Simonov SKS carbine. This prevented soldiers losing their bayonets and also saved money on bayonet scabbards.

The Chinese liked the idea of the folding bayonet and incorporated it into their Type 56 copy of the AK-47 Kalashnikov, which started to roll off the production lines in Red China by the million during the late 1950s. Russian and Chinese folding bayonets drew on the experience of both World Wars, being both short and thin in design. The M1944 had a cruciform bayonet which was ideal for stabbing prone victims rather than slashing standing opponents, while the SKS knife-bayonet had a relatively short, thin blade of twenty-four centimetres, which made it very handy in a scrap and also reduced the risk of it snapping or snagging inside the victim.

The Korean and Indo-China wars would see some

desperate bayonet fighting, made even more unpleasant by the terrible weather conditions in these theatres of war.

Disaster at Unsan – 1950

For three months the position of the American-led United Nations coalition force on the Korean peninsular, was precarious. The Allied troops were penned into a small perimeter at Pusan, on the south-east corner of the peninsula, until the US Marine Corps staged an audacious amphibious landing at Inchon, far behind the communist lines. In the space of a month the North Korean Army had collapsed and the UN forces were racing north towards the Chinese border.

Their approach to the Yalu River, which marked the border between North Korea and Red China, sent alarm bells ringing in Peking. An army of several hundred thousand was dispatched across the Yalu to turn back the unsuspecting Americans.

General Douglas MacArthur, supreme commander of the UN forces, was determined to push his forces to the Yalu and ignored warnings of impending Chinese intervention. A constant stream of orders from MacArthur's headquarters in Tokyo urged his commanders forward. They were to pursue the defeated North Koreans at full speed and not worry about flank security or going firm in defensive positions.

The Chinese were a great unknown. The People's Liberation Army was battle hardened from more than fifteen years of guerrilla warfare against the Japanese and Nationalist Chinese. It was predominantly an infantry army, lacking the sophisticated artillery, armour and air support of the US Army. The Chinese put great store on night movement to gain information on their enemies and to move troops unseen around the battlefield. Armed with good intelligence and the element of surprise, the Chinese would then swarm over their enemy's defences, bayoneting unsuspecting defenders until they met armed resistance. Then their tommy-gunners, armed with Russian PPD 34/38 or PPSh 41 sub-machine-guns, would take over, clearing trenches with sustained fire or barrages of stick grenades (called 'chicoms' by the Americans). Lacking radios, the Chinese coordinated their attacks by bugles, whistles, flutes or shepherd's horns.

The Chinese were also masters of the art of camouflage and deception. They only moved large groups of troops at night and across country. During the daytime they would hide in woods and then emerge at dusk to avoid allied aerial reconnaissance and the roving patrols of fighter-bombers.

The Chinese, however, had almost no logistic back up. Their troops were forced to forage off the land or rely on captured enemy food and ammunition. In the bleak sub-zero winter conditions on the Korean mountains, the Chinese were desperate to overrun UN positions to capture their supplies and shelter. Whole Chinese regiments literally froze to death or disappeared in blizzards. Those who survived fought like men possessed.

During October 1950 the US Eighth Army was responsible for the western flank of the UN forces, with the US 1st Cavalry Division in the van of its advance to the Yalu. Its 8th Cavalry Regiment, a mixed armoured and infantry reconnaissance unit, was assigned to push past the town of Unsan. The 15th Republic of Korea (ROK) Regiment was on its right flank, but a steep hill separated the 8th Cavalry from the nearest US unit, the 5th Cavalry Regiment.

The 8th Cavalry was selected to be the victim of the Chinese First Phase Offensive. Their objective was not to turn back the Americans but test their fighting spirit.

During daylight on 31 October, the Cavalry troopers spotted large smoke clouds drifting over the hills to the north and south of Unsan. Reports were coming in from the South Korean 15th Regiment that enemy troops were attacking, but that they were holding. The Cavalry had no idea that the Chinese had infiltrated troops on the high ground to their south to block the arrival of any reinforcements.

The Chinese attack started on schedule at 17.00 hours on the afternoon of 1 November with a charge against the 8th Cavalry's 1st Battalion, to the north of Unsan itself. Simultaneously another Chinese force infiltrated over the high ground between the Cavalry's 1st and 2nd Battalions, finding a gap in their defences that allowed them to march straight into Unsan town unopposed.

Strong attacks on the 1st and 2nd Battalions now forced them from their positions and they were ordered to fall back on to the town. No one knew it was already in enemy hands. They were ambushed as soon as they arrived, their vehicles were shot up and those who survived had to flee on foot to escape the Chinese ring of steel.

Chinese attention now turned to the 8th Cavalry's 3rd Battalion, which was holding a bridge to the south of Unsan. In spite of being alerted by the battles in the town before midnight, at 03.00 the Chinese launched an audacious attack on the unsuspecting Americans. A company of Chinese infantry calmly marched up to the bridge, and the two squads of GIs guarding it thought the column was American and allowed it to pass. Home and dry, the Chinese commander blew his bugle to signal the start of the assault. His unit stormed into the 3rd Battalion's command post, bayoneting scores of Americans who were in their sleeping bags. All along the battalion's position this story was being repeated as almost half the unit was bayoneted or killed by grenades while asleep.

The remnants of the 3rd Battalion held out in their isolated positions for another day, but the Chinese were able to block all attempts to send help. Only 200 men were able to break out on foot on 4 November. The 8th Cavalry lost 600 men and most of its heavy equipment during its brief encounter with the PLA.

On the other side of the Korean peninsula the US Marine Corps was about to feel the weight of the PLA's First Phase Offensive.

The 7th Marine Regiment was spearheading the 1st Marine Division's advance northwards from its bridgehead at Wonsan into the foggy and snowy wilderness that lay ahead. Their line of advance was the only road north to the Chosin Reservoir. It led through a deep valley dominated by high ridges and ice-covered streams. The road was narrow, winding, and every so often made a deadly hairpin bend.

On 2 November the infantrymen of the 7th Marines attacked up the valley towards the small town of Sudong. They were clearing the high ground either side of the road of small groups of Chinese. After a long and tiring day the regimental commander, Colonel Homer Litzenberg, closed in his troops to a perimeter around the road. He had no idea the battalions of the 124th PLA Division were snaking across the mountains to their start lines.

At midnight, the silence was broken by bugles. Then grenades started detonating and tommy-guns fired in short sharp bursts. A Second World War-vintage T-34/85 tank slowly weaved its way down towards the Marines and began firing. By dawn the Chinese were swarming all over the 7th Regiment, the road was cut in several places and two Marine battalions were surrounded.

For the next day the 7th Regiment fought for its life. Unlike the 8th Cavalry, the Marines stood and fought – there was no panic or rout. Artillery and air strikes blasted the Chinese positions but it would be up to individual Marines to turn the tide.

Two Marines won the Congressional Medal of Honor

near Sudong fighting the Chinese with their bayonets. Corporal Lee Phillips, a squad leader with the 7th Regiment's 2nd Battalion, was in the thick of the action, clearing out Chinese positions from the high ground above the road. Five attempts had been made to clear one enemy strong point but they were beaten back with heavy casualties. He mustered his squad, ordered them to fix bayonets and then led them up the hill into a hail of machine-gun fire. In spite of being pinned down, Corporal Phillips rallied his five uninjured Marines and pressed on. They got to the crest of the hill, only to run into a counter-attack. His accurate rifle fire put paid to that, killing the enemy in the strong point.

With now only three men, Corporal Phillips pressed on with his bayonet charge to clear another strong point, even though his small band was outnumbered two to one. Again his determination paid off and the enemy were cleared from their positions.

For three days the 7th Regiment fought a running battle up the valley with the remnants of the 124th PLA Division. On 4 November the regiment's 1st Battalion was hit by a vicious surprise Chinese counter-attack. Sergeant James Poynter's platoon suddenly found itself surrounded by hordes of Chinese infantry. He quickly pulled his Marines into a tight perimeter to fight off the enemy with concentrated fire. But within minutes the Chinese were on top of the position and Sergeant Poynter was mixing it with his bayonet. Briefly driven back, the Chinese set up three machine-guns only twenty-five metres away. Without hesitating, Sergeant Poynter was charging them, bayonet and hand grenades at the ready. In rapid succession he killed the crews of two of the guns and damaged the third before Chinese fire wounded him mortally. The breathing space gained by this one man's charge allowed the sergeant's platoon to pull back to a better position, from where they saw off the Chinese attack.

The PLA assault had been thwarted and, as if by magic, the Chinese just disappeared. The road north was clear. Three weeks later the first Marine columns trudged northwards and the frozen expanse of the Chosin Reservoir came into view. The road to the Yalu seemed open.

Winter Retreat – Chosin

During the latter half of November 1950, the US 1st Marine Division slowly advanced up the mountain roads to the Chosin Reservoir, until its two advance guard regiments were holding the town of Yudam-ni, on the reservoir's western side. A regiment of the US Army's 7th Division was pushing up the western side of this large water feature, which was now almost totally frozen over.

On 25 November, the Chinese launched their Second Phase Offensive against the Eighth Army, sending it reeling backwards. Two days later three Chinese divisions struck at the 1st Marine Division, which was strung out between Yudam-ni and the sea. The Chinese hoped to slice the Marine Division into digestible chunks and then consume it.

During the night of 27 November, bugle calls urged on Chinese troops around the shores of the reservoir. The Marines pulled into a tight perimeter to hold off the Chinese 'human wave' charges.

Hoping to repeat their successes from the First Phase Offensive, the Chinese moved silently across the hills surrounding Yudam-ni to surprise and overwhelm the Marine outposts. Unlike their US Army counterparts, the Marines' strict discipline meant they were not caught by surprise in their sleeping bags. How a Company of the 7th Marine Regiment turned the tables on the Chinese when they swarmed over a hill towards their lines is legendary. The company was alerted by earlier Chinese attacks and quickly moved to a defensive position on the ridge above its old tented camp.

When a Chinese force moved down the valley, it spotted the tents and moved in for the kill. After the obligatory bugle call, the Chinese charged forward bayoneting the American tents and sleeping bags in the camp. It was now too late for the Chinese. The Marines opened up with everything they had and within a few minutes more than a hundred Chinese were dead. Those left alive fled into the night.

All around the perimeter the Chinese sent charge after charge at the Marines. In one sector, an English-speaking Chinese officer led a charge shouting 'No one lives for ever. You die!' in a crude psychological warfare exercise. As soon as he got into view, a Marine officer shot him dead. As the Chinese waves lapped closer and closer to the Marine lines, platoon commanders and squad leaders started to order their men to fix bayonets. The Chinese were getting closer and they had to be ready to fight hand-to-hand. In some places that night the bayonets would be needed. Mostly, though, the Marines kept the Chinese at bay until daylight.

Across the reservoir, the 1st Battalion of the US Army's 32nd Infantry Regiment was almost overwhelmed by the Chinese attack. The first the GIs knew of the large enemy forces nearby was when hundreds of Chinese soldiers surged over their positions. Trip flares on the perimeter were set off by the Chinese but most of the unit was still struggling out of its sleeping bags when the enemy was among them, bayoneting and grenading the helpless Americans. The forward platoons were killed to a man and the company command post found itself surrounded. For three days the US Army units east of the reservoir were hammered by attack after attack. The two infantry units in the area joined forces but were soon surrounded.

On the morning of 1 December, the battered force was

ordered to break out to the large Marine base at Hagaru-ri. The Chinese ambushed the escaping column, destroyed most of its vehicles and forced the surviving Americans to flee on foot. Swarms of Chinese infantry overran the convoy, bayoneting and shooting any Americans they could find. With the Chinese attacking in force all along the 1st Marine Division's supply route back to the sea, there was no alternative but to fall back. However, the division's no-nonsense commander, Major-General Oliver P. Smith, was not talking about retreating. 'Retreat? Hell! We're attacking in another direction,' he barked at reporters who had the nerve to suggest the US Marine Corps was running from the Chinese.

The Marines sought to avoid the fate of the US Army column by sending their infantry to secure the high ground above the road, before moving the vulnerable truck convoys carrying their ammunition and wounded south. For the cold and hungry Marines this would mean more than a week of desperate fighting on the mountains in sub-zero temperatures. There was little shelter from the elements or chance for sleep. Where possible they set up 'warm-up' tents to allow men to come in from the cold during night-time.

During the retreat this could not be done because of the need to maintain the momentum of 'the advance'. The only shelter came from a sleeping bag which each Marine strapped to his back. Frostbite was rampant but medical facilities were minimal. There was also limited room in the fleet of improvised ambulances that were following behind the advance guard. The Marines had to march or die.

The 1st Battalion, 7th Marine Regiment, made a desperate march across the hills south of Yudam-ni in a daring night assault to seize the key piece of high ground, nicknamed Turkey Hill. The weather conditions were atrocious, with the Marines marching through snowstorms to the objective. The battalion commander kept stopping the march to allow his men to rest and for stragglers to catch up. The terrible weather worked to their advantage. When the Marines assaulted the Chinese position, many were wrapped up asleep in their blankets. The Marines swept into the Chinese camp lobbing grenades, bayoneting and even smashing in heads with entrenching tools.

The first phase of the withdrawal to the Marine supply base at Hagaru-ri was completed successfully, and after a day-long stop to catch some sleep and eat, the Americans pressed south.

On the road south of Hagaru-ri the Chinese put up determined resistance to the Marines. This was to be a fight to the death. The 2nd Battalion, 7th Marine Regiment, was the vanguard force on the road for this phase of the operation. Five kilometres out of Hagaru-ri the Chinese were dug-in in strength across the road. The point company was ordered to assault the position no matter what the cost. To make sure the Marines knew what was at stake, the order 'fix bayonets' was given. This was going to be bloody battle.

As the company commander called in artillery a flight of Marine Corps Corsair fighter-bombers swooped on enemy positions. The Marines charged across an open field with bayonets glistening. By the time the first Marines were among the enemy foxholes, the enemy were starting to waver. A few trenches were grenaded and that was enough for the Chinese. They all broke and ran. As the enemy soldiers fled, the Marines picked off scores of them with well-aimed rifle fire. Thanks to the daring charge the road was open and the 'advance' could continue.

Just outside Hagaru-ri was a large hill that dominated the escape route. It had been taken by the Chinese in their first surprise attack on the Marine base, but repeated counter-attacks had not been able to dislodge them. Marine attacks now pushed them up the sides of the steep feature and kept them at bay as the main force passed by below on its way to safety in the south.

As the Marines started to torch their massive supply dumps in preparation for their retreat, the Chinese became even more determined to capture the valuable supplies.

Their attack reached a climax on the night of 6/7 December. Hundreds of Chinese troops swarmed forward against the 2nd Battalion, 5th Marine Regiment, which was holding a precarious position halfway up the hill. Wave after wave hit Able Company. Its fire kept the Chinese at bay for many hours, but ammunition resupply was dependent on a chain of porters man-packing ammunition up the treacherously slippery mountain side. The resupply effort couldn't keep up with demand and by 03.00 the point platoon was out of ammunition. They resorted to the bayonet to keep the enemy out of their positions. By dawn the crisis had passed. Hundreds of enemy dead were piled two metres deep in front of Able Company's foxholes. Then Marine snipers started to finish off any enemy that showed the slightest sign of movement. More than 800 Chinese died that night.

As the remnants of the 1st Marine Division slowly punched southwards, a Marine unit, 1st Battalion, 1st Marine Regiment, was pushing northwards to seize a key hill, which dominated the final bridge into American-held territory. Its objective, Hill 1081, was held by a strong force of entrenched Chinese troops.

The battalion had climbed across a series of ridges before it approached the enemy in a raging snowstorm. The whiteout blinded both sides. Shrieking and shouting taunts, a platoon of Marines charged forward into the Chinese position. The defenders fled into the storm.

After a cold and dismal night just below the summit of Hill 1081, the 1st Battalion pushed forward again to complete its vital mission. Again the momentum of a bayonet charge was too much for the Chinese defenders, who broke and ran as soon as the Marines got into their positions.

The attack had not been without cost. Almost half of the assault company were either dead, wounded or frostbitten, but as they were clearing the final Chinese positions they were able to see the leading trucks of the 1st Marine Division snake down the valley to safety.

Stalemate in Korea – 1951–53

The successful withdrawal of the 1st Marine Division and US Army units of X Corps to the north-west coast of Korea allowed them to be safely evacuated by sea to the main United Nations positions further south. This, however, was not the end of the war. The Chinese continued their advance southward, capturing the South Korean capital, Seoul, on 4 January 1951.

Three weeks later the Chinese offensive had shot its bolt. UN troops now began a series of limited offensives that clawed back a lot of territory and led to the liberation of Seoul in March. A Chinese spring offensive tried to retake Seoul but it was halted with heavy losses. The Chinese, via the Russians, now indicated they wanted to negotiate an end to the war. For two years the talks continued while the war went on regardless. There were no major movements of the front line, just a continuous series of 'meat grinder' or attritional battles to gain local tactical advantage.

Artillery, armour and airpower were seen as decisive weapons by top UN commanders like General MacArthur, but for the infantrymen at the sharp end, the bayonet was still a vital weapon in close-quarter fighting. There would be plenty more life or death struggles before a veil could be drawn on the UN 'police action' on the Korean peninsula.

During the early hours of 4 February 1951 a force of more than 250 Chinese infantry swarmed out of the night to

surround a small outpost, manned by troops of the US Army's 19th Infantry Regiment. Master Sergeant Stanley Adams and his platoon stood their ground but heavy enemy machine-gun and mortar fire forced them to pull back. They could see more than 150 enemy soldiers silhouetted against the skyline. It seemed like the finish, but Master Sergeant Adams refused to be defeatist. He ordered his men to fix bayonets and with thirteen comrades charged headlong into the mass of the enemy. In spite of being knocked to the ground five times by a bullet wound and grenade blasts, Adams still charged forward. For nearly an hour, the GIs were bayoneting Chinese soldiers in a swirling mêlée until the enemy finally fled, leaving some fifty dead behind them.

The master sergeant then provided covering fire as his depleted platoon moved back to the main battalion position. He was awarded the Congressional Medal of Honor for his actions.

Three days later the 27th Infantry Regiment were attacking a hill in the same sector when their point platoon was pinned down by heavy Chinese fire. The company commander, Captain Lewis Millett, won the Congressional Medal of Honor by rallying the platoon and leading it forward at bayonet point to take the hill. The Captain was the first man into the enemy position, personally bayoneting two Chinese soldiers before continuing to push on, throwing grenades, bayoneting and butt-whipping any enemy who got in his way.

Seeing their leader among the Chinese inspired the rest of the company to make the final dash across open ground to within bayoneting distance of the enemy. With more than fifty bayonet-wielding Americans in their midst, the Chinese immediately fled the hill. As he was clearing the final positions, Captain Millett was injured by a grenade fragment but refused to be evacuated until he had consolidated his troops properly in their positions.

At the end of May 1951 the front lines stabilized along the 38th Parallel, and UN forces began to mount a determined defence of their sectors against the inevitable Chinese counter-attacks. The US 187th Airborne Regiment Combat Team was assigned to defend the Wontong-ni sector of the front, when their troops on Hill 420 came under attack on 31 May. Heavy artillery, mortar and machine-gun fire was used to cover the Chinese advance. G Company put up a determined resistance but it was soon forced to begin a withdrawal because of a lack of ammunition. Corporal Rodolfo Hernandez refused to leave his foxhole and just kept firing at the Chinese human wave as it moved forward. The corporal's M1 Garand then jammed when a cartridge ruptured inside the breach. In wild fury he jumped out of his trench and charged the enemy with nothing but his useless rifle and bayonet. He managed to kill six enemy soldiers before he was himself shot and bayoneted. Left for dead the corporal was now ignored by the enemy who were under counter-attack by the American paratroopers.

This advance drove back the Chinese and allowed Corporal Hernandez to be rescued and evacuated for medical attention. His one-man bayonet charge won him the Congressional Medal of Honor.

Only a month later Lieutenant Benjamin Wilson, of the 31st Infantry Regiment, also won the United States' highest decoration for a lone bayonet charge. After leading his platoon on a bayonet charge that had killed twenty-seven enemy soldiers, the lieutenant's force was in danger of being overrun by an enemy counter-attack. He rushed towards the enemy by himself killing seven Chinese with his bayonet and wounding two more. This dramatic charge forced the rest of the enemy to flee, but they were soon back again and the young lieutenant again charged forward, shooting three of them dead before he was swamped by a squad of Chinese soldiers who wrested his rifle off him. The officer then pulled out his entrenching tool and killed four of his attackers with well-aimed blows. This created a breathing space for all of his platoon to withdraw to safety.

Sergeant Leroy Mendonca, of the 7th Infantry Regiment, single-handedly covered the withdrawal of his platoon during a massive Chinese night attack on 4 July 1951. He stayed in his foxhole firing at the enemy with his rifle. When his supply of ammunition ran out the sergeant started hurling grenades at the enemy. After they were gone, he charged out of his foxhole and started bayoneting any enemy he could find until he was eventually shot down. His comrades later found thirty-seven enemy dead around the fallen sergeant's position.

In June 1952 the 223rd Infantry Regiment was launching a limited attack to secure a key hill feature when the attack stalled under heavy enemy fire. Although already wounded, Corporal Clifton Speicher darted out from under cover to charge the enemy machine-gun nest that was holding up the advance. He was hit again ten metres from the bunker, but pressed on, reaching the rear of the enemy positions. He shot two of the crew and then bayoneted the third. With the enemy machine-gun out of action, the Americans were able to clear the hill with only minimal losses. Corporal Speicher was able to walk to the bottom of the hill, where he collapsed and died. He was posthumously awarded the Congressional Medal of Honor.

Sergeant Donn Porter, of the 14th Infantry Regiment, was manning an outpost with two comrades in September 1952 when they were blasted with artillery and mortar fire. Two enemy platoons then swarmed over the small bunker, cutting its field telephone cable and shooting dead the sergeant's comrades. The sergeant stuck to his position though and picked off fifteen enemy soldiers with rifle fire. The Chinese pulled back to reorganize and then attacked again. This time Porter came out to meet them, killing several with his bayonet before the rest fled. Unfortunately the brave sergeant was killed by an artillery shell before he could get back to the safety of his bunker.

In perhaps the final bayonet charge of the Korean War, Sergeant Gilbert Collier, of the 223rd Infantry Regiment, posthumously won the Congressional Medal of Honor on 20 June 1953. While on patrol in no man's land at night Sergeant Collier's platoon commander slipped and sprained his ankle falling over a twenty-metre cliff. The sergeant decided to remain with the officer while the rest of the patrol returned to the safety of friendly lines. The two men took cover during daylight and tried to get back to friendly territory the following night. They were ambushed, but Sergeant Collier shot dead two of the attackers before being wounded himself. Now out of ammunition, he charged the attacking enemy with his bayonet, killing four of them. The remainder fled into the night and his comrade was able to make good his escape. The heroic sergeant was mortally wounded in the action.

The Legion Dies Fighting – Dien Bien Phu

While the American-led UN forces were being fought to a standstill in Korea, the French were fighting an increasingly bitter battle to retain control of their colonial empire in Indo-China. The French Foreign Legion played an important part in these battles, where they got the chance to demonstrate their love of the bayonet.

The French had controlled Indo-China for a century, until the Japanese occupied the country in 1940 after the surrender of Metropolitan France to the Germans. The pro-German Vichy regime in France then allowed Japanese troops to enter Indo-China and for five years the colonial garrison coexisted with its nominal allies.

In March 1945 the Japanese moved against the colonial administration and its 5,000-strong garrison of Legionnaires. The Japanese tricked the senior French commanders in the colony into attending a dinner and then beheaded them. They then launched surprise attacks on all the French garrisons.

It was a hopeless struggle, but the Foreign Legion garrisons refused to go down without a fight. At Lang Son and Hanoi the Legionnaires fought until they ran out of ammunition; they then fixed bayonets and charged the Japanese. Almost every man died fighting. It was a repeat of the Camerone, but unlike that engagement the Japanese refused to act with chivalry to the survivors. The few wounded who were unable to participate in the Legion's charge were bayoneted or beheaded by the Japanese. One Legion garrison marched 800 kilometres through the jungle to China in order to escape Japanese vengeance.

The Japanese surrender in August 1945 saw British and Nationalist Chinese forces occupying the country until French colonial forces could arrive from Europe. In this power vacuum the Vietnamese nationalist forces under Ho Chi Minh declared independence, but their brief insurrection was put down by the returning French. Ho's guerrilla army, known as the Viet Minh, now retreated to the jungle to wage a hit-and-run battle with the colonial forces, including 30,000 Legionnaires.

The war was particularly brutal with little quarter being shown by either side. At Phu Ton Hoa in July 1947 a force of 110 Legionnaires found themselves in the same position as their forefathers at Camerone. They were surrounded by 3,000 Viet Minh, who were closing in for the kill. Wave after wave of Viet Minh charged the Legion outpost until they were literally climbing on the roof. Fearing they were done for, the Legionnaires chose the only option open to them: they fixed bayonets and charged. The tactic was a success. After a night of bloody bayonet fighting, twenty-three Legionnaires were dead but the enemy had fled.

Over the next five years the Viet Minh grew in strength with the help of the new communist Chinese regime, and slowly began to pick off isolated garrisons. They then started to field regimental- and division-sized formations against the French. By 1953 the French decided to launch a major offensive to bring the Viet Minh to battle and defeat them with their superior air power.

The location for this battle was to be an obscure jungle airstrip called Dien Bien Phu, in a valley in north-west Vietnam (the local name for Indo-China). Beginning in November 1953 a force of 16,000 French colonial troops began to be moved by air into the new base. The majority of these troops were Legionnaires, including a number of the elite Legion parachute battalions. French colonial forces were armed with a mix of weapons, ranging from pre-war MAS 36 rifles, with their cruciform bayonets, to surplus US M1 carbines and modern MAT 49 sub-machine-guns.

The French set about turning the valley into a network of bunker complexes, with interlocking fields of fire, and barbed-wire entanglements. Artillery was flown in to the extended runway. It was intended that the large French presence would entice the Viet Minh into massing their forces around the base, where they would smash themselves against the defences and then be devastated by air power. Unfortunately the Viet Minh's military commander, Nguyen Giap, was not going to oblige the French. He mustered 50,000 troops to encircle the French garrison and then spent four months cajoling tens of thousands of peasants to move hundreds of heavy anti-aircraft guns and artillery into the hills around the base.

On 13 March 1954, the Viet Minh began their offensive with a blistering barrage against the French strong point named 'Beatrice'. Its defences were crushed and several thousand Viet Minh rushed the Legion trenches. Only some 250 of the 1100 garrison escaped back to the main base. The pattern was set for the rest of battle. On 15 March the Viet Minh attacked the 'Gabrielle' strong point. It held out for one night after two companies of Legion paratroopers were sent to its rescue. They charged out of the main base under heavy fire and reached the outpost, but its defences were so battered they were in an untenable position. The base was abandoned. This put the runway out of action, so all supplies and rein-forcements had to be parachuted into the garrison. Its days from then on were clearly numbered, and the Legion would have to fight or die. The Viet Minh now began systematically digging trenches towards the main French perimeter around the airstrip. Day after day they got closer to the base, in spite of raids by the Legion to disrupt the digging. On 12 April two Legion parachute battalions jumped into the base to bolster its faltering defences. Scores of Paras were blown away from their drop zones, landing in Viet Minh territory where they were killed before they could get out of their harnesses.

The survivors of the parachute battalions were assigned to defend the outer ring of strong points, 'Huguette', 'Elaine' and 'Claudine'. On 23 April the Viet Minh swept towards Huguette to be met by fanatical resistance from the Legion Paras. At the climax of the battle two companies of Paras counter-attacked, charging out of the strong point with bayonets fixed. Viet Minh machine-gunners wiped them out in minutes. The strong point, though, remained French.

General Giap now turned up the pressure. More than 7,000 Viet Minh troops surged forward against Claudine and Huguette on 3 May. The first attack left 1500 Viet Minh dead around the wire. They attacked again and again. The fight raged within the strong point for three days, the Legionnaires counter-attacking against every Viet Minh advance. The defenders were desperate. They were short of food, ammunition and air support. All they had in sufficient numbers were bayonets and they used them to deadly effect. By 6 May the strong points were lost for good. The following day the Legion Paras made a last counter-attack to try to save Elaine. It was beaten back with heavy losses.

The French base commander, Colonel Christian de Castries, now threw in the towel and raised the white flag over his command post. The Legion Paras however were not going to go into captivity without a fight and they staged a final bayonet charge against the Vietnamese. It was a brave gesture, but ultimately futile. They were all mown down by enemy machine-gun fire.

To the south of them, the main base, the Isobelle strong point, was still holding out but its commander, Colonel André Lalande, realized the end had come. He too chose to lead his men out in a last bayonet charge during the early hours of 8 May. Three large groups of Legionnaires surged out of the trenches towards the Viet Minh. Only twelve men managed to hack their way past their attackers into the jungle and make their way back to French lines.

After this final charge, the French garrison at Dien Bien Phu just ceased to exist. Out of the 16,000 defenders more than 9,000 were killed in the battle; 7,000 were captured but only 2,000 survived captivity at the hands of the Viet Minh. General Giap lost 22,000 killed or wounded. He had broken the will of the French Government to resist, and within eight weeks they had concluded an armistice with Ho Chi Minh. French rule was over for good.

FOUR

THE BAYONET IN LOW-INTENSITY WARFARE – VIETNAM AND ADEN

Introduction

The 1960s saw a proliferation of wars in Asia and Africa as the West's colonial empires began to unravel, and poor and developing countries found themselves at the centre of the global struggle between capitalism and communism.

This was the age of the nuclear stand-off between the superpowers, so it is hardly surprising that the role of basic infantry weapons, such as the bayonet, was not high on the agenda of military high commands around the world.

However, for the thousands of Western soldiers who were sent to fight in Vietnam, and other conflicts during this period, the bayonet proved to be an invaluable weapon in close-quarter combat. When 'Victor Charlie' (Viet Cong) got inside the wire, the bayonet was ideal for killing him. Company and battalion officers also found that the bayonet was a great tool for steadying and boosting the morale of troops in the heat of combat. For those officers who had not served in Korea or the Second World War the morale factor was a revelation.

The heavy firepower of modern weapons meant it was rare during this era for two opposing units to get within bayonet-fighting distance. When bayonets did cross, the age-old principles of aggression, strength and determination always prevailed.

The proliferation of wars in tropical regions also saw increasing requests from front-line troops for multi-purpose blades that could be used to hack through jungle canopies, open ration tins, skin animals and slit the throats of enemy soldiers. These requirements were reflected in the two most popular assault rifle bayonets of this era. The American Colt 5.56mm M16 was fielded with a 16cm blade and dagger-style grip, while the Belgian Fabrique Nationale (FN) FAL and its British version, the L1A1 Self Loading Rifle, also sported a knife-style bayonet with a blade just under twenty centimetres long.

Russian designers created the most revolutionary bayonet of the era when they fielded the AK-47 bayonet, which when clipped to the end of the bayonet scabbard became a wire-cutter.

Vietnam – Search and Destroy 1967–68

America's involvement in the conflict in South-east Asia began to escalate in 1959 when the first United States military advisers were sent to South Vietnam to help build up its army against attacks from communist North Vietnam.

Over the next six years, communist guerrillas steadily gained strength throughout South Vietnam in spite of increasing US military aid. By 1965 US President Lyndon B. Johnson dramatically escalated the war by ordering American combat troops to Vietnam, along with the bombing of North Vietnam by the US Air Force and Navy. In the space of just three years, more than 500,000 US troops would be in-country and South-east Asia would be engulfed in a seemingly endless war.

Within South Vietnam, US ground forces soon found themselves facing an elusive foe who would appear from the jungle to launch surprise attacks on their bases and then disappear again. American commanders started to establish a network of heavily defended bases around the country from which aggressive forays could be launched, with the aim of bringing the enemy into battle. Then the Americans' massive firepower would be brought to bear and the enemy destroyed. Well, that was the theory.

This 'search and destroy' strategy quickly led to a war of attrition developing. It became a life or death struggle between the communists and Americans to see who could take more casualties and still keep on fighting. Eventually the Americans gave up, under the weight of public opinion, which was not prepared to bear 59,000 war dead.

The war was at its climax in 1967–68, when the US troop presence was at its height and the American high command was aggressively pursuing 'search and destroy'. There was no more aggressive American military contingent in Vietnam than the US Marine Corps. Its III Marine Amphibious Force (III MAF) was concentrated in the north of South Vietnam, opposite the so-called Demilitarized Zone (DMZ) with the communist North. The 3rd Marine Division was the most northerly Marine formation, and its job was to secure a number of fortified fire support bases (FSBs) along the DMZ. These were supplied by truck convoys, which weaved their way along roads, known as main supply routes (MSRs) surrounded by paddy-fields or tropical jungle.

Of the twenty-one Marine infantry battalions serving with III MAF, the majority were tied down on static guard duty protecting the FSBs. A major effort had to be made to 'thin out' units to gather together the large number of troops required for 'search and destroy' sweeps.

The main enemy unit on the opposite side of the DMZ

was the 324B Division of the North Vietnamese Army (NVA). It was a cunning and devious opponent whose commanders realized that frontal attacks on the Marine bases would end in bloody failure because of mutual artillery support from neighbouring FSBs. They therefore concentrated on attacking the vulnerable supply convoys. This further forced the Marines to devote more resources to protecting themselves rather than taking the war to the enemy.

Towards the end of August 1967 the 3rd Marine Division's intelligence began to pick up indications that the NVA would try to cut the supply route between the Con Thein FSB and the Cam Lo road junction. The 3rd Battalion, 26th Marine Regiment was ordered to move into position halfway along the MSR on 7 September, to pre-empt any enemy ambush operations. Over the next five days the battalion would be fighting for its life after being surprised by a full NVA regiment.

The battalion had been in-country for almost a year on mainly company-sized operations near Hue, until it got involved in a battle with a Viet Cong battalion just before Christmas. In June 1967 it had been sent to bolster the Marine garrison at Khe Sanh, where it was involved in a number of small skirmishes with NVA units. By September many of the battalion's personnel were counting the days until their tour was up and they could return home.

On 6 September it moved out to relieve another Marine battalion that had been securing the MSR, taking over a piece of ground known as 'the Churchyard'. The following day the 812th NVA Regiment struck. With artillery support from across the DMZ, it sent two battalions to attack the 3rd Battalion, but thanks to heavy artillery and air support the enemy was beaten off for the loss of more than a hundred dead. The Marines lost twenty dead and seventy wounded in a vicious firefight, which found the M16 rifle prone to jamming. By nightfall on 7 September the Marines had pulled back into a tight perimeter and awaited reinforcements. On the morning of 10 September they began to move to a new and more defensible position a few kilometres to the south.

India and Lima Companies led the move, sweeping along a small ridge, while Mike Company was sent through a large rice paddy. Battalion headquarters and Kilo Company took up the rear. By 16.00 the battalion was strung out in column when two NVA battalions surged over a hill to the west, running towards the Marines. AK-47 fire and salvos of rocket-propelled grenades (RPGs) started raking through the Marines. To the surprised Marines it looked as if the whole hillside was moving – there were more than 400 NVA soldiers in close formation. Some were even wearing captured Marine uniforms and flak jackets.

Survivors of the attack recounted how many Marines just froze at the sight of enemy troops advancing in the open. Then the officers and more experienced men started spraying the enemy with their M16s on automatic. All hell broke loose. Within minutes the enemy were only a few metres away. Scores of Marines were hit and some of their supporting tanks were hit by RPGs.

Now a third NVA battalion attacked the front of the Marine column, hitting Lima Company as it moved up a scrub-covered hill to the south of the rice paddy. Captain Dick Camp, the company commander, and his men threw themselves to the ground to try to get under cover from the storm of AK-47 rounds that had erupted around them. Dozens of Marines were hit. Those left alive tried to disappear below ground, quickly gouging improvised ditches. The enemy continued to advance, with the AK-47 and RPG fire getting closer by the minute.

No one issued the order, but all around Lima Company's shrinking perimeter, Marines started to fix bayonets. This was the first time the 3rd Battalion had ever needed to fix bayonets in its Vietnam tour. The Marines realized they were in deep trouble. This act seemed to steel the nerves of Lima Company: their rate of fire increased and so did enemy casualties.

The NVA now surged forward in a 'human wave' attack. They just charged towards the Marines firing from the hip as they ran. A large thicket of scrub was providing cover for the enemy advance but two Marine non-commissioned officers, Sergeant David Brown and Gunnery Sergeant Marvin Bailey, decided to take them on. They blasted the enemy moving up a trail through the thicket with M16 rounds and 40mm grenades fired from M79 grenade launchers. Their valiant efforts held off the NVA for thirty minutes, though Sergeant Brown was shot in the head. Half a dozen NVA now started to crawl through the thicket towards Lima Company's line of improvised foxholes. Out of the thicket a cloud of 'Chicom' stick grenades started to shower on the Marines who crouched even deeper into their foxholes. Captain Camp ordered a counter-barrage of M26 grenades which killed all the enemy grenadiers.

Sergeant Marshall Jesperson had mustered his squad near the thicket and had briefed them on how to deal with another incursion by enemy grenadiers. They would be bayoneted. On cue the enemy moved back into the thicket to resume the bombardment. Sergeant Jesperson led his men forward. No orders were given, the Marines just followed their leader when he got up and ran forward. They showed no mercy. The enemy squealed like pigs as the Marines finished them off with bayonets, rifle butts and knives.

With the thicket secure, Lima Company had broken the back of the NVA attack. Captain Camp began to reorganize his defences and administer first aid to his wounded. One of the casualties was Sergeant Jesperson who was screaming that he was blind. It was only a temporary blindness after an RPG had blown the head off another Marine and human debris had been blasted into the sergeant's face.

By 19.00 the 3rd Battalion's position had stabilized. AC-47 'Spooky' gunships were raking the NVA positions with thousands of rounds a minute. They broke contact, leaving the remains of 144 of their soldiers in the paddy-field. The Marines lost 34 dead and 192 wounded – almost half the complement.

Throughout the remainder of 1967, III MAF continued its 'search and destroy' mission. The Tet Offensive, the battle of Hue and siege of Khe Sanh temporarily forced the Marines on to the defensive, but by the late spring of 1968 'search and destroy' was back on the agenda.

The 2nd Battalion, 4th Marine Regiment was operating as a battalion landing team (BLT) conducting amphibious assaults along the coast to surprise the NVA. On 1 May, the battalion was sent to secure the village of Dai Do. Golf Company, commanded by Captain Jay Vargas, was the first unit ashore. As soon as the Marines hit the beach from the landing craft and started to move across a rice paddy to the objective, they came under artillery, rocket and mortar fire.

The enemy fire increased as the Marines approached the fortified village. Captain Vargas was wounded by grenade fragments as his men fought for each hut. A long firing line was established by the Marines to tear apart the enemy defences. Switched to automatic, the Marines' M16s let rip. They then stormed into the village. Once inside they secured a perimeter for the inevitable NVA counter-attack. The enemy kept probing during the night but the Marines' firepower kept them at bay. Captain Vargas called down artillery fire to within fifty metres to stop the enemy getting too close. This did not stop small groups of enemy getting into the village, so at dawn a sweep was organized to clear them out.

In the morning the Marines called in air strikes to allow

them to advance into a neighbouring village. Three companies of Marines took the village but they were all heavily under-strength and could not hold it in the face of a massive enemy counter-attack. Golf Company reorganized and pressed forward to retake the village. As they were moving out, a full NVA battalion launched itself into the battle. Captain Vargas had no choice but to call off the attack. Golf Company was now surrounded and fighting for its life.

The Marines and NVA were trading M16 and AK-47 fire at point-blank range. Then the NVA started firing volleys of RPGs and throwing stick grenades at the Marines. Captain Vargas kept moving around his shrinking perimeter in spite of being wounded by shrapnel from a rocket. He would direct the fire of Marines, resupply ammunition and clear jammed M16s. Golf Company lacked the firepower to hold off the enemy, and soon the two sides were brawling in the paddy-field. Bayonets and knives slashed and stabbed. The aggressive Marines fought to gain the upper hand and were able to break free from the enemy. Captain Vargas used one platoon to establish a firing line while the wounded were dragged to safety.

This stiff fight made the enemy cautious, and now the 2nd Battalion was locked into a blistering firefight with the remnants of the NVA force on the outskirts of the village. By noon, reinforcements had arrived and the enemy withdrew after suffering some 800 casualties. The 2nd Battalion had 72 dead and 297 wounded.

During the Marines' 'search and destroy' operations the bayonet played its part as a weapon of last resort. Such fighting was rare during the Vietnam War, where infantry combat was dominated by automatic weapons and grenades. In a tight corner, however, every Marine would keep his bayonet at the ready to keep 'Charlie' at bay.

BAYONET BATTLE

Bayonets at Khe Sanh

For just over four months in 1968 the US Marine Corps garrison of Khe Sanh held at bay a vastly superior force of more than 20,000 North Vietnamese Army (NVA) troops. The siege grew into the largest set-piece battle of the Vietnam War and saw the biggest artillery duels of the conflict. A massive American air bombardment and air resupply effort turned the battle in their favour and prevented a repeat of the Battle of Dien Bien Phu, where the Vietnamese overwhelmed the besieged garrison of French Foreign Legionnaires.

The siege of Khe Sanh was won by the 6,000 US Marines who burrowed themselves deep into the earth and endured day after day of constant artillery and mortar fire. Anyone that emerged from cover could be seen and killed by fire directed by enemy observers on the hills around the base. At night the Marines had to watch their perimeter for infiltration by North Vietnamese sappers, who could disarm trip flares with ease and then move silently in for the kill. Where the enemy managed to make encroachments the Marines swiftly counter-attacked and regained the lost ground. On two occasions these incursions were so serious the Marines had to resort to the bayonet to expel them.

The first US troops arrived in Khe Sanh in 1962 to set up a Special Forces camp to keep watch on communist infiltration routes across the nearby border with Laos. They began recruiting local tribesmen to fight the communists, but the area remained a bit of a backwater in the war until 1966 when the enemy mortared the camp. By January 1966 a full Marine battalion had reinforced the area and began constructing defences high above the small village of Khe Sanh. During 1967 US Navy Seabee construction units arrived and began to build a 1,170 metre-long runway.

All through the year there was an increasing number of

contacts between the Marines and the North Vietnamese in the area around Khe Sanh. Intelligence reports, aerial reconnaissance, radio intercepts and prisoner/defector debriefs all pointed to a major enemy build-up aimed at taking the base. Marine commanders in the region began to intensify preparations to repulse any attack. By the end of the year a full Marine regiment, the 26th Marines, was occupying the base. Contrary to popular image, most of the Marines were not dug in around the airstrip but were positioned on a series of hilltop outposts to the north of the base, dominating the surrounding terrain. In the main Khe Sanh base itself was one Marine battalion, a battalion of South Vietnamese Rangers, and a Marine artillery regiment of twenty-four guns, along with USAF personnel operating the airfield. US Army artillery units outside the perimeter had the range to offer fire support, and several hundred US aircraft could be called upon to provide air cover.

Surrounding the Marines were elements of four NVA Regular divisions and several thousand locally recruited Viet Cong (VC) guerrillas. They boasted some 100 artillery pieces, rocket launchers and 200 mortars. The communists had laid careful plans to take the US base, with most of their guns being positioned in jungle caves to prevent US fighter-bombers finding them.

The communist infantry also dug themselves deep into the hillsides around Khe Sanh and started digging towards the American lines. It was a modern form of ancient siege warfare, with the besiegers digging trenches, or saps, as a way to protect themselves from the enemy's firepower.

On 17 January 1968 an ambush escalated into a major battle on the outer edge of the US defence perimeter. A Marine patrol was ambushed and two Americans were killed. A platoon was sent to investigate. It was ambushed, and a company was sent to get it out of trouble. The company bumped into a dug-in North Vietnamese battalion and had to make a fighting withdrawal back to its hilltop base.

Then, in the early hours of 21 January, the serious attack began. NVA sappers got through the wire and mine obstacles on Hill 861, and broke into the Marines' position under cover of darkness. Only a swift counter-attack and some vicious hand-to-hand fighting defeated the enemy. All the sappers who broke through the perimeter were killed, but it was an unpleasant surprise for the Marines who had previously felt secure inside their wire.

Next, at first light, the North Vietnamese gunners began a snap artillery, mortar and rocket barrage against the main American base. Trucks, helicopters and bunkers were all hit in the attack. The VC spy network in the base had also been active, and the communist gunners scored a direct hit on the main ammunition bunker. Almost all the Marine artillery and mortar ammunition – 1500 tonnes – blew up in a massive explosion. Six helicopters were hit on the airfield and the runway was peppered with holes, making it impossible for the large USAF C-130 transport aircraft to land. The North Vietnamese seemed to have Khe Sanh at their mercy – it was cut off from the outside world and had no means of defence.

The fate of the Marines was now firmly in the hands of the USAF, US Navy and Marine Corps fliers who had promised to protect the base if it was isolated. Boeing B-52s started to mount round-the-clock airstrikes on communist positions near the base. Tactical fighters were in action during daylight hours, dropping thousands of tonnes of napalm. At night AC-47 gunships circled over the base pumping fire from their 7.62mm mini-guns into suspected targets. The AC-47s also had special flare dispensers, which meant they could light up the night around the Marine positions and prevent the VC sappers sneaking up on the wire undetected.

While the Seabees struggled to repair the runway, the

USAF started the largest airlift of supplies since the Berlin Airlift to replenish the Marines' ammunition stockpile. Small C-123 transports braved the communist fire to land on what was left of the runway. The C-130s made low-level parachute drops and began using the new low altitude cargo extraction system to deliver pallets of ammunition. This involved the aircraft flying low across the drop zone with the rear ramp open. A parachute attached to the cargo pallet was released out of the back and then the loadmaster cut loose the securing strap and the cargo was pulled out of the aircraft by the parachute. While all this was going on, Marine helicopters made daily flights into the base bringing in troops and supplies, as well as resupplying the outlying outposts with underslung loads.

All the aircraft and helicopters flying into the base were subject to communist anti-aircraft fire on their approach and mortar and artillery fire as they unloaded. Scores of aircraft and helicopters were hit but the pilots kept open the vital airbridge.

The launch of the countrywide Tet Offensive by the communists saw fighting intensify around Khe Sanh. On 5 February there was another assault against Hill 861. Here the Marines had to resort to the bayonet. Hill 861 was held by the 2nd Battalion, 26th Marine Regiment, which had been fighting for its life since the siege had begun two weeks before. During the early hours the massive acoustic sensor field sown around the main base began detecting a large enemy force advancing on the Hill 881S outpost, held by a Marine unit next to the 2nd Battalion. The units on Hill 881S were alerted and a massive artillery barrage, plus supporting air strikes, was brought to bear. In the hail of hot metal, the communist attack was stopped in its tracks.

Unfortunately for the 2nd Battalion, there was a gap in the sensor field so a breakaway group of enemy were not detected moving towards Hill 861. The 2nd Battalion itself had an outpost on a small hill nearby, called Hill 861A, defended by its E Company under the command of Captain Earle G. Breeding.

At 03.05 the storm broke over E Company's small perimeter. AK-47 and RPG fire broke over the base. The Marines tried to hold the communists on the wire with M60 machine-gun fire, M79 grenade launchers and tear gas. In 1st Platoon's sector the weight of attack was too heavy and its young commander, Second Lieutenant Donald E. Shanley, had to pull his men back into the centre of the position, where Captain Breeding was organizing a counter-attack.

Shanley's men led the charge back into their old positions. Here the fight turned into what was called a 'bar-room brawl'. The Marines were fighting with every weapon they had – M16s on automatic, knives, bayonets and rifle butts. One NVA soldier, while locked in a life or death struggle with a Marine, was caught in a burst of crossfire. The Marine was saved by his flak jacket and the communist was cut in half. Their body armour saved other Marines in this action, which saw a number of NVA soldiers getting their throats cut.

Captain Breeding now launched his 2nd and 3rd Platoons into the battle. 'Charlie' didn't know how to cope – 'We walked all over them,' said the captain later. The remaining NVA fled after thirty minutes of vicious fighting, leaving Echo Company back in control of its positions. When they started to comb 1st Platoon's positions for any concealed enemy the Marines found 109 dead. Not one Marine was killed in the hand-to-hand fighting, but E Company lost seven dead and thirty-five seriously wounded during the first phase of the battle. Shortly after dawn the enemy attempted to regroup and attack again, but this time E Company was ready. The NVA met a wall of mortar and artillery fire and their attack got nowhere.

Elsewhere the US Special Forces camp at Lang Vai, five

kilometres to the west of the Marine base, came under a two-day sustained attack by North Vietnamese troops backed by PT-76 light tanks. The twenty-four Green Berets and a couple of hundred local tribesmen were soon desperately calling for help. American aircraft swarmed around the beleaguered camp but the outpost was doomed. The Marines in Khe Sanh could not launch a rescue mission because of the danger of ambush. A small Green Beret rescue force landed by helicopter and recovered fourteen of their comrades who managed to escape from the base under cover of an air strike.

All through this attack, the communists kept up the pressure on the Marines. Their outposts were being continuously probed and the main base itself was being bombarded round the clock, with a record 1300 impacts in the base being recorded on 23 February alone. Some shells found their mark, hitting ammunition dumps and key bunkers. One shell detonated 1500 90mm and 106mm mortar rounds. On some days no one was killed but on others the death toll was high. In one engagement a Marine patrol was ambushed and twenty-five Americans were killed.

In spite of the bombardment, the USAF kept open the air bridge, and the Marines were never short of ammunition or supplies. When danger threatened, fire could always be brought down to kill any enemy massing to attack. Thanks to the airlift, the Marine artillery and mortar batteries in Khe Sanh were always supplied with enough ammunition to repel with heavy losses any communist attacks.

The North Vietnamese slowly built up for their big attack but they never launched an all-out effort against the main Marine base. Their trench line pushed to within 105 metres of the US outer defences, and on one occasion they dug a trench to within a few metres of the American wire. The only major attack came on the last night in February in the sector held by the South Vietnamese Rangers. Communist sappers managed silently to clear a path through the wire and Claymore mines, but when they charged the Rangers, the VC were met by a hail of machine-gun and mortar fire. Some seventy enemy were left dead. This was the high-water mark of the communist offensive against Khe Sanh. American firepower had broken the back of their attacks.

During March 1968, the Americans began preparations to lift the siege of Khe Sanh in an operation known as 'Pegasus'. The 1st Cavalry Division (Airmobile) was brought up to Da Nang and the Marines in Khe Sanh got ready to break out.

To keep the enemy pinned down around the main Khe Sanh base a series of raids were made on the NVA positions. The 26th Marine Regiment's 1st Battalion was ordered to launch an attack on an NVA trench position just outside the perimeter of the main base, near the runway, on the morning of 30 March. Captain Kenneth W. Pipes' B Company was to lead the assault at 09.00 after a ten-minute artillery barrage. Early morning fog covered the advance out of the base and the enemy were taken totally by surprise. Two platoons of B Company swarmed over the enemy trenches with bayonets fixed. Those who were caught in the open by the Marines were shot or bayoneted.

Captain Pipes then set about systematically clearing the position with grenades, satchel charges and flame-throwers. By the time they had finished three hours later some 113 NVA were entombed in their old positions. Captain Pipes, however, had been wounded and three Marines killed when his command bunker was hit by a lone mortar round late in the morning.

On 1 April Operation Pegasus began, with heavy artillery and an air strike against communist positions. The 1st Cavalry Division, 'Air Cav', then began landing at strategic positions behind the communist front line, and the Marines in Khe Sanh staged a series of raids to pin the enemy in his positions.

Behind the 'Air Cav' came combat engineers to repair the road into Khe Sanh, which had been all but destroyed by B-52 strikes. By 7 April, the 'Air Cav' had opened up a route into Khe Sanh and its troopers began to relieve the Marines who had been cut off for seventy days. The North Vietnamese just melted away into the jungle. The 'Air Cav' and Marines only managed to capture twenty-one enemy soldiers. They were all exhausted and shell-shocked after being on the receiving end of the biggest air and artillery bombardment since the Second World War.

In total some 200,000 shells had been fired in support of the base and US aircraft – from small T-28s to giant B-52s – dropped more than 100,000 tonnes of bombs. Some 1,124 air resupply sorties had kept the base going by delivering 12,430 tonnes of supplies in the most successful combat airlift operations ever. In the seventy days of the siege 199 Americans had been killed and 1600 wounded. Communist casualties are impossible to estimate, though the Marines did capture fifty enemy troops. The best guess by US Intelligence was that 10,000 enemy soldiers were killed or wounded during the siege. In spite of their detailed preparations to take the base, the communists held back from an all-out assault. The massive firepower brought to bear by the Americans meant that such an attack would have been unlikely to succeed and would have ended in a bloodbath. There was no repeat of Dien Bien Phu.

The siege of Khe Sanh has entered US Marine Corps folklore, with the 26th Marines receiving a Presidential Unit Citation for their efforts.

Battle for Hue

Three years after the United States committed combat troops to defend South Vietnam, the country was rocked by a massive communist offensive that threatened to overwhelm allied positions from the Demilitarized Zone (DMZ) in the north, to the capital Saigon in the south. The communist attack on 31 January 1968 – the Tet national holiday – took the free world forces by surprise. More than 100,000 North Vietnamese and Viet Cong (VC) troops attacked 36 out of 44 provincial capitals, 23 major airbases, and numerous small outposts around the country, in a coordinated attack that stretched Allied forces to the limit. In Saigon, a small team of VC sappers entered the US Embassy compound, before 101st Airborne Division troops were helicoptered on to the roof of the building and managed to kill them.

In most places throughout the country, the offensive was short-lived, with the defenders holding their ground and successfully repulsing the attackers and inflicting heavy casualties. Throughout the country, 45,000 communist troops were killed and almost 7,000 taken prisoner. In the northern city of Hue, the 4th and 6th North Vietnamese Army (NVA) Regiments, supported by six VC battalions, scored a major success. They quickly overran the city and surrounded the compounds of the South Vietnamese 1st Division, and the region's American military advisers. For over three weeks, they held the city, as four US Army, three US Marine Corps, and eleven South Vietnamese battalions first surrounded the city, and then cleared it, house by house.

Hue was the ancient capital of Vietnam, and it contained numerous historic buildings; to save them, air strikes and artillery support fire were banned. The 1st and 5th Marine Regiments had to clear the city with only their tanks to provide heavy firepower. They had to fight for every metre against a dug-in enemy. It took ten days for the Marines to punch a corridor to the American compound, and clear the southern part of the city.

South Vietnamese troops were making no progress, so on

12 February the Marines went to their assistance, and soon made a breach in the massive old fortress walls surrounding the city centre. Even without the usual fire support, the city was devastated, 5,800 civilians were killed and 116,000 were made homeless. While 500 Allied troops had been killed, the communists lost 5,000 troops.

Large numbers of communist troops managed to break out through the thinly manned US siege lines. While the Marines took the brunt of the fighting in the city, US Army units were drafted in to sweep up any escaping communists. During these bloody operations a further 3,000 enemy troops were killed, in a number of desperate battles.

Elements of the 101st Airborne Division were part of this effort, and on 21 February, the 2nd Battalion (Airborne), 501st Infantry Regiment was caught in a bloody battle with a strong group of communists holding a river bank. The battalion's D Company was ordered to assault the position, when it came under fire from machine-guns and rocket-propelled grenades (RPGs).

Leading the point squad was 29-year-old Sergeant Joe Hooper. Seeing that the attack was faltering, he rallied several men and stormed across the river. This move cleared several enemy bunkers, and the rest of the company moved forward, but lost several men to heavy enemy fire that was still coming in. Hooper again ran forward and pulled back the wounded into the cover of the river bank. During this heroic action he was wounded, but refused medical assistance.

With the attack still stalled, Sergeant Hooper embarked on a one-man bayonet charge that later earned him the Congressional Medal of Honor. He charged out of the river, and single-handedly destroyed three enemy bunkers with hand grenades before shooting dead their occupants. Two enemy soldiers who were attacking the battalion's chaplain were also killed by the sergeant.

The advance continued. Sergeant Hooper and his squad were now sweeping a built-up area, when an NVA officer charged out of a building. Hooper then squared-up to the communist and bayoneted him. His squad now came under fire from another building, so the sergeant charged it. Once inside, he killed the occupants with grenades and M16 fire.

Despite losing a lot of blood from his wounds, Sergeant Hooper was still leading his men forward when they came to the rear edge of the enemy position. Four bunkers were holding up the advance. Hooper grabbed several grenades from his men and ran along the length of a communications trench behind the bunkers tossing grenades into each of them. Not content with this, on his way back to his squad, he rescued a wounded American soldier trapped in a trench. He first had to kill an NVA soldier with his pistol before he could carry the wounded comrade to safety. In the final phase of the attack, Hooper shot dead three enemy officers who were manning one of the last bunkers.

Fortunately Sergeant Hooper survived his wound, and later rose to the rank of staff sergeant. According to his citation, 'His supreme valor, inspiring leadership and heroic self-sacrifice were directly responsible for the company's success, and provided a lasting example of personal courage for every man on the field. Staff Sergeant Hooper's actions were in keeping with the highest traditions of the military service, and reflect great credit upon himself and the US Army.' He had also proved himself to be very handy with the bayonet.

The Last Australian Bayonet Charge

Australia's involvement in the Vietnam conflict began in 1962 when a small Australian Army Training Team was dispatched to South Vietnam to help train the country's small and poorly equipped forces in their struggle against the communist North. Six years later Australian troops would be called upon to make the last bayonet charge in the country's history.

Over the next three years the conflict escalated, and in early 1965 the Americans decided to commit combat troops to prop up the anti-communist South. It was not surprising that the Australians soon afterwards sent a battalion of infantry and supporting units to fight alongside the Americans.

The 1st Battalion, the Royal Australian Regiment (1 RAR) began deploying to South Vietnam in June 1965, to operate as part of the US Army's 173rd Airborne Brigade (Separate) in the Bien Hoa region. During its tour the battalion was heavily engaged in 'search and destroy' sweeps through the jungles around the large American base at Bien Hoa, losing some twenty-three men killed in action. The 'Diggers' were far from happy working as part of an American brigade, and by March the following year had expanded their force to task force (brigade) size and won agreement that it be assigned its own area of responsibility.

During April and June 1966, the 1st Australian Task Force (1 ATF) began establishing itself in Phoc Tuy Province, to the south-east of the South Vietnamese capital Saigon. Unlike 1 RAR which was made up exclusively of long-service regular soldiers, 1 ATF included units containing large numbers of National Servicemen (conscripts). The two Australian infantry battalions, backed by their own artillery, armour and air support, began setting about dominating their area with aggressive patrolling and humanitarian aid support for the local population. A mixture of Australian and American weapons were used by 1 ATF, the main rifles in use being the US-made Colt 5.56mm M16 rifle, and Australian-made versions of the Belgian Fabrique Nationale (FN) FAL, designated L1A1 Self Loading Rifle (SLR). The M16s had American 16cm M7 knife bayonets while the SLRs had a version of the standard FAL bayonet, which had a blade of just under twenty centimetres in length.

In August 1968 the locally recruited Viet Cong (VC) guerrillas surrounded and attempted to overrun a company of the 6th Battalion, The Royal Australian Regiment, but they were beaten back with heavy losses. This defeat made the VC treat the Australians with great respect.

Over the next three years 1 ATF made great progress in its campaign to defeat the VC in its area, and in the spring of 1968 communist activity was significantly lower than in other parts of South Vietnam. So when the communists launched the countrywide Tet Offensive in January 1968 the Australians were called upon to send troops to help the hard-pressed Americans and South Vietnamese in other operational areas.

Within a few days the VC and North Vietnamese Army (NVA) offensive had been contained and over the next three weeks Allied forces largely destroyed the first wave of communist assault troops. After two months spent licking their wounds the NVA launched another offensive on 4 May aimed at capturing Saigon. The enemy assault was launched from the north-west of Saigon with eleven regiments, and gathered momentum until the large US logistic base at Long Binh, outside the city, was under threat.

It was decided that 1 ATF would take part in a major US operation to pre-empt the communist offensive and move units by helicopter into the Long Binh area to set up fire support bases (FSBs). After establishing themselves, the Australian and US forces would conduct aggressive sweeps into the plantations and scrub around the area to bring the communists into battle. Superior allied air power and artillery would then inflict devastating casualties on the enemy.

Area of Operations (AO) 'Surfers' was assigned to 1 ATF as its objective and plans were made to helicopter in two battalions of infantry and an artillery regiment with the mission of 'interdicting' enemy withdrawal routes to the north of Long Binh. Intelligence estimated that five main force regiments of NVA Regulars were in the Australians' AO and they could muster some 3,000 troops. The plan called for a two-day operation to fly in 1 ATF and establish FSB 'Coral' from 12 May. In the first wave were 1 RAR and its sister unit, 3rd Battalion, the Royal Australian Regiment (3 RAR). A battery of artillery was to support each infantry battalion until the full task force could be deployed.

The first infantry unit to hit the landing zone at Coral was to be 1 RAR, then on its second tour in Vietnam. It was commanded by a Korean War veteran, Lieutenant-Colonel Phil Bennett. The unit had been in-country for two months so had plenty of experience of taking on the VC, but had yet to cross paths with the NVA. The battalion now contained a strong contingent of National Servicemen, but there were also many veterans of its previous tour in Vietnam.

As the battalion's officers started to prepare for the operation they became increasingly concerned that they were being sent into a hornets' nest of battle-hardened enemy troops. Coordinating an air assault operation was a complex matter and it took several days for all the Australian units to be briefed and prepared. Advance units of 1 ATF then had to move into American bases near AO Surfers, ready for the fly-in. The Americans were already heavily engaged with NVA units in neighbouring areas so they were not in a position to provide the Australians with much help.

The insertion phase began early in the morning with 3 RAR leading in the first waves of UH-1D Huey helicopters. An advance party had been sent ahead to join up with American units of the 1st Infantry Division, 'The Big Red One', which was operating in the area. It had been in contact with the NVA throughout the morning, so a US infantry battalion secured the landing zone while 3 RAR choppered in. The proximity of the US engagement meant that the second wave of helicopters carrying 1 RAR had to be reorganized. It was switched to the larger Boeing-Vertol CH-47A Chinooks which meant the organization of its landings had to be changed at the last minute. The battalion's lead element, D Company, under Major Tony Hammett also had its assigned landing zone changed. This caused the company some stressful moments as it tried to work out where it was. The presence of decomposing NVA bodies all around the position further added to the sense of foreboding. An American general then landed in his gleaming personal command 'Huey' to break the good news to 1 RAR, that they would not have to worry about finding the enemy – they would soon come looking for them!

By early afternoon 1 ATF was on the ground in strength at FSB Coral and was beginning to build up its defences. The first shallow trenches had been dug, artillery gun pits pre-pared, command posts set up, Claymore mines sited on the perimeter, and clearance patrols and ambush patrols sent out around the FSB.

D Company was operating on the northern edge of the perimeter and had an early brush with a small NVA scout team, killing one enemy. Like the other ATF infantry elements, it then moved into an ambush position beyond the main artillery, ready to stand guard for the night. Just after 03.00 on 13 May D Company's ambush position was suddenly engulfed in AK-47 and rocket-propelled grenade (RPG) fire. Within minutes the fire stopped and the enemy withdrew, leaving two Australians dead. A Royal Australian Air Force 'Huey' made a daredevil night casualty evacuation ('dust-off') flight to lift out D Company's three seriously wounded men. The dead were left until morning. Then the jungle was strangely quiet until around 04.00 when the NVA mounted their first attack on artillery positions in the centre of the FSB. Some 800 enemy infantry had managed to move around the infantry ambush positions and charge the gun pits of 102 Field Battery Royal Australian Artillery and mortar pits of 1 RAR. The attack began with a well-aimed mortar barrage into Australian positions. As the enemy pressed forward they threw in heavy machine-gun fire and salvos of RPG. Soon they were at close quarters, trading AK-47 fire and grenades with the 'Diggers'. Colonel Bennett's battalion, however, was not caught up in this maelstrom and he calmly stood on top of his trench calling AC-47 'Spooky' gunships on to the NVA.

By dawn the enemy attack had been broken; their fire slowly fell away and they began to melt back into the jungle. Seven Australians had been killed and twelve wounded during the brief but violent engagement. The bodies of thirty-eight enemy soldiers were found around the gun and mortar pits. More enemy were killed at close quarters as the Australian gunners swept their positions for any NVA who had not retreated.

Colonel Bennett now decided to pull in his rifle companies to provide close protection for the guns and prevent a repeat of the night's unfortunate events. Before they got back to FSB Coral though, D Company would make Australian military history.

In the company's position, Major Hammett tried to distract his men's minds from their two casualties by ordering the morning routine to proceed as normal. Clearance patrols were sent out to make sure no enemy were lurking nearby, while the rest of the company cooked breakfast, shaved, cleaned weapons and boots.

As morning progressed a group of enemy soldiers was seen moving northwards away from the main FSB, survivors of the previous night's attack. Major Hammett ordered a section to go and investigate, but before they got very far at least three machine-guns opened up on them. This changed the situation and the major now decided to clear out the enemy with a full-scale company attack. He hoped this would also snap his troops out of their black mood caused by their casualties.

Quickly looking over the ground, Major Hammett spotted a large ditch or drain that ran up the right flank of the enemy position. The company's three platoons were to move up under cover of the ditch to a forming-up point and attack the enemy from the flank. One platoon was to set up a fire support position, while the other two went in to clear out the enemy. This was classic infantry assault tactics straight out of the training manual, but it didn't stop the men from thinking that their commander was mad.

A flight of helicopter gunships appeared overhead and the attack had to be stalled while they let rip. The rockets missed and the requested artillery fire was also way off target. D Company seemed to hesitate as it lay in the drainage ditch 200 metres from the NVA, who were still blasting away with their machine-guns from an old abandoned American FSB.

Now Major Hammett shouted along the ditch the classic order 'fix bayonets'. All along the position his men started to pull their bayonets out of their webbing and click them on their rifles. The mood changed in an instant. With their commander in front, D Company climbed over the three-metre-high ditch and headed for the enemy. The tactics book was thrown out of the window. There was no pepper-potting or fire and manoeuvre skirmishing, just a long line of men moving through the waist-high grass, stooping so as not to be seen on the skyline.

In response the enemy raked the line with poorly aimed fire. No one was hit but Major Hammett radioed for the fire support platoon to keep the enemy's heads down. In their excitement they fired off all their rounds and for what seemed like an age the fire ceased as every man changed his magazine at the same time. The company commander ordered his advancing line to start firing 'aimed shots' at the enemy. The

'Diggers' were having none of it. They were firing their M16s from the hip on automatic, spraying the enemy line.

Now the Australians were nearing the enemy positions. Grenades started to be thrown and two groups of NVA soldiers emerged from a concealed trench to fire into the backs of the lead platoon. One of the positions was silenced with a well-aimed M79 grenade launcher round that blasted the enemy trench.

Two 'Diggers' then closed in on the other three enemy soldiers who were hiding in a shell crater. Lance Corporal 'Jock' McDonald and Corporal 'Greasy' Jones took them on. McDonald put an M79 grenade into the crater to cover Jones as he went forward. The corporal jumped on the crater rim, filled one NVA soldier with bullets but then his M16 had a stoppage, so he bayoneted the second enemy, and without hesitating butt-whipped the third. While the NVA soldier was stunned, Jones finished him off with a powerful bayonet thrust. That threat neutralized, D Company continued with the task at hand.

The 'Diggers' were only a few metres from the enemy and heavy fire was still coming from their main position. An M60 machine-gun was set up and more than 500 rounds pumped into enemy positions. A derelict M113 armoured personnel carrier was also spotted, so an M72 66mm anti-tank rocket was fired off. This caused a massive explosion and D Company cheered as they swept forward. Within minutes they were in the old fire base only to find it empty. The enemy had fled in the face of Australian 'cold steel'. One participant said later that it was just like the First World War. The company had not lost a single man in the charge, but had killed some NVA and chased off the rest. Not surprisingly, morale was now sky high. However, the war was not over and the company had to reorganize itself, replenish its ammunition and then march back to FSB Coral in blistering heat.

Now 1 ATF pulled back into a tight perimeter around FSB Coral to await the inevitable NVA night attack. At just after 02.00 on 16 May the NVA started to mortar, then RPG salvos began to land around their trenches. About half an hour later assault infantry started to move forward towards 1 RAR A and C Companies. In an instant the front of the position erupted into a killing field. Claymore mines, machine-gun fire, mortars, artillery and napalm from air strikes were all put down on the advancing NVA. The effect was devastating but for the 'Diggers' in their trenches it was a terrifying experience.

To steady morale A Company's 3 Platoon were ordered to 'fix bayonets' in their trenches, ready to repel any NVA who got through the wall of fire and steel being laid in front of the position. None did.

An NVA battalion was sent into action against D Company just after 06.00 and was met by the same massive firepower. Again to steady morale, the order was given to 'fix bayonets' by a platoon commander in a voice loud enough to be heard all round the company position.

It had the desired effect, though not before one enthusiastic man had 'fired' off his bayonet towards the enemy, after incorrectly fastening it to his rifle in the excitement. Morale was so high at this point that the 'Diggers' started singing 'Waltzing Matilda' in their trenches. Major Hammett was reportedly not impressed, complaining that they should be fighting rather than singing.

By dawn the attack had run its course. Five Australians were dead and nineteen wounded. The bodies of thirty-four NVA were found around the perimeter. There would be no more all-out attacks on FSB Coral. The battles around the fire base are usually remembered for the aggressive use of tanks by 1 ATF, but they must also go down in Australian military history as the last recorded occasion in which 'Diggers' charged the enemy with bayonets fixed.

Aden 1967 – Border Bayonets

While the US and Australian Armies were waging warfare on a massive scale in Vietnam during the late 1960s, the British were fighting an imperial rearguard action in an obscure corner of the Middle East. In June 1967 British soldiers carried out a daring bayonet charge on the outskirts of Aden, in what is now the Yemen, which would be the last use of the bayonet by the British Army until the 1982 Falklands War.

The Aden conflict is long forgotten now, but in the 1960s it was at the centre of British strategy in the Middle East. The then South Arabian Federation was formed in the 1960s in the hope of allowing a pro-British group of local leaders to develop and then assume control of the colony. This was a forlorn hope in the hothouse atmosphere of Arab nationalism that was sweeping the region at the time. Egypt's President Abdel Nasser was fomenting unrest against British colonialism, supporting scores of like-minded guerrilla groups and political hotheads.

By 1964 the mountainous hinterland of South Arabia was awash with rebellious tribesmen, sporting Egyptian-supplied weapons. Brigade-sized British forces were sent into the mountains to pacify the region in a series of operations beginning in May 1964. Six months later the conflict had spread to the colony's capital, Aden, engulfing the large modern city in a bloody urban guerrilla campaign.

This was a war which pitted British troops and locally recruited security forces against an unseen enemy, who merged with the local population. Only when they were throwing grenades into British bases or assassinating off-duty special branch policemen did the Arab guerrillas emerge from the shadows. In 1966 alone there were 510 terrorist-type incidents in the city of Aden and nearly five times as many in the following year.

To cope with this ever-increasing rise in tension during 1965 and 1966, the British garrison in the city had grown to some five battalions of infantry and an armoured reconnaissance regiment with Alvis Saladin armoured cars, and a group of supporting engineers, signallers and logistic troops. There were also strong contingents of the locally recruited, but British officered, South Arabian Army (SAA) and armed police.

The British Government's announcement in February 1966 that it would withdraw UK forces from Aden by the end of 1968 effectively pulled the rug from attempts to build pro-British Arab political structures and locally recruited security forces. No Arab who valued his life would now side with the British. Those already in British service quickly opened contact with the nationalists and most began to assist them from within the colonial administration.

By the spring of 1967 the security situation was getting out of hand. The families of British servicemen were all evacuated to the UK and the British Army became the only dependable force of law and order in the city.

Aden town was a large and modern city, which had grown thanks to British interest in developing its port and airfield as strategic bases for operations in the Middle East. The main residential and commercial districts were on a peninsula. The port and government district was on the eastern edge of this, but the Royal Air Force's main airfield, Khormaksar, was built astride the peninsula's thin neck. Surrounding the airfield was a series of some half-dozen British and SAA barracks or 'lines' as they were known. These were a mix of modern permanent facilities built from stone and concrete, and temporary accommodation of tents for the thousands of British troops on temporary duty. Some of these camps, such as the large Radfan Camp, were used by units on security duty in the local area, while some were used to house units back from duty 'up-country'. There were also a number of SAA bases where British officers and senior non-commissioned officers (NCOs) were trying to lick the locally recruited force into shape. Champion Lines was the main training base for the SAA, and lay between Radfan Camp and the Khormaksar runway.

To the north of Khormaksar was the suburb of Sheikh Othman. It was a nest of National Liberation Front (NLF) guerrillas; dozens of British soldiers were killed or injured in its rabbit warren of back alleys. On 24 May the 1st Battalion, The Parachute Regiment, took over control of Sheikh Othman and set up its main operating base in Radfan Camp. Within a week the Paras had staged a major operation to win back control of the district from NLF guerrillas, resulting in six Arab gunmen being killed and five captured. To reinforce the strength of the paratroopers an additional rifle company was brought into Aden from the British garrison in Bahrain, in the peaceful Arabian Gulf.

Under the command of Major David Miller, C Company of the 1st Battalion, The King's Own Royal Border Regiment, was in for an interesting time in Aden. Only eight years before, the regiment had been amalgamated, bringing together the King's Own Royal and Border Regiments. Life for the soldiers from Cumbria and North Lancashire was very different in Aden. There were no cocktail parties or beating retreats. They manned watch-towers and machine-gun posts in blistering heat and went on foot and vehicle patrols in dusty Arab townships. The enemy could strike at any moment, and the company suffered grenade, knife, mortar, bomb and machine-gun attacks.

In the months running up to the British withdrawal, political intrigue among the local Arabs was running very high. On 16 June 1967 a group of senior Arab SAA officers objected to the appointment of a new commander for the force. This caused them to be suspended from duty pending an investigation of their complaints. Rumours were rife in the colony, and on 20 June the word started to spread that the Arab officers had been arrested by the British and dismissed. The story was false but it was enough to make many SAA soldiers think the British were about to swoop and seize their barracks and immediately began to place them in a state of defence. British officers inside were isolated in their offices or messes. Champion Lines was taken over by its garrison and when a truckload of British soldiers drove past on their way back to Radfan Camp after some rifle training on a nearby range, the SAA rebels opened fire. Eight British soldiers were killed and another eight wounded. The fire was totally random, killing a British officer and a civilian in Radfan Camp. The chaos swiftly spread through the colony, and a total of twenty-two British soldiers were killed and thirty-one injured in the day of madness.

When news of the mutiny at Champion Lines reached the South Arabian Federal Government, they promptly asked for British troops to be sent in to restore order and to protect the lives of seconded British and loyal Arab officers and men in the camp. The request was accepted and at 10.00 hours on 20 June 1967 the Paras' commanding officer Lieutenant Colonel Michael Walsh ordered Major Miller and C Company, which was the battalion's stand-by reserve force for the area, to carry out this unenviable task. Major Miller takes up the story:

I was ordered to secure the guard room and main armoury in Champion Lines, but with instructions not to open fire unless absolutely necessary lest the news that British troops were firing on Arab troops might cause even wider unrest and lead to a general disintegration of the Federal Government and its military forces. A troop of Saladin armoured cars from the Queen's Dragoon Guards were placed in support for the operation.

Having given out preliminary instructions to my platoon

commanders, I moved out with a small protection party to make contact with the senior British officer in Champion Lines before completing my plan. However, the situation worsened before I had time to complete this task and the company was ordered to move immediately. The move was made in three-ton vehicles which came under fire from Champion Lines shortly after leaving Radfan Camp. The machine-gunner on the leading vehicle was shot dead before the column had moved more than a few hundred yards and a further eight men were wounded before the column reached the main entrance to Champion Lines where the platoons debussed. This was a very critical point in the operation: there was still considerable weight of fire coming from Champion Lines; the company was still largely unbriefed; fire was not to be opened unless absolutely necessary; wounded had to be attended to; and having just seen some of their comrades becoming casualties the soldiers were not feeling particularly sympathetic towards the Arab mutineers. The main burden of surmounting this awkward situation fell on the platoon commanders and their sergeants who all carried out their tasks most bravely and efficiently.

Morale of C Company was considerably improved when they started fixing their L1A1 knife bayonets on to their L1A1 Self Loading Rifles (SLRs).

To begin with, 10 Platoon under Second Lieutenant Tony Davidson secured the area of the main guardroom and were able to give protection to the British and Arab officers and soldiers who had taken refuge in the building. Meanwhile, Sergeant Frank Roberts of 9 Platoon was taking care of some of the wounded who had been moved to safety a short distance beyond the main entrance. The majority were to wait to be evacuated by helicopters. One casualty was judged by Sergeant Roberts to need immediate evacuation to Radfan Camp. He called for volunteers to take the wounded man back. Immediately Lance Corporal Vickers, a Royal Corps of Transport driver with C Company, and Private John Dickenson volunteered to drive and escort the wounded man in a three-tonner back to Radfan Camp. Both knew the personal risk to which they would be exposing themselves. The vehicle came under fire as it passed Champion Lines and Private Dickenson was wounded.

The guardroom having been secured, 9 Platoon under Second Lieutenant Bill Bird passed through 10 Platoon to take over the main armoury. Subsequently Second Lieutenant Simon Addy with 11 Platoon were positioned to cover the main armoury and act as a reserve. During these moves within the barracks, the platoons had been subjected to machine-gun and rifle fire from the mutineers. However, the sudden appearance of British troops with fixed bayonets had quickly restored law and order in Champion Lines. None of C Company actually bayoneted any Arab mutineers that morning – they did not need to. As soon as they got close, the Arabs raised their hands in surrender. They had no fight in them when faced by cold steel wielded by C Company's aggressive and determined soldiers.

The securing of Champion Lines was achieved without any fire being returned by C Company, while the armoured cars resorted to only a limited amount of fire. Unfortunately a further four British soldiers were wounded when a force from the Parachute Regiment came out of Radfan Camp to help C Company recover their wounded.

The quick and decisive action by Major Miller and his men undoubtedly prevented a great deal of bloodshed, saved the lives of a number of British officers and played a major part in preventing the mutiny of the SAA spreading throughout Aden and the Federation.

For his leadership and courage during this dangerous operation Major Miller was awarded the Military Cross. Lance Corporal Vickers and Private Dickenson were mentioned in dispatches.

The British garrison in Aden was very impressed by C Company's use of the bayonet and whenever morale needed lifting, reference to the weapon usually did the trick.

The most famous British unit in Aden during 1967 was the 1st Battalion, the Argyll and Sutherland Highlanders, led by their flamboyant commanding officer, Lieutenant-Colonel Colin Mitchell. In July 1967 they reoccupied the Crater region of Aden which had been occupied by NLF guerrillas after the SAA revolt on 20 June. During that day three Argylls had been killed in an ambush but a rescue mission was vetoed by the British high command. Colonel Mitchell was determined that none of his men would be left to their fate during the move into Crater. He told his battalion that if any men went down they were to be rescued at all costs. 'If you have no ammunition you are to go in with the bayonet. It is better the whole battalion dies in Crater to rescue one Jock than any one of us come out alive.' Fighting talk, but it put steel in the backs of the Argylls and the NFL quickly learned to respect the Scots.

Major Miller and C Company provided covering fire for the final evacuation, and was the final sub-unit of the British Army to withdraw from Aden in November 1967. He and his company were ferried by Wessex helicopter on to the aircraft carrier HMS *Albion* and later transferred by small landing craft to L(anding) S(hip) T(ank) *Empire Guillemot* for the voyage to Bahrain in the Persian Gulf, to rejoin the rest of the 1st Battalion. Earlier on the final day of the withdrawal operation Admiral Sir Michael Le Fanu, the commander-in-chief, sent a letter to Major Miller addressed 'Somewhere in or near Aden', saying, 'It has been very agreeable to have your Charlie Company round my location. They have struck me as a very cheerful, on the ball, smart outfit. Please present my compliments to your Colonel when you meet him, show him this letter and thank him for all that his fine Regiment has done for us in this rather hairy situation.'

FIVE

THE FALKLANDS 1982

Introduction

Britain and Argentina found themselves at war in 1982 over the fate of the Falkland Islands, an archipelago some 800 kilometres from South America and over 10,700 kilometres from the UK. Argentina had long claimed the islands and the British Government by the 1980s gave every impression of wanting to be rid of the sleepy colonial backwater. In a comic-book invasion in March 1989 Argentine scrap metal merchants seized the British dependent territory of South Georgia, which was close to the Antarctic circle. Events then spiralled out of control when the British sent a party of Royal Marine Commandos to arrest the scrap metal merchants who had raised the Argentine flag and turned out to be Argentine Marines. In a few days the Argentines invaded the Falklands, seizing the small British garrison. In response a large naval task group and amphibious force were dispatched by British Prime Minister Margaret Thatcher to recapture the islands.

Once ashore at San Carlos on East Falkland, the 10,000-strong British ground force began a four-week campaign that would see them march across a mountain range in treacherous weather and then fight a night battle to dislodge the 12,000 Argentine defenders from around the island's capital, Port Stanley. The final battle for the town would see bloody hand-to-hand combat for control of key mountain ridges, involving the use of the bayonet by many attacking British soldiers.

The insignia of the British Infantry Branch is the upright bayonet against a red shield. It adorns all the institutions controlled by the Director of Infantry, which run specialist training courses for infantry officers, non-commissioned officers and private soldiers.

British infantry tactics had progressed considerably since the First World War, but the bayonet was still a prized weapon during the final phase of an assault. In the early 1980s the Parachute Regiment was perhaps the British Army's premier infantry force. Its three battalions were fully recruited and trained for dismounted combat, in harsh weather and terrain. Two battalions of Paras spearheaded the British campaign to retake the Falklands.

Aggression, firepower and physical fitness were the key to the success of the British Paras in their brief but violent contacts with the Argentine defenders of the Falklands.

The average front-line paratroopers were nineteen or twenty years old. They had been moulded into tough and resourceful professional combat soldiers in the Parachute Regiment's rigorous 22-week-long selection and training process. This seemed to have been purposefully designed to prepare paratroopers for combat in the Falklands, with endurance marches carrying full combat equipment building up their fitness, and boxing (called 'milling') sessions to bring out their fighting spirit. Physically weak and poorly motivated recruits soon fell by the wayside. Parachute training had a reputation for brutality, but one Falklands veteran said the training kept him alive in combat. The 'humanely' trained Argentine conscripts were like lambs being led to the slaughter, he said.

The Royal Marine Commandos were the most numerous British infantry unit to participate in the Falklands campaign, with three commandos or battalions participating in it. Although part of the Royal Navy, the green-bereted Commandos had an equally gruelling selection and training procedure as the Paras.

The Royal Marines, Paras and line infantry units all used standard tactics devised by the Infantry Branch and taught at its School of Infantry at Warminster and NCO Tactics Wing at Brecon. The latter institution in the Welsh mountains had a reputation for toughness that was second to none throughout NATO. Every British Army infantry sergeant had to pass Brecon. Even the Royal Marines grudgingly send NCOs on the course.

As they advanced to combat across the Falklands, British infantrymen and Marines were loaded down with weaponry. Their personal weapon was the 7.62mm L1A1 Self Loading Rifle (SLR), which was the British version of the famous Belgian FN FAL. Its effective battlefield range was 600 metres; when fitted with an Improved Weapon Sight it could be fired accurately at night up to around 300 metres. Five twenty-round magazines were carried in webbing pouches and several hundred more rounds were usually stuffed into pockets or rucksack. The weapon was completed by an L1A1 bayonet with a 19cm-long blade for close-quarter killing. Four L2 fragmentation grenades were usually carried; a good grenadier could throw them up to thirty-five metres. Two white or coloured smoke grenades were carried to create smoke screens or mark targets for artillery, mortar or close air support. Each soldier also had a 66mm Light Anti-Tank Weapon (LAW) HEAT rocket, which could punch through 300 millimetres of tank armour at up to 300 metres. This throwaway rocket could quickly be brought into action by extending the launch tube. It was easy to aim with a simple flip-up sight system.

While the infantryman's weapons were deadly and easy to use, his personal equipment and uniform was not so efficient in standing up to the rigours of the unforgiving Falklands climate and waterlogged terrain. The British soldier's boot was designed in the 1950s and easily let in water, causing trench foot and other problems. Sleeping bags and uniforms were equally poorly designed, so the British soldiers were constantly fighting the elements to survive. At this point their training and physical toughness took over. The Royal Marines were slightly better off because of their NATO Arctic Warfare role, which meant they already had special cold weather equipment.

The British infantrymen and Marines fought in an eight-man section, broken down into a six-man rifle group and a two-man gun group. The rifle group was commanded by the section corporal, while the gun group was run by a lance corporal. The gun group provided the section's firepower with a 7.62mm General Purpose Machine Gun (GPMG), based on the Belgian FN MAG.

Section battle drills were simple but flexible, to allow the section commander to fight according to the terrain and enemy. When the section came under effective fire the gun group would put down suppressive fire to win the firefight. The section commander then had to plan his assault, either flanking the enemy or charging them frontally. Under covering fire from the rifle group, the gun group would approach the enemy and then fight through the position in pairs. The 'battle pair' was fundamental to success.

Two soldiers would close on the enemy and assault individual trenches. One would provide covering fire with his SLR or 66mm LAW, while the other crawled up, posted a grenade in the enemy trench and then cleared out any remaining enemy with bullet or bayonet.

These were the textbook tactics. In the Falklands they would be put to the test in demanding circumstances. Improvisation in the face of the enemy would be necessary to ensure victory.

BAYONET BATTLE

Top Malo House

Before the British could fight the battle for Stanley, the Falkland Islands' capital, they had to move across 80 kilometres of mountain ranges that stood between their beach-head at San Carlos and their objective. This was a bleak wilderness of high mountains, largely unpopulated save for a few remote sheep farms.

It had been intended that the British would fly their troops across this terrain by helicopter and then attack. On 25 May the Argentine Air Force had sunk the SS *Atlantic Conveyor* and sent her precious cargo of three Chinook and six Wessex helicopters to the bottom of the South Atlantic. Now the British, led by 3 Commando Brigade, would have to march across the mountains. To maintain the element of surprise they set about deploying covert reconnaissance patrols from the Army's Special Air Service Regiment (SAS), Royal Marines Special Boat Service (SBS) and Royal Marines Mountain and Arctic Warfare Cadre (M&AW) ahead of the advancing troop columns. Their mission was to find and then destroy any Argentine Special Forces observation posts that might be able to give the enemy commanders in Port Stanley early warning of the British advance.

To watch the northern route, between San Carlos and Teal Inlet, 3 Commando Brigade dispatched M&AW. It first deployed a number of its own covert observation post teams, however, to watch for signs of enemy activity.

The Cadre was set up to provide 3 Commando Brigade with its own dedicated deep reconnaissance capability, unlike the SBS which had a 'strategic' mission. In addition its personnel also worked as the brigade's specialist winter warfare instructors running 'mountain leaders' courses for the Royal Marines during their annual deployments to North Norway. Late in the afternoon of 30 May a Cadre four-man observation patrol spotted two Argentine UH-1 helicopters approach a remote farm building, called Top Malo House, and land sixteen special forces soldiers. The patrol commander requested an air strike to take out the enemy troops, but it was starting to get dark, so other methods were needed to deal with the Argentines.

The Cadre's commander, Captain Rod Boswell, was ordered to muster his troops and mount an assault on the position. He initially intended to fly in at night and then strike at dawn. Luck was not with the Cadre and its Royal Navy Sea King helicopter failed to arrive on time. An hour late, the nineteen-man assault team began its 45-kilometre low-level flight to the drop-off point in a gully, only some 1,000 metres from the objective. Out of sight of the enemy, Captain Boswell split his team into a seven-man fire support team and a twelve-man assault squad. The fire team moved to the left to get into position to shoot in the assault team, led by Captain Boswell.

They moved under cover of a ridge for most of the way until they had to leave its shelter to approach the objective. They crawled over the crest on their stomachs until they were only a couple of hundred metres from the house but the Argentine sentry never saw them.

Captain Boswell ordered his men to 'fix bayonets' and then fired off a green signal flare. On cue the fire support team blasted the house with six M72 66mm LAW rockets. An Argentine soldier who moved to the window to engage the assault team as it ran forward was taken out by a well-aimed shot from a Cadre sniper rifle. The assault team briefly stopped to allow two more LAWs to be fired into the house and then they were off again.

The Argentines didn't wait to trade cold steel with the Royal Marines. They fled the house, a wise move because an ammunition store inside promptly blew up and set the building on fire. Taking cover in a stream bed fifty metres from the burning house the Argentines traded fire with the assault team, which kept pressing forward into bayonet range.

All resistance ceased when the Argentine commander was felled by two well-aimed 40mm M79 grenade launcher rounds. Five of the enemy were dead and seven were wounded. Three Cadre members were slightly wounded. The speed of the Cadre's charge had totally put the enemy off balance and panicked them. The Argentines told their captors that they thought they were under attack by a full company. Two other Argentine observation post teams had watched the attack and were so keen not to be on the receiving end of another such charge that they immediately surrendered to the nearest British units.

Mount Longdon

By the second week in June 1982 the British had successfully moved their two brigades to within striking distance of Port Stanley. They were now poised to launch their final assault against the Argentine main forces deployed to defend the islands' small capital.

The Argentines had been in the hills overlooking Port Stanley for almost two months. Most of the soldiers were conscripts with no experience of modern combat. Although the officers were long-service professionals, they too were lacking in combat experience and training. Their logistic support left a lot to be desired. Few of the Argentine soldiers had eaten a hot meal in several weeks, ammunition resupply was difficult in the mountainous terrain and communications were almost non-existent.

However, the Argentine high command had a good eye for ground. They had placed their troops on all the high ground of tactical importance around Port Stanley, and placed minefields in low ground to channel the British into their main defensive positions. The hilltop defensive positions chosen were all natural fortresses, with overhanging rocks to protect trenches from artillery, and large open fields of fire on the approach routes.

Defending the feature known as Mount Longdon was B Company of the 7th Mechanized Infantry Regiment and an engineer platoon – at most 200 men. They were to be attacked by the 3rd Battalion, The Parachute Regiment (3 PARA) – one of the British Army's toughest and most aggressive units.

The British plan to take Port Stanley envisaged a two-phase operation carving into the Argentine defences in two large bites. On the night of 11/12 June, 3 Commando Brigade would slice into the eastern sector of the defences, to allow 5 Infantry Brigade to attack from the south and crack open the heart of the enemy position.

For this attack, 3 Commando Brigade was assigned command of 3 PARA and the battalion was allocated Mount Longdon as its objective. This was on the extreme left of the position and they were to kick off the brigade assault, crossing their start line half an hour before the next battalion was due to go into action.

Lieutenant Colonel Hew Pike commanded 3 PARA. He had an aura about him – it was obvious that he was going to come out of the Falklands without so much as a scratch and make the grade for promotion to general (both in fact happened). The whole battalion was affected by the Para 'self-image'. They called themselves the 'green-eyed boys', an allusion to what they saw as their superiority in all things military. The plan devised by Colonel Pike was simple. A and B Companies were to move up the mountain in silence, and in pincer movements assault two positions, designated Full Back and Half Fly. C Company would be in reserve, providing fire support along with the mortar, anti-tank and machine-gun platoons.

BAYONET BATTLE

Colonel Pike and his company commanders held the Argentines in low regard and did not expect them to put up much resistance. For this reason the colonel hoped to surprise them by advancing as close to their positions as possible under cover of darkness, before storming into their trenches with bayonets fixed. The tactical term was 'silent night attack'. In the rocky crags that ran the length of Mount Longdon the Argentines were waiting. It was thirteen degrees below freezing, with rain and sleet falling. Their commanders were expecting the British to attack at dawn so they switched off their ground surveillance radar. The first they knew of 3 PARA's attack was when a corporal in B Company stepped on a mine, blowing his foot off.

The enemy sentries had been asleep, allowing B Company to get within fifty metres of their main defensive position on the crest of the mountain. All hell now broke loose as both sides started trading small-arms and machine-gun fire. B Company charged forward, overrunning the first Argentine platoon and grenading several bunkers.

Once the initial shock had passed, the Argentine in-depth positions started fighting back with determination. Their heavy machine-guns and night-sighted sniper rifles began taking an increasing toll of the advancing paratroopers who, using the darkness and folds in the rocks, began to crawl up on the enemy positions.

Privates Dominic Gray and Ben Gough managed to crawl undetected up to an Argentine bunker and crouched beside it as the soldiers inside blasted away into the night. In unison the two Paras each pulled the pin out of a grenade and posted it through the firing slit of the enemy bunker. The instant the grenade exploded the two jumped in the trench and started to bayonet the three surviving enemy. Private Gray killed an enemy soldier by sticking his bayonet through his eye socket.

The battle was going badly for B Company. Argentine

238

resistance was strong and well organized. Sergeant Ian McKay was shot dead as he single-handedly charged an enemy machine-gun nest, winning the paratrooper the Victoria Cross.

All around the mountain, small groups of paratroopers were fighting for survival. Lieutenant Mark Cox and Private Kevin Connery took out another enemy bunker in the same way as Gray and Gough. Private Connery first hit the bunker with an M72 66mm LAW rocket. Then the two threw in grenades before finishing the enemy off with the bayonet. For good measure they also put two 7.62mm rounds – double-tapping in Para vernacular – in each of the four enemy.

By 03.00 B Company's attack had clearly stalled. It had suffered more than 50 per cent casualties and was unable to get any further. Colonel Pike therefore ordered A Company to halt its advance and swing back to help B Company.

The commanding officer was now forward with B Company and he was determined to get the attack going before daylight made the battalion vulnerable to enemy artillery fire, directed from nearby hills. 'I shall never forget the sight that morning, of A Company advancing through a thick mist with bayonets fixed,' recounted Colonel Pike. A Company dropped their heavy webbing and stuffed everything they needed for the assault into the pockets of their Para smocks.

A Company first set up a fire base with its 7.62mm General Purpose Machine-Guns (GPMGs) at the eastern edge of the ridge. The artillery forward observation officer attached to the company got into position and started to bring down 105mm shells on the enemy positions. With this fire support falling, 1 Platoon started to crawl forward on their stomachs towards the enemy bunkers. When they were close enough, they blasted the bunkers with 66mm rockets and lobbed grenades ahead. They then dashed into the enemy, slashing and stabbing with bayonets.

This was slow but systematic work because of the need to ensure no enemy were left behind to shoot the Paras in the back. The platoon used up almost all its 66mm rockets and hand grenades during its attack. It was now 2 Platoon's opportunity to join the advance, which they did using similar tactics in their sector, although the supporting artillery fire had to be stopped when the Paras got close to the enemy positions.

Under the weight of this systematic advance, the Argentines broke and started running off the mountain. A Company's 3 Platoon was now launched forward to complete the rout and secure the far end of the mountain, ready for any Argentine counter-attack. It never came. The company's slow but systematic tactics paid off, and it only suffered one man slightly wounded during this phase of the battle.

At just after 08.00, with dawn breaking, Mount Longdon was in British hands. The ten-hour battle had cost 3 PARA twenty-three killed and forty-seven wounded, the majority from B Company. Around thirty Argentine defenders were killed in the battle and fifty were captured, many of them wounded. The remaining fifty or so escaped to fight another day. There was no mass surrender, a testament to the bravery of Argentinian conscripts that night. The battle was an epic bayonet charge, which had ended in victory for the aggressive and determined paratroopers.

Mount Tumbledown

While 3 PARA were storming Mount Longdon at bayonet point, 42 and 45 Commando Royal Marines were clearing the Argentine defenders from Mount Harriet and Two Sisters. They used massive firepower to support their assaults – artillery and MILAN anti-tank missiles. The Argentines cracked early, so the 'Royals' were not required to clear them out of their positions with bayonets. Some 400 surrendered to the Commandos who suffered only minimal casualties.

A day of reorganization followed as the British prepared for the final battle for Stanley. During the evening of 13/14 June, 3 PARA's sister battalion, 2 PARA, employed artillery, mortars, MILANs and General Purpose Machine-Guns (GPMGs) to clear Wireless Ridge. Some 400 enemy fled and 17 were captured, with 100 being killed in the barrage. As the Paras set about reorganizing, they were counter-attacked and ordered to fix bayonets to repel the enemy. British artillery turned back the enemy before 2 PARA could get to blood its bayonets.

It was now the turn of the 2nd Battalion, the Scots Guards, to attack Mount Tumbledown. The battalion was to spearhead 5 Infantry Brigade's operation to clear the southward-facing section of the Argentine defences. The battalion had not been part of the original task force, which had landed at San Carlos Water on 21 May. It had been on public duties guarding Buckingham Palace in London, wearing red coats and bearskins. When the war broke out the battalion had been assigned to 5 Infantry Brigade as an afterthought as it was meant to garrison the islands after the Argentine surrender, rather than actually fight. The Brigade had sailed to the South Atlantic in the liner *Queen Elizabeth II*. After an abortive attempt by the Welsh Guards to march to Stanley via Goose Green, 5 Infantry Brigade was moved by sea to the Bluff Cove and Fitzroy area, losing many men when the Argentines bombed two Royal Fleet Auxiliary landing ships.

The Scots Guards may not have been as highly trained in amphibious warfare as the Royal Marines but they were very definitely 'hard' men. Recruited from the slums of Glasgow and Edinburgh, the guardsmen knew all about close-quarter combat.

Many of the officers were not of Scottish origin, being

so-called 'Surrey Highlanders'; they did, however, know their trade and were keen to get in action before 3 Commando Brigade 'won' the war by themselves. From their forward base at Bluff Cove, the Scots Guards were ordered forward to their assembly area below Mount Tumbledown on the morning of 13 June. Royal Navy helicopters lifted them into position by midday and the commanding officer Lieutenant Colonel Mike Scott issued his final orders for the attack at 14.00. To provide identification at night the battalion's password was that well-known Scottish phrase, 'Hey, Jimmy'. It was thought that no Argentine would be able to mimic the accent properly. Berets rather than steel helmets would be worn during the approach to Tumbledown – helmets were awkward and uncomfortable when climbing over rocks.

Just one company of Argentine Marines – only a hundred Regulars at the most – occupied the summit of the mountain. Like the defenders of Mount Longdon they were well prepared to defend themselves, hiding in a series of rocky crags along the mountain's crest line.

Colonel Scott correctly assumed that the Argentines would think his main axis of advance would be from the south, following the track from Bluff Cove to Port Stanley, so he organized a diversionary force made up of the battalion's 'odds and sods' to push up the road with help from Scorpion light tanks of the Blues and Royals. Bang on schedule the diversion began at 08.30 and distracted Argentine attention while the battalion formed up ready to attack.

The main assault was simple, with G Company first assaulting the left edge of the mountain, to allow Left Flank and then Right Flank Companies to clear their objectives (the unique designation of the Scots Guard companies comes from the position they occupy on ceremonial parades). Each company would have to clear out an enemy platoon position, which was considered an achievable objective under the

British Army doctrine that stated a superiority of three to one was needed to assure victory in infantry combat.

Five batteries of 105mm artillery, two additional mortar platoons and naval gunfire from HMS *Active* and *Yarmouth* were laid on ready to support the attack after the first troops crossed the start line at 21.00. G Company moved in two columns towards its objective through rain and snow flurries. There were irregular mortar and artillery strikes during the eight-kilometre advance but the enemy did not detect them. The Guardsmen found their objective abandoned, but further up the mountain voices could be heard speaking in Spanish. They began securing the area and preparing to give fire support for the next phase of the operation. Left Flank Company under Major John Kiszley now got the word to move, and at 10.30 it had passed through G Company on its way forward.

Kiszley, who like Colonel Pike of 3 PARA was to become a senior general after the war, deployed his company in text-book fashion with two platoons up (in line abreast) and the third hanging back in reserve. The assault platoons spread out in extended line and swept up the mountain, but they found the going difficult on the huge boulders that cover it. About 300 metres from the first Argentine position, the enemy opened fire with a .50 calibre heavy machine-gun. Both forward platoons started to take casualties from the well-sited enemy machine-guns and sniper rifles.

Lieutenant Alastair Mitchell's platoon put in a section attack on an enemy machine-gun post but was beaten back. For three hours Left Flank Company was pinned down on the slopes of the mountain. The Guardsmen traded 66mm LAW rocket and M79 grenade-launcher fire with the enemy. Protected in their rock bunkers, the Argentines refused to budge and were not running away, as had been predicted by senior British officers. It was taking an age for the artillery and mortar fire controllers to adjust their fire.

At 02.30 the shells at last began to slam into the enemy bunkers. Kiszley now ordered Lieutenant Mitchell's platoon to charge forward with fixed bayonets. The guardsmen got in among the rocks and started grenading and bayoneting the surviving defenders. The company commander advanced close behind the platoon, weaving through the mayhem, shouting encouragement; all around Kiszley could see Guardsmen fighting for their lives; he was soon alone on a small ridge line.

The officer called out repeatedly, 'Fifteen Platoon, are you with me?' Eventually a Scottish voice replied, 'Aye, sir, I'm f---ing with you.' He rallied the platoon and set off for the summit of the mountain. Kiszley was in the thick of the action. He led a group of Guardsmen up a gully, throwing hand grenades at an enemy position ahead. Storming into the position he shot two enemy soldiers and bayoneted a third, his bayonet breaking in two while the hapless Argentine expired.

The Argentine defences were now completely unhinged and the Guardsmen began taking prisoners. Kiszley suddenly found himself standing on the summit, looking down on Port Stanley under street lighting and with traffic still moving around.

Left Flank Company's hold on Tumbledown was precarious; Kiszley only had six men with him at the summit. He was described as looking like 'the Monarch of the Glen' by Lieutenant Robert Lawrence, when he met him on the summit. The remainder of Left Flank Company was now spread over the slopes of the mountain, tending to wounded and guarding prisoners. For his dash and bravery Kiszley was awarded the Military Cross.

The battle for Tumbledown was far from over. On the eastern edge of the mountain the Argentines were still holding out, so Colonel Scott ordered Right Flank Company to push on to clear the final positions.

Major Simon Price sent two platoons forward, preceded by

a barrage of 66mm rocket and M79 grenade-launcher fire to clear a machine-gun post. One platoon held its position to provide fire support for the assault troops. Lieutenant Lawrence led the assault troops round to the right of the enemy in the hope of taking them by surprise. The enemy gunner saw them coming and turned his weapon to bring them under heavy fire. Guardsmen hit the dirt and started to return fire. The young officer now started to crawl forward on his belly to clear out the enemy post with a phosphorous grenade. In a bizarre episode the pin of the grenade stuck so he had to crawl back to his troops and get a corporal to pull out the pin. After another nerve-racking crawl he hurled the grenade and it took out the enemy gunner.

This was the signal for the rest of Lawrence's platoon to charge forward. Every man in the platoon moved as one and with bayonets to the fore, the enemy were overwhelmed. The Guardsmen burst into an enemy position and the Argentines started surrendering. After rounding them up and disarming them, the platoon commander led his men forward again only to run into a wall of enemy fire. To keep up the momentum of the attack, Lieutenant Lawrence ordered his men to skirmish forward in pairs, one man providing covering fire as the other doubled forward to the next piece of cover.

During this advance the lieutenant found a body behind a rock. To see if it was alive he stuck his bayonet into its arm. The Argentine was very much alive and suddenly spun around on the ground. This violent movement caused the officer's bayonet to break and he also found he was out of ammunition. The Argentine was trying to grab his pistol so Lieutenant Lawrence stabbed him repeatedly with the stump of his snapped bayonet. It took a long time for the soldier to die.

Now Lieutenant Lawrence and his men had broken the back of the enemy defences. Right Flank Company was fanning out on the far side of Tumbledown just as dawn was breaking. In his moment of victory an Argentine sniper's bullet found Lieutenant Lawrence's head. He was left permanently disabled but was awarded the Military Cross.

By 08.15 the Scots Guards were in control of Tumbledown. The battalion lost seven dead and forty-one injured. Around twenty Argentines were killed and fourteen captured. The rest worked their way back into Port Stanley, where within a few hours the Argentine garrison would surrender. The bayonet charges of the Scots Guards had broken the back of the last Argentine defence line.

SIX

A CENTURY OF BAYONET FIGHTING

Conclusion

In a century that has seen tremendous advances in military technology, with tanks, machine-guns, jet aircraft, submarines and nuclear weapons all making decisive appearances, it comes as a great surprise to many people that the bayonet still crops up again and again in accounts of battles.

From the Boer War through to the Falklands, the bayonet was used by soldiers on every continent, in every major war. Infantry soldiers the world over demand bayonets. They use them to kill their opponents in close combat or just to intimidate their enemies into fleeing the battlefield.

No infantry soldier worth his salt would go into battle without his bayonet. While the British in the First World War and Japanese in the Pacific War placed special emphasis on the bayonet, most infantrymen saw it as just one of the weapons in their armoury, to be used in certain circumstances. Time and again, it proved a vital weapon in close-quarter fighting. When the enemy are within a few metres, the bayonet has often proved itself to be the quickest and most effective way to dispatch them. Some people have called the bayonet a 'weapon of last resort', to be used only when all else fails. Automatic weapons have been known to jam, or else run out of ammunition because soldiers get carried away in the heat of battle and fire it all off. In confined spaces it may also endanger comrades to fire off automatic weapons – unlike in the movies real bullets often go straight through bodies and keep going for several hundred metres. Grenades are effective for clearing buildings, trenches and fortifications but they are not infallible. Defenders may shelter behind sandbags or dead comrades. Steel helmets and body armour can also protect defenders from grenade splinters. In these circumstances the only thing to do is go in with the bayonet to make sure defenders are dead.

For these reasons the infantryman loves his bayonet. It provides an insurance policy if all his high-tech weaponry fails. The very act of fixing bayonets is a psychological milestone in a battle – it tells soldiers that hand-to-hand combat is near and that they must steel themselves to do or die. Numerous veterans of bayonet charges say the very order 'fix bayonets' has transformed the morale of a unit, making it perform extraordinary feats of bravery.

The bayonet also provides commanders with tactical flexibility because bayonets allow soldiers to kill silently. In many circumstances it is necessary to maintain the element of surprise by dealing with opponents in silence rather than reveal your position. In jungle fighting or during night attacks this is a vital consideration.

Bayonet designs have gone through considerable evolution during the twentieth century to match the changing perceptions of the weapon's tactical employment. The long sword bayonets of the first decade of the century were a throwback to the use of the weapon as the infantry's main means of keeping cavalry at bay. Experience in the trenches of the First World War, however, led most nations to look to shorter blades, designed principally for killing other infantrymen at close quarters.

During the Second World War, most Western armies modified their bayonet-fighting tactics, seeing the bayonet charge simply as the last phase of an assault as troops go in for the kill against enemy troops in prepared positions. To get to that stage in the battle, infantry would be supported by artillery, machine-guns, mortars and tanks to keep the enemy's head down, so allowing the assault troops to get close without suffering unnecessary losses.

The one exception to this trend was the Imperial Japanese Army, which for uniquely oriental reasons gave the bayonet charge a quasi-religious significance. Japanese generals just did not care how many soldiers died charging enemy positions heavily defended by artillery and machine-guns. Indeed, death in battle was considered the ultimate honour. In the first months of the Pacific War Japanese bayonet charges carried all before them. Allied troops in Malaya, Singapore, Hong Kong, the Dutch East Indies and the Philippines were badly led, poorly equipped, half starved and not trained to live in tropical conditions. The sight of hundreds of mad Japanese charging out of the jungle was too much for many Allied soldiers, who either raised the white flag or ran for their lives.

This infected the Japanese with a syndrome known as 'victory disease'. Time and again they resorted to the same arrogant tactics until they started to come up against Allied troops who were prepared to stand and fight. The result was mass slaughter. In defeat, the 'dishonoured' Japanese would then resort to bayonet charges into the face of the enemy as a route to an early death, and redemption for the previous failure. To Westerners, the Japanese belief in the moral superiority of their soldiers' bodies over the .50-calibre bullet seems bizarre, but for millions of Japanese during the Second World War it was an act of faith. It also led to the country's inevitable defeat, as the Japanese Empire's best troops were killed by the thousands for no tactical or strategic advantage whatsoever.

Throughout the previous chapters the details of numerous bayonet charges and combat have been recounted. It is clear that success depends on many factors. There are two distinct phases of a bayonet engagement: the mass assault by a unit to seize an objective and the hand-to-hand fighting by individual soldiers.

To get into close contact with the enemy requires in varying degrees the following factors: good planning, a covered approach to protect troops from enemy fire, surprise, and determination once committed to push on through. By far the most important factor is protection from the enemy's firepower.

The inability to understand this factor led to mass slaughter on the Western Front during the First World War, as British generals kept sending their troops forward against prepared German defences despite the glaring evidence that bayonet charges only ever worked when the troops could get to within a few dozen metres of the enemy without being seen. They called this 'dash' tactics.

Bad weather or dead ground would be used to cover the forward movement of troops until they were close enough to the enemy to allow them to surge forward into their trenches. Good use of artillery by forward observers could also help by keeping the enemy penned inside their bunkers until the British infantry were almost on top of them. The timed rolling barrages used at the Somme were too inflexible, and allowed the Germans to man their firing positions unmolested and machine-gun thousands of British troops, for in some cases no loss to themselves.

The sudden appearance of hundreds of bayonet-wielding troops in front of or behind a position has often been enough to send an enemy scurrying to the rear. While the Japanese banzai war cries and British First World War 'killing faces' are often mocked by saloon bar generals, the morale factor in warfare is too often underestimated. An individual soldier's motivation to fight is determined by many factors. As long as he perceives he is part of a bigger unit that will protect him from whatever the enemy does, he will keep fighting. This is often called unit cohesion or *esprit de corps*. If this can be broken and the soldier made to feel he is alone and vulnerable on a dangerous battlefield, then he will opt to save himself rather than fight.

If the bayonet charge comes at the culmination of a series of events designed to undermine morale of an enemy, such as artillery fire, air strikes or a long siege, then it is often the straw that breaks the back of an opponent's will to resist.

If hundreds of enemy troops come running and screaming towards a half-starved and shell-shocked opponent, more often than not the enemy soldiers will begin to think they, personally, are the intended target. This will force them to think only about saving their own skin, which can take many forms: a rapid exit to the rear, hiding at the bottom of a dugout hoping they will not be found, surrender, or in some cases shooting off-target in the perverse belief that the attackers will spare them because the defenders have not killed any of their comrades. The mere act of charging forward with a bayonet can spread fear and panic in weak-willed opponents.

It is usually the case that some defenders will stand and fight. Success then depends on good teamwork to break enemy resistance quickly. Assaults usually only succeed if the attacker uses imaginative tactics, with some providing covering fire as others go in for the kill. This prevents the assault wave being mown down by small groups of defenders, as on the Somme.

In close-quarter battle, the bayonet is king when the attacker can take an enemy by surprise, striking before the target has time to bring his firearm to bear or parry the thrust. Unless he gets the first thrust in to an opponent, it becomes a trial of strength to see who can emerge alive. Butt-whipping, kicking, biting and punching will then all come into play. Time and again there have been cases of individual soldiers making lone charges into enemy positions, and bayoneting their way through numerous positions after killing many enemy soldiers. More often than not this results in an early death and the award of a posthumous decoration for valour. Why do soldiers do these foolhardy but brave acts? Many observers talk of 'battle rage' or 'battle madness'. After seeing comrades shot or killed and their unit pinned down by murderous enemy fire all 'normal' reasoning goes. Extreme solutions and ideas take over. It seems logical to charge straight at the enemy. Once the 'battle-mad' have bayoneted or grenaded their first enemy soldier they start to consider themselves invulnerable and just cannot stop.

The apparent absence of bayonet fighting in major conflicts over the past fifteen years would seem to indicate that the weapon is losing its place on the battlefield. History would suggest that it is only a matter of time before bayonets see action again. The truth is bayonets have never really gone out of fashion.

Almost every army in the world still provides its soldiers with bayonets, and teaches bayonet fighting in basic infantry training. Advanced infantry skills involve the extensive prac-tising of assault tactics, including the use of the bayonet to clear enemy bunkers and buildings.

Before Desert Storm in 1991, British, American, French, Egyptian and Kuwaiti troops carried out regular bayonet training in preparation for eliminating the massive Iraqi trench works along the Saudi Arabian border. Coalition commanders were expecting the Iraqis to put up fanatical resistance, requiring assault troops to go in and take them out with grenade and bayonet.

When Coalition land forces actually advanced into Kuwait

A CENTURY OF BAYONET FIGHTING

and southern Iraq, Saddam Hussein's hapless forces had been so weakened by a month of incessant artillery and air strikes they invariably surrendered as soon as a Coalition armoured personnel carrier drew up alongside their trench. During the summer of 1995, as troops of the United Nations Rapid Reaction Force prepared to break the three-year-old siege of the Bosnian capital Sarajevo, they carried out a number of high-profile exercises clearing trenches at bayonet point. British troops of the 1st Battalion, The Devonshire & Dorset Regiment constructed a mock Serb trench system and practised moving through it bayoneting a selection of improvised dummies.

After the UN and NATO launched the Operation Deliberate Force air offensive, the Rapid Reaction Force prepared a ground offensive to take and clear Serb checkpoints blocking aid convoy routes into Sarajevo. Warrior armoured cars carrying the British infantry had their engines running and crews mounted when the Serbs backed down and relinquished their iron ring around the city.

In both the Gulf and Bosnia, the bayonet training of Western troops was carried out in the full spotlight of CNN, so potential opponents got a good look at what was coming their way. This was a not very subtle form of psychological warfare, but it served to scare opponents and reassure the folks back home that their enemies would be shown no mercy.

Showing your opponents an uncovered bayonet blade has long been a way of warning them they are about to face death. So why not do the same thing on television? It certainly is less risky to one's own troops who do not have to go within rifle range of the enemy.

Bayonets have also surprisingly proved their worth in humanitarian aid missions in Africa. When US troops were deployed in Somalia, during Operation Restore Hope, they were called on to use their bayonets to restore order in the famine-ravished country. The 10th Mountain Division began arriving in Somalia in December 1993, and then moved into the countryside to secure airfields, so aid supplies could be flown in to remote locations. Its troops were then deployed to protect international aid agency food warehouses, which were being attacked and looted by hungry Somalis.

Two platoons of the 87th Infantry's 2nd Battalion were securing the remote town of Wanwaylen when they were alerted that a mob was attacking the local Red Cross food warehouse. The troops rushed to the scene to find mayhem. Their rules of engagement prevented them opening fire and they had no riot gear. The answer: fix bayonets. Major Martin Stanton described the scene:

> I gave the word to Lieutenant Christiansen to advance and clear the warehouse. The troops advanced with bayonets fixed at a fast walk that broke into a jog. As they approached the warehouse, they began shouting at the top of their lungs. The sight of this line of shouting soldiers closing with fixed bayonets was enough to cause most of the looters to bolt. Only a few stayed to try to get food. They were ejected by Lieutenant Christiansen's people. We managed to clear the warehouse with only one soldier slightly cut (on a piece of corrugated iron) and no major wounds to any Somali, although a few required a few blows with rifle butts before they would stop resisting.

This is perhaps the last recorded instance of US troops carrying out a bayonet charge though few would expect it to be the last.

So what does the future hold for the bayonet? The development of modern lightweight body armour poses both challenges and opportunities for bayonet advocates. Body armour provides a great deal of protection against slashing and stabbing. New lightweight, low-cost materials are likely to become more widely available. Traditional bayonets may have to be redesigned to enable them to penetrate the artificial fibres used in body armour.

The fitting of metal or ceramic plates to body armour has provided its wearers with very high levels of protection against gunshots. To kill these new 'knights' of the battlefield could require soldiers to have to close on them to dispatch them with the bayonet, striking at unprotected areas like the face, neck, arms, legs and groin. It may even be necessary for the attacker to stun the victim with a powerful butt stroke and then rip off protective clothing to make him vulnerable to the killer bayonet thrust. Special hooks or spikes may have to be added to bayonets to allow the rapid stripping away of a victim's body armour.

While close-quarter combat may seem 'politically incorrect' in the casualty-conscious environment of the current era, it has to be remembered that this is purely a Western phenomenon. Armies in eastern Europe, the Middle East, Asia and Africa have no such scruples, so the prospect of bayonet fighting should not be considered too outrageous. It would take a very brave man to predict the demise of the bayonet. Over the next hundred years the order 'fix bayonets' will still reverberate around the battlefield when the going gets tough.

BIBLIOGRAPHY

James Bancroft, *Devotion to Duty*, Aim High Productions, Manchester, 1990.

D.S. Banting and G.A. Embleton, T*he Western Front 1914–1918*, Altmark Publishing, 1971.

Eddy Bauer, *World War II*, Orbis Publishing, London, 1979.

I.F.W. Beckett, *Victoria's Wars*, Shire Publications, 1974.

Antony Beevor, *Crete: The Battle and the Resistance*, John Murray (Publishers) Ltd, London, 1991.

Ray Bonds (ed.), *The Vietnam War*, Salamander Books, London, 1979.

Vincent Branley, *Two Sides of Hell*, Bloomsbury Publishing, London, 1994.

Christopher Buckley, *Greece and Crete 1941*, HMSO, London, 1952.

Anthony Carter, *World Bayonets: 1800 to the Present*, Arms & Armour Press, London, 1996.

Christopher Chant, *Gurkha*, Blandford Press, Poole, 1985.

Richard Connaughton, John Pimlott, Duncan Anderson, *The Battle for Manila*, Bloomsbury, 1995.

James Cooper and Matthew Cooper, *Hitler's Elite*, Macdonalds and Jane's, London, 1975.

——, *Panzer Grenadiers*, Macdonalds and Jane's, London, 1977.

R.B. Crosse, *A Record of H.M. 52nd Light Infantry*, Spennell Press, Warwick, 1956.

Martin Davidson and Adam Levy, *Decisive Weapons*, BBC, London, 1996.

Peter Dennis, Jeffrey Grey, Ewan Morris, Robin Prior, *The Oxford Companion to Australian Military History*, Oxford University Press, Oxford, 1995.

Director Public Relations (Army), *The British Army in the Falklands 1982*, HMSO, London, 1983.

Anthony Farrar-Hockley, *The British Part in the Korean War*, Vol. 1, HMSO, London, 1990.

Simon Foster, *Okinawa 1945*, Arms & Armour Press, London, 1994.

R.W. Gould, *Epic Actions of the First World War*, Tom Donovan Publishing, Brighton, 1997.

Ian Gow, *Okinawa 1945: Gateway to Japan*, Grubb Street, London, 1986.

Paddy Griffiths, *Battle Tactics of the Western Front*, Yale University Press, New Haven, 1994.

Eric Hamel, *Chosin*, Presidio, Novato, 1981.

——, *Ambush Valley*, Presidio, Novato, 1990.

BIBLIOGRAPHY

Max Hastings, *Overlord*, Michael Joseph, London, 1984.

Max Hastings and Simon Jenkins, *The Battle for the Falklands*, Michael Joseph, London, 1983.

Michael Hickey, *The Unforgettable Army*, Spellmount, Staplehurst, 1992.

Richard Holmes, *War Walks*, BBC, London, 1996.

Robin Hunter, *True Stories of the Foreign Legion*, Virgin, London, 1997.

Christopher Jennings and Adrian Weale, *Green-Eyed Boys*, HarperCollins, London, 1996.

Curt Johnson, *Battles of the American Revolution*, Roxby Press Ltd, Maidenhead, 1975.

Kenneth N. Jordan, *Heroes of Our Time*, Schiffer Military Library, Atglen, 1994.

——, *Forgotten Heroes*, Schiffer Military Library, Atglen, 1995.

——, *Yesterday's Heroes*, Schiffer Military Library, Atglen, 1996.

——, *Men of Honor*, Schiffer Military Library, Atglen, 1997.

Charles T. Kemps, *The History of the Vietnam War*, Hamlyn, London, 1988.

Leo Kessler, *The Iron Fist*, Futura Publications, London, 1997.

Dr Michael King, *Rangers*, Combat Studies Institute, Fort Levenworth, 1985.

John Laffin, *Australian Battlefields of the First World War*, Kangaroo Press, Kenthurst, 1992.

John and Robert Lawrence, *Tumbledown*, 22 Books, Rochester, 1988.

Stewart Lone, *Japan's First Modern War*, St Martin's Press, London, 1994.

James Lucas, *Battlegroup*, Arms & Armour Press, London, 1993.

Lyn MacDonald, *They Called it Passchaendale*, Penguin, London, 1978.

——, *1914*, Penguin, London, 1987.

Lex McAulay, *The Battle of Coral*, Hutchinson, Victoria, 1988.

Scott McMichael, *A Historical Perspective on Light Infantry*, Combat Studies Institute, Fort Levenworth, 1987.

James Marchington, *Knives: Military Edged Tools & Weapons*, Brassey's, London, 1997.

Henry Maule, *The Great Battles of World War II*, Hamlyn, London, 1972.

Lida Mayo, *Bloody Buna*, Purnell Book Services, London.

Martin Middlebrook, *The First Day of the Somme*, Penguin, 1971.

——, *The Kaiser's Battle*, Penguin, 1978.

——, *The Fight for the Malvinas*, Viking, London, 1989.

P.J.R. Mileham, *Fighting Highlanders*, Arms & Armour Press, London, 1993.

Colin Mitchell, *Having Been a Soldier*, Hamish Hamilton, London, 1979.

Harold Moore and Joseph Galloway, *We Were Soldiers Once . . . and Young*, Random House, New York, 1992.

William Moore, *See How They Ran*, Leo Cooper, 1970.

Eric Morris, *Circles in Hell*, Hutchinson, London, 1993.

Bernard C. Nalty, *Air Power and the Fight for Khe Sanh*, USAF, Washington DC, 1986.

Bryan Perrett, *Last Stand*, Arms & Armour Press, London, 1991.

——, *Against All Odds*, Arms & Armour Press, London, 1995.

——, *Impossible Victories*, Arms & Armour Press, London, 1996.

Bruce Quarry, *German Paratroopers in the Med*, Patrick Stephens, Cambridge, 1979.

David Rissuk, *The DLI at War*, DLI, Durham, 1952.

Gordon Rottman, *US Army Airborne 1940–90*, Osprey, London, 1990.

Lee Russel, *The US Marine Corps since 1945*, Osprey, London, 1984.

Siegfried Sassoon, *Memoirs of an Infantry Officer*, Faber and Faber, London, 1930.

Peter Simpkin, *et al.*, *Regiments of the Scottish Division*, Macmillan Press, Basingstoke, Hampshire, 1973.

Tony Spagnoly and Ted Smith, *Salient Points*, Leo Cooper, 1995.

Shelby L. Stanton, *Ten Corps in Korea 1950*, Presidio, Novato, 1989.

Donn A. Starry, *Armoured Combat in Vietnam*, Blandford Press, Poole, Dorset, 1981.

J.W.Thomason, *Fix Bayonets!*, Greenhill Books, London, 1989.

Julian Thompson, *No Picnic*, Leo Cooper, London, 1985.

Masanobu Tsuji, *Japan's Greatest Victory, Britain's Worst Defeat*, Spellmount, Staplehurst, 1997.

Merrill B. Twining, *No Bended Knee*, Presidio, Novato, 1996.

John Watts and Peter White, *The Bayonet Book*, John Watts and Peter White, Birmingham, 1975.

Roy Westlake, *British Battalions on the Somme*, Leo Cooper, 1994.

Charles Whiting, *Hunters from the Sky*, Leo Cooper, London, 1975.

——, *The Poor Bloody Infantry, 1939–45*, Century Hutchinson, London, 1987.

——, *The Battle of Hurtgen Forest*, Leo Cooper, London, 1989.

Gordon Williamson, *SS: the Blood-Soaked Soil*, Brown Books, London, 1995.

Chester Wilmot, *The Struggle for Europe*, Collins, London, 1952.

S. Woodburn Kirby, *Singapore*, Cassel, London, 1971.

Hiromichi Yahara, *The Battle for Okinawa*, John Wiley, New York, 1995.

Periodicals

Army; After the Battle; Combat & Survival Magazine; The Falklands War, Marshall Cavendish, London, 1983; *The London Gazette; The Lancet; Purnell's History of the Second World War; The Elite; Strategy & Tactics; War Monthly*

INDEX

INDEX

INDEX